American Ethnic Writers

American Ethnic Writers

Volume 1

Ai – Adrienne Kennedy

Edited by
David Peck
University of California, Long Beach

Project Editor
Tracy Irons-Georges

SALEM PRESS, INC.
Pasadena, California
Hackensack, New Jersey

Most of these essays originally appeared in *Identities and Issues in Literature*, 1997, edited by David Peck. The remainder were adapted from *Magill's Literary Annual*, from *Masterplots, Revised Second Edition*, 1996, and from the following *Masterplots II* series: *Drama*, 1990; *Poetry*, 1992; *African American Literature*, 1994; *Women's Literature*, 1994; and *American Fiction, Revised Edition*, 2000. All bibliographies and lists of published works have been updated.

∞ The paper used in these volumes conforms to the American National Standard for Permanence of Paper for Printed Library Materials, Z39.48-1992 (R1997).

Library of Congress Cataloging-in-Publication Data

American ethnic writers / David Peck; project editor Tracy Irons-Georges.

    p.   cm. — (Magill's choice)

    Includes bibliographical references and index.

    ISBN 0-89356-157-6 (set : alk. paper). — ISBN 0-89356-172-X (v. 1 : alk. paper). — ISBN 0-89356-184-3 (v. 2 : alk. paper)

    1. American literature—Minority authors—Bio-bibliography—Dictionaries. 2. Minority authors—United States—Biography—Dictionaries. 3. Authors, American—Biography—Dictionaries. 4. Ethnic groups in literature—Dictionaries. 5. Minorities in literature—Dictionaries. 6. Ethnicity in literature—Dictionaries. I. Peck, David R. II. Irons-Georges, Tracy. III. Series.

PS153.M56 A414 2000
810.9'920693—dc21

00-059529

First Printing

PRINTED IN THE UNITED STATES OF AMERICA

Table of Contents

Publisher's Note

There was a time not long ago in American literature when virtually the only experience explored in the literary canon was that of white Europeans from the mainstream of society. Rarely was the voice of a writer from another ethnic background heard. Then in the twentieth century came the Harlem Renaissance, and African American writers were suddenly in demand. By mid-century, Jewish American writers reexamined their ethnic heritage in the light of the Holocaust. By century's end, American Indian writers redefined their place in the nation's cultural history, and Asian American and Latino writers depicted the immigrant experience in the United States. Ethnic writers had joined the ranks of critically celebrated authors.

American Ethnic Writers explores the rich tradition of these writers and the ways in which they have expressed their sense of identity through literature, both fiction and nonfiction. This set profiles 136 writers and one or more of their works. Thus, 217 essays provide an analysis of literary works—novels, plays, short stories and collections, poems and collections, autobiographies, and essays. Most of these 353 articles were first published in *Identities and Issues in Literature* (1997); others were adapted from the *Masterplots* and *Magill's Literary Annual* series. All essays address the theme of personal and cultural identity. Articles on writers emphasize how the theme of race and ethnicity relates to the writer's life and how this theme is expressed through their writings. Articles on literary works discuss the work in terms of issues of identity. Most essays are accompanied by photographs.

Each author essay begins with birth and death information, including dates and places. Then, in one sentence, the author's central achievement in literature is stated. One or more ethnic traditions with which the writer is associated is given. Next is a list of the author's principal works in all genres, with publication dates. The text that follows concentrates on the theme of ethnic or racial identity, especially as it is explicitly, concretely treated in that individual's literature.

After the author profile comes one or more essays analyzing the writer's literary works that are especially pertinent to a discussion of race, ethnicity, and identity. Each of these essays is defined by type of work. Then the year in which the title was first published is provided. Additional information—such as when a drama was first performed, original language title if other than English, or dates of republication with a different title—are included when applicable.

For every writer, a list of "Suggested readings" appears after the last literature essay. These sources, publications useful for further study of the author's life and works, have been updated to include the most recent scholarship. Every writer profile concludes with a byline, with names separated by slashes when the authors contributed different parts of the essay.

At the back of both volumes are three useful features. An Author Index lists all 136 profiled writers, and a Title Index includes all 217 covered works. The Ethnic Identity List categorizes the authors by one or more groups: African American writers, American Indian writers, Asian American writers, Jewish writers, and Latino writers.

We wish to thank all the scholars who wrote these essays. Their names and affiliations are listed at the beginning of volume 1.

Contributor List

Amy Allison
Independent Scholar

Gerald S. Argetsinger
Rochester Institute of Technology

Angela Athy
Bowling Green State University

Lisa R. Aunkst
Independent Scholar

JoAnn Balingit
University of Delaware

Jack Vincent Barbera
University of Mississippi

Paula C. Barnes
Hampton University

Henry J. Baron
Calvin College

Margaret W. Batschelet
University of Texas

Carol F. Bender
Alma College

Jacquelyn Benton
Edgewood College

Milton Berman
University of Rochester

Cynthia A. Bily
Adrian College

Margaret Boe Birns
New York University and The New School for Social Research

Sandra F. Bone
Arkansas State University

Muriel W. Brailey
Wilberforce University

Wesley Britton
Grayson County College

Susan Butterworth
Independent Scholar

Emmett H. Carroll
Seattle University

Leonard Casper
Boston College

Russ Castronovo
University of Miami

Christine R. Catron
St. Mary's University

Nancy L. Chick
University of Georgia

C. L. Chua
California State University, Fresno

J. Robin Coffelt
University of North Texas

David Conde
Metropolitan State College of Denver

Holly Dworken Cooley
Independent Scholar

Virginia M. Crane
California State University, Los Angeles

Shira Daemon
Independent Scholar

Joyce Chandler Davis
Gadsden State Community College

Barbara Day
City University of New York

Frank Day
Clemson University

Mary Jo Deegan
University of Nebraska–Lincoln

Frenzella Elaine De Lancey
Drexel University

Bill Delaney
Independent Scholar

Francine Dempsey
The College of Saint Rose

Don Evans
Trenton State College

Grace Farrell
Butler University

Edward A. Fiorelli
St. John's University

T. A. Fishman
Clemson University

Anne Fleischmann
University of California, Davis

Robert Frail
Centenary College

Tom Frazier
Cumberland College

Chris Freeman
St. John's University

Janet Fujimoto
California State University, Fresno

Constance M. Fulmer
Pepperdine University

Jill B. Gidmark
University of Minnesota

Craig Gilbert
Portland State University

Joyce J. Glover
Independent Scholar

Charles A. Gramlich
Xavier University of Louisiana

James Green
Arizona State University

Robert Haight
Kalamazoo Valley Community College

Betty L. Hart
University of Southern Indiana

David M. Heaton
Ohio University

Terry Heller
Coe College

Diane Andrews Henningfeld
Adrian College

Kay Hively
Independent Scholar

Arthur D. Hlavaty
Independent Scholar

Pierre L. Horn
Wright State University

E. D. Huntley
Appalachian State University

Andrea J. Ivanov
Azusa Pacific University

Martin Japtok
University of California, Davis

Helen Jaskoski
Independent Scholar

Andrew O. Jones
University of California, Davis

Jane Anderson Jones
Manatee Community College, South

Theresa M. Kanoza
Eastern Illinois University

Leela Kapai
University of the District of Columbia

Jacquelyn Kilpatrick
Governors State University

Christine H. King
University of California, Davis

Judith Kitchen
State University of New York, College at Brockport

Laura L. Klure
Independent Scholar

Lynne Klyse
Independent Scholar

Gregory W. Lanier
The University of West Florida

Douglas Edward LaPrade
University of Texas–Pan American

Richard M. Leeson
Fort Hays State University

Leon Lewis
Appalachian State University

Janet E. Lorenz
Independent Scholar

Bernadette Flynn Low
Dundale Community College

R. C. Lutz
University of the Pacific

Joanne McCarthy
Tacoma Community College

Grace McEntee
Appalachian State University

Ron McFarland
University of Idaho

A. L. McLeod
Rider University

Anne B. Mangum
Bennett Collge

Lois A. Marchino
University of Texas at El Paso

Julia M. Meyers
North Carolina State University

Michael R. Meyers
Shaw University

Laura Mitchell
California State University, Fresno

Robert A. Morace
Daemon College

Rafael Ocasio
Agnes Scott College

Patrick O'Donnell
West Virginia University

Cynthia Packard
University of Massachusetts–Amherst

David Peck
University of California, Long Beach

Andrew B. Preslar
Lamar University, Orange

R. C. S.
Independent Scholar

Josephine Raburn
Cameron University

Brian Abel Ragen
Southern Illinois University–Edwardsville

Ralph Reckley, Sr.
Independent Scholar

Rosemary M. Canfield Reisman
Independent Scholar

Barbara Cecelia Rhodes
Central Missouri State University

Janine Rider
Mesa State College

Christy Rishoi
Michigan State University

Larry Rochelle
Johnson County Community College

Mark Sanders
College of the Mainland

Richard Sax
Madonna University

Daniel M. Scott III
Rhode Island College

Chenliang Sheng
Northern Kentucky University

Amy Beth Shollenberger
Independent Scholar

Debra Shostak
The College of Wooster

R. Baird Shuman
University of Illinois at Urbana-Champaign

Thomas J. Sienkewicz
Monmouth College, Illinois

Charles L. P. Silet
Iowa State University

Carl Singleton
Fort Hays State University

Joseleyne Ashford Slade
Michigan State University

Marjorie Smelstor
University of Wisconsin–Eau Claire

Pamela J. Olubunmi Smith
University of Nebraska–Omaha

Virginia Whatley Smith
University of Alabama–Birmingham

Brian Stableford
Independent Scholar

Trey Strecker
Ball State University

Philip A. Tapley
Louisiana College

Australia Tarver
Texas Christian University

Judith K. Taylor
Northern Kentucky University

Julie Tharp
*University of Wisconsin Center–Marshfield
 Wood College*

Lorenzo Thomas
University of Houston–Downtown

Tony Trigilio
Northeastern University

Richard Tuerk
East Texas State University

William Vaughn
Independent Scholar

Martha Modena Vertreace
Kennedy-King College

Kelly C. Walter
Southern California College

Qun Wang
California State University, Monterey Bay

Patricia L. Watson
University of Georgia

Gary Westfahl
University of California, Irvine

Kathryn Ervin Williams
Michigan State University

Pat M Wong
Binghamton University

American Ethnic Writers

Ai

(Florence Anthony)

BORN: Albany, Texas; October 21, 1947

Ai has renewed the poetic dramatic monologue in poems that record moments of public and private history.

TRADITIONS: African American, American Indian, Japanese American
PRINCIPAL WORKS: *Cruelty*, 1973; *Killing Floor*, 1979; *Sin*, 1986; *Fate*, 1991; *Greed*, 1993; *Vice: New and Selected Poems*, 1999

Ai is a multiracial American woman. Her mother's immediate ancestors were African American, Native American (Choctaw), and European American (Irish and Dutch). Her father's ancestors were Japanese. Ai has said that the history of her family is the history of America. She does not find her identity in any racial group. She insists on the uniqueness of personal identity. One of the aims of her work is to destroy stereotypes. She has said that she is "irrevocably tied to the lives of all people, both in and out of time." Consequently, whoever "wants to speak" in her poems "is allowed to speak regardless of sex, race, creed, or color."

Ai grew up in Tucson, Arizona. When she was seven, her family moved to Las Vegas, Nevada, for a year, then spent two years in San Francisco, California, before returning to Tucson. They moved again when Ai was twelve, this time to Los Angeles, California, returning again to Tucson three years later, when Ai was fifteen. Ai attended Catholic schools until the seventh grade. Her first poem, written when she was twelve, was a response to an assignment by the nuns to write a letter from the point of view of a Christian martyr who was going to die the next day. When she was fourteen, intending to enter a contest for poems about a historical figure, Ai began writing poems regularly.

History was Ai's best subject in high school, which she attended in Tucson. At the University of Arizona, also in Tucson, Ai found her identity in the "aesthetic atmosphere" of intellectual life. She was graduated from the university in 1969 with a degree in Oriental studies. She earned an M.F.A. degree in creative writing from the University of California at Irvine in 1971. When Ai published her first book of poetry, *Cruelty*, in 1973, she became a nationally known figure, so striking were her grimly realistic and violent poems. Ai married the poet Lawrence Kearney in 1976. In 1979, her second book, *Killing Floor*, won the Lamont Poetry Prize. She separated from Kearney in 1981, and

1

the couple divorced in 1984. In 1986, her third book, *Sin,* won an American Book Award from the Before Columbus Foundation. She has since published *Fate* in 1991 and *Greed* in 1993.

Cruelty
TYPE OF WORK: Poetry
FIRST PUBLISHED: 1973

Ai is more concerned with social class than with racial identity or gender in *Cruelty.* The book is a series of poetic dramatic monologues spoken by members of the underclass in America. It is a searing indictment of societies that permit the existence of poverty.

Life, itself, is cruel for the speakers in *Cruelty.* The speaker in "Tenant Farmer" has no crops. The couple in "Starvation" have no food. In "Abortion," a man finds the fetus of his son wrapped in wax paper and thinks: "the poor have no children, just small people/ and there is room for only one man in this house." Men and women become alienated from each other in these conditions. The speaker in "Young Farm Woman Alone" no longer wants a man. In "Recapture," a man finds and beats a woman who has run off from him. In "Prostitute," a woman kills her husband, then goes out to get revenge on the men who use her.

Out of the agony of their lives, some of Ai's characters achieve transcendence through love. The couple in "Anniversary" has managed to stay together, providing a home for their son for many years, in spite of never having "anything but hard times." In "The Country Midwife: A Day," the midwife delivers a woman's child for "the third time between abortions." Beneath the mother "a stain . . . spreads over the sheet." Crying out to the Lord, the midwife lets her bleed. Ending the cycles of pregnancy for the woman, in an act of mercy, the midwife takes upon herself the cross of guilt and suffering.

Ai extends her study of the causes and consequences of poverty to other times and places in the second half of *Cruelty.* The figure in "The Hangman" smells "the whole Lebanese coast/ in the upraised arms of Kansas." In "Cuba, 1962" a farmer cuts off his dead wife's feet, allowing her blood to mix with the sugar cane he will sell in the village, so everyone can taste his grief. Medieval peasants are evoked by "The Corpse Hauler's Elegy," although the plague victims he carries could also be contemporary.

Violence increases in the final poems of the book, a sign of the violence in societies that perpetuate social injustice. In "The Deserter," a soldier kills the woman who gave him shelter in order to leave everything of himself behind. In "The Hitchhiker," a woman is raped and killed by a psychopath in Arizona. In "The Child Beater," a mother beats her seven-year-old daughter with a belt, then gets out her "dog's chain leash." Ai has compassion for all of these people—including the killers—and she demands compassion for them from her readers.

Greed

TYPE OF WORK: Poetry
FIRST PUBLISHED: 1993

Greed is a collection of poems about the identity of America in the late twentieth century. In dramatic monologues spoken by famous or obscure Americans, Ai exposes amorality in the institutions of society, business, and private life. For most of the speakers, America has not kept its promises. Truth and justice are illusions in a society made more vicious, because of greed, than the Darwinian struggle for survival among animals. Money, power, drugs, sex—these are the gods of late twentieth century America.

To the African American speakers, slavery is still alive in the "big house" of white America. Violence is the result. In "Riot Act, April 29, 1992," a black man, going to get something on the day the wealth "finally trickled down," threatens to "set your world on fire." In "Self Defense," Marion Barry, mayor of Washington, D.C., trapped using crack cocaine by the FBI, warns: "The good ole days of slaves out pickin' cotton/ ain't coming back no more." In "Endangered Species," a black university professor, perceived as "a race instead of a man," is stopped by police while driving through his own neighborhood.

In "Hoover, Edgar J.," Ai indicts the director of the FBI for abuse of power. Hoover admits he has "files on everybody who counts" and "the will to use them." Deceptions by government are implicated in poems concerning the assassination of President John F. Kennedy. In "Jack Ruby on Ice," Ruby is refused sanctuary, in exchange for his testimony, by the Chief Justice of the United States. In "Oswald Incognito and Astral Travels," Oswald finds himself "trapped/ in the palace of lies,/ where I'm clothed in illusion/ and fed confusion with a spoon."

Other poems explore domestic violence and sexual abuse of children. In "Finished," a woman kills her husband after repeated episodes of physical abuse. In "Respect, 1967," such a man expresses rage "against the paycheck that must be saved for diapers/ and milk." The speaker in "Life Story" is a priest who sexually abuses young boys. As a child, he was abused by his uncle, also a priest. In "The Ice Cream Man," the speaker lures a little girl inside his truck to sexually molest her. He tells of his own abuse by his stepfather and his mother.

Ai offers little hope for the promise of America in *Greed*. She closes the book with the title poem, about the savings and loan scandal of the 1980's. The responsible working man in "Family Portrait, 1960" has little chance to succeed. Even so, he takes care of his sick wife, cooks dinner, oversees the baths of his young daughters, then dozes—"chaos kept at bay" for one more day.

SUGGESTED READINGS

Ai. "An Interview with Ai." Interview by Catherine French, Rebecca Ross, and Gary Short. *Hayden's Ferry Review* 5 (Fall, 1989): 11-31.

_____. "On Being One-Half Japanese, One-Eighth Choctaw, One Quarter Black, and One-Sixteenth Irish." *Ms.* 6 (May, 1978): 58.

Cuddihy, Michael, and Lawrence Kearney. "Ai: An Interview." *Ironwood* 12 (Winter, 1978): 27-34.

Leavitt, Michele. "Ai's 'Go.'" *The Explicator* 54 (Winter, 1996): 126-127.

Wilson, Rob. "The Will to Transcendence in Contemporary American Poet Ai." *Canadian Review of American Studies* 17, no. 4 (Winter, 1986): 437-448.

—*James Green*

Meena Alexander

BORN: Allahabad, India; February 17, 1951

*Alexander's work examines women in society from the perspective of an
expatriate feminist.*

TRADITIONS: South Asian
PRINCIPAL WORKS: *Stone Roots*, 1980; *House of a Thousand Doors: Poems and Prose
   Pieces*, 1988; *Women in Romanticism: Mary Wollstonecraft, Dorothy Wordsworth,
   and Mary Shelley*, 1989; *Fault Lines: A Memoir*, 1993; *Manhattan Music*, 1997

Meena Alexander spent her early life in Kerala, a state at the southwestern
tip of India. She received her English education in the Sudan, traveling
between her parents' home in Africa and her grandparents' home in India.
She received her bachelor's degree in 1969 from the University of Khartoum
and a Ph.D. from the University of Nottingham in 1973. After teaching at
universities in Delhi and Hyderabad, she moved to New York City in 1979.
By the age of forty-four, she had published six volumes of poetry, a novel, a
play, two volumes of literary criticism, and an autobiography.

Alexander describes herself as a "woman cracked by multiple migrations,"
acted on by the disparate and powerful influences of the languages and
customs of the four continents on which she has lived. Although her works
are written in English, she grew up speaking Malayalam, a Dravidian language of southwest India, and Arabic, the language of her Syrian Christian
heritage, spoken in North Africa. Her writing reflects the tension created by
the interplay of these influences and serves as a way to derive meaning from
her wide range of experience.

The most prominent theme of Alexander's work is the difficulty inherent
in being a woman, of having a woman's body and coping with the societal,
physiological, and personal pressures on and responses to that body as it
develops through childhood into maturity and middle age. Her grandmothers
serve as mythical figures with whom Alexander closely identifies. Her perspective is further complicated by her alienation from the language and
culture of her childhood, and by her need to recover something of that past.
The images of fecundity and beauty with which Alexander's work is suffused
derive from her youth in Kerala; these images may be juxtaposed with images
of infirmity, sterility, or brutality, underscoring the writer's need to integrate
the fragmented components of her life as an expatriate woman.

The imagination provides a synthesis of the elements of history and
personality in Alexander's work. Her poems "begin as a disturbance, a

jostling in the soul" which prompts her to write, seeking "that fortuitous, fleeting meaning, so precious, so scanty."

House of a Thousand Doors
TYPE OF WORK: Poetry
FIRST PUBLISHED: 1988

House of a Thousand Doors: Poems and Prose Pieces is a collection of fifty-nine poems and prose pieces. Alexander's poetry reflects her multicultural heritage and the tension it creates. The book is organized into three sections, the first and third sections serving as a synthesis for the wide variety of subjects and themes treated in the body of the work. Many of the poems reflect the writer's subjective response to her experience; many also project or create new experiences that underscore the importance of imagination as a lens through which to focus the inner life into poetry.

The title poem of *House of a Thousand Doors* uses the title metaphor to describe the variety of forces that operate on the persona: gender, heritage, language, experience, ideology, and the search for meaning. A complex array of images embodies these forces in the book, reflecting the author's sensitivity to their influence. Alexander uses her writing to integrate the diversity of her experience.

Dominating the persona's early life is the figure of her grandmother, a powerful member of the family who learned to exercise some control over the many lines of force that affected her life. The mature awareness of the persona is imposed on the re-created memory of herself as a girl watching the figure of the grandmother kneel in turn before each of the thousand doors on a never-ending pilgrimage, "a poor forked thing" praying for the favor of her ancestors. The grandmother becomes a figure of myth and a symbol of tradition serving as the focus of many of the poems in the collection. Conciliation and unity with the culture and solidity of the past are central to *House of a Thousand Doors.*

The three major sources of imagery in the book are family, culture, and nature. Family images, though literal, have a universal quality—she describes finding her grandmother's letters "in an old biscuit box" and wonders if her grandmother was, like herself, "inventing a great deal." Other images reflect the diminution of women at the behest of a patriarchal society; a cell door closing on a woman raped by the police clangs "like an old bell left over by the British," while a portrait of the pacifist leader Mohandas Gandhi looks down from the wall. A third class of imagery, the imagery of nature, reflects the persona's romantic theory of art; she laments, "My body/ part water/ part rock/ is searching for heaven." This searching brings her back to her past, real and mythical, and ultimately back to herself and her need for meaning.

SUGGESTED READINGS

Dave, Shilpa. "The Doors to Home and History: Post-Colonial Identities in Meena Alexander and Bharati Mukherjee." *Amerasia Journal* 19 (Fall, 1993): 103.

Duncan, Erika. "A Portrait of Meena Alexander." *World Literature Today* 73, no. 1 (Winter, 1999): 23-28.

Perry, John Oliver. Review of *House of a Thousand Doors*, by Meena Alexander. *World Literature Today* 63 (Winter, 1989): 163.

_____. Review of *Nampally Road*, by Meena Alexander. *World Literature Today* 65 (Spring, 1991): 364.

Rao, Susheela N. Review of *Fault Lines*, by Meena Alexander. *World Literature Today* 68 (Autumn, 1994): 883.

—Andrew B. Preslar

Sherman Alexie

BORN: Spokane Indian Reservation, Wellpinit, Washington;
October 7, 1966

*Alexie, an accomplished writer of poetry and fiction, is a spokesperson
for the realities of reservation life.*

TRADITIONS: American Indian
PRINCIPAL WORKS: *The Business of Fancydancing: Stories and Poems,* 1992; *First
Indian on the Moon,* 1993; *The Lone Ranger and Tonto Fistfight in Heaven,* 1993;
Old Shirts and New Skins, 1993; *Reservation Blues,* 1995; *Indian Killer,* 1996;
The Toughest Indian in the World, 2000

Sherman Alexie is a Spokane-Coeur d'Alene Indian who grew up in Wellpinit, Washington, on a reservation. He acknowledges that his origin and
upbringing affect everything that he does in his writing and otherwise.

Alexie's father retired from the Bureau of Indian Affairs and his mother
worked as a youth drug and alcohol counselor. The first of their five children
to leave the reservation, Alexie attended Gonzaga University in Spokane for
two years before entering Washington State University, where he studied
creative writing with Alex Kuo. He was graduated in 1991.

Among the five books Alexie produced between 1992 and 1995, the
seventy-seven-line free verse poem "Horses," from *Old Shirts and New Skins,*
typifies the passion, anger, and pain in some of his most effective poems.
Focused on the slaughter of a thousand Spokane horses by General George
Wright in 1858, the long lines echo obsessively: "1,000 ponies, the United
States Cavalry stole 1,000 ponies/ from the Spokane Indians, shot 1,000
ponies & only 1 survived." The poem is one of Alexie's favorites at readings,
where it acquires the incantatory power of the best oral poetry.

Although Alexie's poems often have narrative and dramatic qualities, he
is also adept at the short lyric, and his published work includes examples of
the sestina and the villanelle. "Reservation Love Song," from *The Business of
Fancydancing,* reflecting on the poverty of reservation life, with its govern-
ment-built housing and low-quality food, begins:

> I can meet you
> in Springdale buy you beer
> & take you home
> in my one-eyed Ford.

Sherman Alexie (Marion Ettlinger)

First Indian on the Moon is largely composed of prose poems. "Collect Calls" opens with an allusion to Crazy Horse, who appears often as a mythic figure in Alexie's writing: "My name is *Crazy Horse*, maybe it's *Neil Armstrong* or *Lee Harvey Oswald.* I am guilty of every crime; I was the first man on the moon." As in his fiction, Alexie tempers the anger and pain of his poems with satiric wit, as in "The Marlon Brando Memorial Swimming Pool," from *Old Shirts and New Skins,* in which activist Dennis Banks is imagined as "the first/ Native American real estate agent, selling a 5,000 gallon capacity dream/ in the middle of a desert." Not surprisingly, there is no water in the pool.

The Lone Ranger and Tonto Fistfight in Heaven

TYPE OF WORK: Short fiction
FIRST PUBLISHED: 1993

Alexie's initial foray into fiction (except for a few stories sprinkled among his poems), *The Lone Ranger and Tonto Fistfight in Heaven* appeared before his twenty-seventh birthday and was awarded a citation from the PEN/Hemingway Award committee for best first book of fiction in 1993. Praising his "live and unremitting lyric energy," one reviewer suggested that three of the twenty-two stories in the book "could stand in any collection of excellence."

Alexie grew up in Wellpinit, Washington, on the Spokane Indian Reservation; he is Spokane-Coeur d'Alene. Critics have noted that the pain and anger of the stories are balanced by his keen sense of humor and satiric wit. Alexie's readers will notice certain recurring characters, including Victor Joseph, who often appears as the narrator, Lester FallsApart, the pompous tribal police chief, David WalksAlong, Junior Polatkin, and Thomas Builds-the-Fire, the storyteller to whom no one listens. These characters also appear in Alexie's first novel, *Reservation Blues* (1995), so the effect is of a community; in this respect, Alexie's writings are similar to the fiction of William Faulkner. One reviewer has suggested that *The Lone Ranger and Tonto Fistfight in Heaven* is almost a novel, despite the fact that Alexie rarely relies on plot development in the stories and does not flesh out his characters. It might more aptly be said that the stories come close to poetry, just as Alexie's poems verge on fiction. The stories range in length from less than three to about twenty pages, and some of the best, like "The First Annual All-Indian Horseshoe Pitch and Barbecue," leap from moment to moment, from one-liner to quickly narrated episode, much like a poem.

That story begins, "Someone forgot the charcoal; blame the BIA." The next sentence concerns Victor playing the piano just before the barbecue: "after the beautiful dissonance and implied survival, the Spokane Indians wept, stunned by this strange and familiar music." Survival is a repeated theme in Alexie's work. The story then jumps to a series of four short paragraphs, each beginning "There is something beautiful about. . . ." Then we are told that Simon won at horseshoes, and he "won the coyote contest when he told us that basketball should be our new religion." A paragraph near the end is composed of a series of questions, each beginning "Can you hear the dreams?" The last paragraph features a child born of a white mother and an Indian father, with the mother proclaiming: "Both sides of this baby are beautiful."

Beneath the anger, pain, and satiric edge of his stories, often haunted by the mythic figure of Crazy Horse and tinged with fantasy, Alexie offers hope for survival and reconciliation.

Reservation Blues
TYPE OF WORK: Novel
FIRST PUBLISHED: 1995

Alexie's first novel, *Reservation Blues*, was published before his thirtieth birthday and after the striking success of *The Business of Fancydancing* (1992), a collection of poems and stories published by a small press when he was twenty-six. By the time his novel was being reviewed, nearly eight thousand copies of *The Business of Fancydancing* were in print, along with two additional collections of poetry, *Old Shirts and New Skins* and *First Indian on the Moon*, and a heralded book of short stories, *The Lone Ranger and Tonto Fistfight in Heaven*, all published in 1993.

In his novel Alexie reasserts an equation that he formed in "Imagining the Reservation," from *The Lone Ranger and Tonto Fistfight in Heaven:* "Survival = Anger ' Imagination. Imagination is the only weapon on the reservation." *Reservation Blues* is arguably the most imaginative of his works to date, blending, among other things, the Faust myth with life on the "rez" and the dream of making it big in the music world. Alexie has performed in his own blues band.

The novel is haunted by the bad memories (the essence of the blues) and by several characters' nightmares, including Junior Polatkin, Victor, and Thomas Builds-the-Fire, all of whom are familiar from other stories and poems by Alexie. The role of the deity in the novel is played by Big Mom, who lives atop a mountain on the reservation and has powerful magic. The story gets underway when a black blues guitarist from Mississippi, Robert Johnson (a historical personage) who has sold his soul to the devil (a white man known as "The Gentleman") for a magic guitar wanders onto the reservation and passes his literally hot guitar to Victor.

On their way to success and fame the group acquires a pair of vocalists in Chess and Checkers, two Flathead women, and two groupies, Indian "wanna-be's," Betty and Veronica, named after characters in the Archie comic series. When Betty observes that white people want to be like Indians so they can live at peace with the earth and be wise, Chess says, "You've never spent a few hours in the Powwow Tavern. I'll show you wise and peaceful."

The destruction of the dream comes when the group goes to New York, where they find that their exploitative agents are none other than Phil Sheridan (source of the words "The only good Indian is a dead Indian") and George Wright (who commanded the soldiers that slaughtered the Spokane ponies in 1858, a recurring motif in Alexie's work). They work for Calvary Records. This novel encompasses broad humor, but the laughter is almost always painful. The satiric thrust, the travel, and the ironies attendant on innocents abroad suggest that *Reservation Blues* belongs to the tradition of Voltaire's *Candide* (1759).

SUGGESTED READINGS

Bellante, John, and Carl Bellante. "Sherman Alexie, Literary Rebel." *Bloomsbury Review* 14 (May-June, 1994): 14-15, 26.

Busch, Frederick. "Longing for Magic." *The New York Times Book Review,* July 16, 1995, 9-10.

Kincaid, James R. "Who Gets to Tell Their Stories?" *The New York Times Book Review* 97 (May 3, 1992): 1, 24-29.

Price, Reynolds. "One Indian Doesn't Tell Another." *The New York Times Book Review* 98 (October 17, 1993): 15-16.

Silko, Leslie Marmon. "Big Bingo." *Nation* 260 (June 12, 1995): 856-858, 860.

Teters, Charlene. "Poet, Novelist, Filmmaker Sherman Alexie: Spokane, Coeur d'Alene." *Indian Artist* 4, no. 2 (Spring, 1998): 30-35.

—Ron McFarland

Paula Gunn Allen

BORN: Cubero, New Mexico; October 24, 1939

As a novelist, poet, literary critic, and scholar, Allen preserves and creates Native American literature.

TRADITIONS: American Indian

PRINCIPAL WORKS: *The Blind Lion,* 1974; *Coyote's Daylight Trip,* 1978; *A Cannon Between My Knees,* 1981; *Star Child,* 1981; *Shadow Country,* 1982; *The Woman Who Owned the Shadows,* 1983; *Studies in American Indian Literature,* 1983; *The Sacred Hoop: Recovering the Feminine in American Indian Traditions,* 1986; *Wyrds,* 1987; *Skins and Bones: Poems 1979-87,* 1988; *Spider Woman's Granddaughters: Traditional Tales and Contemporary Writing by Native American Women,* 1989 (editor); *Off the Reservation: Reflections on Boundary-Busting, Border-Crossing Loose Canons,* 1998

Paula Gunn Allen, as an American Indian woman, sees her identity in relation to a larger community. She is proud to be part of an old and honored tradition that appreciates the beautiful, the harmonious, and the spiritual. She also recognizes that since in the United States there are more than a million non-Indians to every Indian, she must work to stay connected to her Native American heritage.

Allen frequently refers to herself as "a multicultural event"; people of many ethnicities are related to her. Her mother was a Laguna Indian whose grandfather was Scottish American. Allen says that she was raised Roman Catholic, but living next door were her grandmother, who was Presbyterian and Indian and her grandfather, who was a German Jew. Her father's family came from Lebanon; he was born in a Mexican land-grant village north of Laguna Pueblo. She grew up with relatives who spoke Arabic, English, Laguna, German, and Spanish. Her

Paula Gunn Allen (Tama Rothschild)

relatives shared legends from around the world.

Even with such cultural diversity in her family, as a teenager Allen could find no Native American models for her writing. Consequently, she read Charlotte Brontë's *Jane Eyre: An Autobiography* (1847) about twenty times; her other literary favorites were Louisa May Alcott, Gertrude Stein, and the Romantic poets John Keats and Percy Bysshe Shelley. When she went to the University of New Mexico and wanted to focus on Native American literature in her Ph.D. program in English, it was impossible. The scholarship was not there to study. She came to write the books that she wanted to read and teach the courses that she wanted to take.

Allen has taught at San Francisco State University, at the University of New Mexico, in the Native American Studies Program at the University of California at Berkeley, and at the University of California, Los Angeles.

In enumerating the influences that have made her who she is, Allen first honors her mother, who taught her to think like a strong Indian woman and that animals, insects, and plants are to be treated with the deep respect one customarily reserves for high-status humans. She honors her father for teaching her how to weave magic, memory, and observation into the tales she tells. Finally, the Indian collective unconscious remains the source of her vision of spiritual reality.

The Sacred Hoop
TYPE OF WORK: Essays
FIRST PUBLISHED: 1986

The collection of essays *The Sacred Hoop: Recovering the Feminine in American Indian Traditions* documents the continuing vitality of American Indian traditions and the crucial role of women in those traditions. The title comes from a lesson Allen learned from her mother: that all of life is a circle—a sacred hoop—in which everything has its place. These essays, like tribal art of all kinds, support the principle of kinship and render the beautiful in terms of the harmony, relationship, balance, and dignity that are the informing principles of Indian aesthetics. Indians understand that woman is the sun and the earth: She is grandmother, mother, thought, wisdom, dream, reason, tradition, memory, deity, and life itself.

The essays are all characterized by seven major themes that pertain to American Indian identity. The first is that Indians and spirits are always found together. Second, Indians endure. Third, the traditional tribal lifestyles are never patriarchal and are more often woman-centered than not. Tribal social systems are nurturing, pacifist, and based on ritual and spirit-centered, woman-focused worldviews. The welfare of the young is paramount, the complementary nature of all life forms is stressed, and the centrality of powerful, self-defining, assertive, decisive women to social well-being is unquestioned. Fourth, the physical and cultural destruction of American

Indian tribes is and was about patriarchal fear and the inability to tolerate women's having decision-making capacity at every level of society. Fifth, there is such a thing as American Indian literature, and it informs all American writing. Sixth, all Western studies of American Indian tribal systems are erroneous because they view tribalism from the cultural bias of patriarchy. Seventh, the sacred ways of the American Indian people are part of a worldwide culture that predates Western systems.

These powerful essays are divided into three sections: "The Ways of Our Grandmothers," "The Word Warriors," and "Pushing Up the Sky." All of them testify to the value of American Indian traditions and the strength of the voices of Indian women. Allen identifies the Indian roots of white feminism as well as the role of lesbians in American culture, and she projects future visions for American Indian women, tribes, and literature.

Spider Woman's Granddaughters
TYPE OF WORK: Biography and short fiction
FIRST PUBLISHED: 1989

Spider Woman's Granddaughters: Traditional Tales and Contemporary Writing by Native American Women, edited by Allen, is a collection of two dozen traditional tales, biographical writings, and short stories by seventeen accomplished American Indian women writers. All the women follow the tradition of Grandmother Spider, who, according to the Cherokee, brought the light of thought to her people, who were living as hostages in their own land. These stories are war stories, since all American Indian women are at war and have been for five hundred years.

Some of the selections are old-style stories; others deal with contemporary issues. All are by women intimately acquainted with defeat, with being conquered, and with losing the right and the authority to control their personal and communal lives. They have experienced the devastating destruction of their national and personal identities. They powerfully demonstrate the Indian slogan: We shall endure.

The first selection, "The Warriors," contains eleven stories of strong women who are self-defining, fearless, respectful, prayerful, and self-assertive. Their warpath is an odyssey through a brutal and hostile world. Each recognizes that the Indian family must continue to cling to tradition. A warrior must remember where she comes from; beauty is what gives human beings dignity; and the young must be taught how to keep their sense of value intact. These women warriors do not give up hope, even when they are dying, their children are stolen, and they are undergoing emotional and physical battering. They continue to resist when all the forces of a wealthy, powerful, arrogant, ignorant, and uncaring nation are mustered against them in order to coerce their capitulation.

The second section, "The Casualties," contains five selections about Indian women who have been wounded in the continuing war that seeks to destroy rather than enhance their individual and collective spiritual power. For example, Linda Hogan's "Making Do" is about a mother's powerlessness in the face of loss and grief. She clings to her tribal traditions and carves wooden birds, hoping to regain the power, healing, and grace that were traditionally put into carvings.

The third section, "The Resistance," contains eight selections that are more hopeful. Since the 1960's, Native Americans have become more involved in the administration of the economic and legal affairs of their tribes. "Deep Purple," by Allen, a Native American urban lesbian who loves a white woman, addresses the issue of colonization in the women's movement and tries to reclaim her connection to the spiritual powers of the past. Like all the granddaughters of Spider Woman, she is aware of her responsibilities, gifts, and identity.

SUGGESTED READINGS

Albers, Patricia, and Beatrice Medicine. *The Hidden Half: Studies of Plains Indian Women.* Lanham, Md.: University Press of America, 1983.

Allen, Paula Gunn, ed. *Studies in American Indian Literature.* New York: Modern Language Association of America, 1983.

Bataille, Gretchen M., Kathleen Mullen Sands, and Charles L. P. Silet, eds. *The Pretend Indians: Images of Native Americans in the Movies.* Iowa City: University of Iowa Press, 1980.

Brandon, William. *The Last American: The Indian in American Culture.* New York: McGraw-Hill, 1974.

Bruchac, Joseph, ed. *Survival This Way: Interviews with American Indian Poets.* Tucson: University of Arizona Press, 1987.

Chapman, Abraham. *Literature of the American Indians: Views and Interpretations.* New York: New American Library, 1975.

Coltelli, Laura. *Winged Words: American Indian Writers Speak.* Lincoln: University of Nebraska Press, 1990.

Deloria, Vine, Jr. *God Is Red.* New York: Grosset & Dunlap, 1973. Reprint. New York: Dell Books, 1983.

Etienne, Mona, and Eleanor Leacock, eds. *Women and Colonization: Anthropological Perspectives.* New York: Praeger, 1980.

Fisher, Dexter, ed. *The Third Woman: Minority Women Writers of the United States.* Boston: Houghton Mifflin, 1980.

Hanson, Elizabeth I. *Paula Gunn Allen.* Boise State University Western Writers Series 96. Boise, Idaho: Boise State University Press, 1990.

Keating, AnaLouise. *Women Reading Women Writing: Self-Invention in Paula Gunn Allen, Gloria Anzaldúa, and Audre Lorde.* Philadelphia: Temple University Press, 1996.

Swann, Brian, and Arnold Krupat, eds. *I Tell You Now: Autobiographical Essays by Native American Writers.* Lincoln: University of Nebraska Press, 1987.

—Constance M. Fulmer

Isabel Allende

BORN: Lima, Peru; August 2, 1942

*Allende brings a feminist perspective to the traditions of Latin
American literature.*

TRADITIONS: Latino

PRINCIPAL WORKS: *La casa de los espíritus,* 1982 (*The House of the Spirits,* 1985);
De amor y de sombra, 1984 (*Of Love and Shadows,* 1987); *Eva Luna,* 1987
(English translation, 1988); *El plan infinito,* 1991 (*The Infinite Plan,* 1993);
Paula, 1994 (English translation, 1995); *Hija de la fortuna,* 1999 (*Daughter of
Fortune,* 1999)

The daughter of a Chilean diplomat, Isabel Allende was born in Lima, Peru.
Following her parents' divorce, she lived first with her grandparents in
Santiago and later with her mother and stepfather in Europe and the Middle
East. She returned to Chile as a young woman and began her career as a
television and newsreel journalist and as a writer for a feminist journal.

In 1973, Allende found herself at the center of Chile's turbulent political
life when her uncle and godfather, the country's Marxist president Salvador
Allende, was assassinated during a military coup. In the months that followed, Allende worked to oppose the new dictatorship headed by General
Pinochet until fears for her safety led Allende to move to Venezuela with her
husband and two children.

Allende's first novel, *The House of the Spirits,* was published to international
acclaim. It is a family saga set against a backdrop of political upheaval in an
unnamed South American country. Her second book, *Of Love and Shadows,*
followed two years later and also drew on her country's troubled history. Both
works placed Allende firmly within the Latin American tradition of novels
that take a strong stand in their fictionalized portrayals of political events.
Allende's third novel, *Eva Luna,* traces the extraordinary life of its title
character and the Austrian journalist who becomes her lover. All three novels
are examples of the literary style known as Magical Realism, in which
strange, supernatural occurrences are intermingled with everyday events.
Allende's work, however, brings a distinctly feminist perspective to a literary style that is predominantly male.

Following her divorce from her husband of twenty years, Allende moved
to the United States in the 1980's, where she remarried and settled in
California. Her next novel, *The Infinite Plan,* draws on her American experience in its story of a man's life from his childhood in the barrios of Los

Angeles to his adult search for meaning and happiness. In 1995, Allende published one of her most personal works, *Paula*, a chronicle of her daughter's death following a long illness. Allende examines her experience as a woman and a mother in her portrayal of love, pain, and loss.

Allende's position as a woman working within the traditions of Latin American literature has led her to create strikingly original stories and characters, and she remains a consistently intriguing and rewarding writer.

The House of the Spirits
TYPE OF WORK: Novel
FIRST PUBLISHED: *La casa de los espíritus*, 1982 (English translation, 1985)

The House of the Spirits, Allende's first novel, established her international reputation and remains her best-known work. Drawing on the Latin American literary style known as Magical Realism, the book tells the story of the Trueba family over several generations. Set in an unidentified South American country that resembles Allende's homeland, the novel chronicles the social and political forces that affect the family's fate.

The story begins with Esteban Trueba and his marriage to Clara del Valle, a young woman who possesses clairvoyant gifts and communicates easily with the spirit world. Their marriage produces a daughter, Blanca, and twin sons. Esteban also fathers a son by one of the peasant women on his family estate; years later his illegitimate grandson, a member of the secret police, will torture his legitimate granddaughter, Alba, a political prisoner. Esteban's political ambitions take him to the country's senate, where he opposes left-wing reform efforts, while Blanca's affair with an idealistic peasant boy results in Alba's birth. The boy becomes a populist songwriter and a leading figure in the Socialist movement. A subsequent leftist victory is short-lived, however, and the elected government is deposed in a military coup. Alba, who has married one of the leftist leaders, is arrested and tortured before her grandfather can secure her release. In an effort to come to terms with all that has happened to her and to her family, she sets about writing the book that will become *The House of the Spirits*.

Allende's novel has been compared to Gabriel García Márquez's masterpiece *Cien años de soledad* (1967; *One Hundred Years of Solitude*, 1970) in style and structure and in the use of Magical Realism, a technique that combines ordinary events with the fantastic and miraculous, giving rise to startling and vivid imagery. Allende herself maintains that much that seems incredible in the book is drawn from memories of her childhood. The characters of Esteban and Clara Trueba are based on her own maternal grandparents, and she began the book not as a novel but as a letter to her aging grandfather meant to reassure him that the family stories would live on through her. The book's political themes are also taken in part from Allende's family history;

her uncle was Salvador Allende, the Socialist president slain in Chile's 1973 military coup.

The House of the Spirits brings a strong female voice to the forefront of Latin American literature and offers a collection of vital female characters who embody the book's spirit of endurance, resilience, and courage.

The Infinite Plan

TYPE OF WORK: Novel
FIRST PUBLISHED: *El plan infinito,* 1991 (English translation, 1993)

The Infinite Plan was Allende's first novel following her move to the United States. Although it was written in Spanish, the book is set in California and chronicles the life of a European American man. Allende uses her character's experiences to examine the factors that shaped the United States' social history in the decades following World War II. Her focus is the Latino culture in California, in which the main character comes of age.

As the book opens, young Gregory Reeves and his family are living a nomadic life as his father preaches a spiritual doctrine he calls the Infinite Plan. When the elder Reeves falls ill in Los Angeles, the family settles in the barrio (although they are not Latino). Gregory grows up experiencing life as a member of a minority group within the community. His closest friend is Carmen Morales, whose family comes to regard him as an honorary son. Following high school, Gregory leaves home for Berkeley and college while Carmen remains in the barrio until an unwanted pregnancy and near-fatal abortion make her an outcast.

Gregory leaves an unhappy marriage to serve a harrowing tour of duty in Vietnam, while Carmen lives abroad and begins designing jewelry. Both meet again in Berkeley, where Gregory embarks on an ambitious quest for success that leads him away from his youthful idealism and into a second failed marriage and problems with alcoholism. Carmen adopts her dead brother's half-Vietnamese son and discovers a strong sense of herself, marrying an old friend and settling in Italy. Gregory begins at last to take stock of his life and to see the pattern—the infinite plan—that has shaped it.

Allende's first novel set in her adopted country reflects her perspective on the United States as an immigrant. Her delight in tolerance and open-ness—matters of great importance to a writer whose life was marred by the repressive military coup in Chile in 1973—is apparent in her affectionate portrait of the freewheeling Berkeley of the 1960's. Her cultural identity as a Latina also comes into play in her portrayal of life in the barrio and the effect that religion and a patriarchal society have on Carmen.

Allende makes use in the novel of some aspects of the Latin American literary style known as Magical Realism, bringing a kind of heightened realism to the story, which blends realistic events with exaggerated or improbable ones. The result is a book filled with memorable characters that brings a fresh perspective to the post-World War II history and culture of the United States.

SUGGESTED READINGS

Allende, Isabel. "Writing as an Act of Hope." In *The Art and Craft of the Political Novel,* edited by William Zinsser. Boston: Houghton Mifflin, 1989.

Bly, Robert. Review of *The Infinite Plan,* by Isabel Allende. *The New York Times Book Review,* May 16, 1993, 13.

Foster, David William, ed. *Handbook of Latin American Literature.* New York: Garland, 1987.

Meyer, Doris, and Margarite Fernandez Olmos, eds. *Contemporary Women Authors of Latin America.* New York: Brooklyn College Press, 1983.

Rodden, John, ed. *Conversations with Isabel Allende.* Austin: University of Texas Press, 1999.

Zinsser, William, ed. *Paths of Resistance: The Art and Craft of the Political Novel.* Boston: Houghton Mifflin, 1989.

–Janet E. Lorenz

Julia Alvarez

BORN: New York, New York; March 27, 1950

Alvarez expresses the complexities of being cross cultural and an immigrant to the United States.

TRADITIONS: Caribbean, Dominican American

PRINCIPAL WORKS: *Homecoming: Poems,* 1984; *How the García Girls Lost Their Accents,* 1991; *In the Time of the Butterflies,* 1994; *The Other Side-El Otro Lado,* 1995; *Something to Declare,* 1998

Although she was born in New York City, Julia Alvarez spent much of her childhood in the Dominican Republic. Her parents were from the island. Her mother came from a well-positioned and wealthy family, but her father was rather poor. The family's divided economic position was tied to political problems within the Dominican Republic. Her father's family, which once was wealthy, supported the losing side during the revolution, while her mother's family benefited from supporting those who gained power. Julia's family, although poorer than most of their relatives, enjoyed a privileged position in the Dominican Republic.

Although she was raised in the Dominican Republic, Alvarez describes her childhood as "an American childhood." Her extended family's power, influence, American connections, and wealth led to Alvarez's enjoying many of the luxuries of America, including American food, clothes, and friends. When Alvarez's father became involved with the forces attempting to oust the dictator of the Dominican Republic, Rafaél Leonidas Trujillo Molina, the secret police began monitoring his activity. Immediately before he was to be arrested in 1960, the family escaped to the United States with the help of an American agent. In an article appearing in *American Scholar* ("Growing Up American in the Dominican Republic") published in 1987, Alvarez notes that all her life she had wanted to be a true American girl. She thought, in 1960, that she was going to live in her homeland, America.

Living in America was not quite what Alvarez expected. As her fictional but partly autobiographical novel *How the García Girls Lost Their Accents* hints, Alvarez was faced with many adjustments in America. She experienced homesickness, alienation, and prejudice. Going from living on a large family compound to living in a small New York apartment was, in itself, quite an adjustment. Alvarez's feeling of loss when moving to America caused a change in her. She became introverted, began to read avidly, and eventually began writing.

Alvarez attended college, earning degrees in literature and writing. She took a position as an English professor at Middlebury College in Vermont. She has published several collections of poetry, but her best-known work is her semiautobiographical novel *How the García Girls Lost Their Accents.* Alvarez can be praised for her portrayal of bicultural experiences, particularly for her focusing on the women's issues that arise out of such an experience.

Julia Alvarez (Algonquin Books)

How the García Girls Lost Their Accents

TYPE OF WORK: Novel
FIRST PUBLISHED: 1991

Set in New York City and the Dominican Republic, Alvarez's novel traces the lives of the four García sisters—Carla, Sandra, Yolanda, and Sofia—as they struggle to understand themselves and their cross-cultural identities. The novel is structured in three parts, focusing on the time spans of 1989-1972, 1970-1960, and 1960-1956. Throughout these years the García girls mature and face various cultural, familial, and individual crises. The sisters' mother, Laura, comes from the well-known, wealthy de la Torres family, who live in the Dominican Republic. The third part of the novel narrates the Garcías' flight from their homeland due to political problems within the country.

The Garcías emigrate to the United States, planning to stay only until the situation in their homeland improves. Once arriving in America, the sisters struggle to acclimate themselves to their new environment. The second part of the novel traces the sisters' formative years in the United States. Included among the numerous stories told are Yolanda's struggle to write an acceptable speech for a school event, Carla's trial of attending a new public school where she is bombarded by racial slurs, and Sandra's hatred of an American woman who flirts with her father during a family night out. In addition, part 2 narrates the García girls' summer trips to the Dominican Republic—their parents' way to keep them from becoming too Americanized. During these trips the García sisters realize that although they face great struggles as immigrants in the United States, they have much more freedom as young women in the United States than they do in the Dominican Republic.

Part 1 of the novel begins with Yolanda, who is known as the family poet, returning to the Dominican Republic as an adult. She discovers that the situation in her country has not changed. When she wants to travel to the coast alone, her relatives warn her against it. This early chapter sets Yolanda up as the primary narrator and introduces the tension between the traditions of the island and the new and different culture of the United States. In this first part readers learn about the girls' young adult lives, primarily about their sexual awareness, relationships, and marriages. Virginity is a primary issue, for the sisters' traditions and customs haunt them as they negotiate their sexual awakenings throughout their college years in the United States. In short, it is in this first part in which readers learn precisely how Americanized the García girls have become, and throughout the rest of the novel readers learn how the girls have lost their "accents" gradually, throughout the years.

SUGGESTED READINGS

Alvarez, Julia. "An American Childhood in the Dominican Republic." *The American Scholar* 56 (Winter, 1987): 71-85.

Garcia-Johnson, Ronie-Richele. "Julía Alvarez." In *Notable Hispanic American Women*, edited by Diane Telgen and Jim Kamp. Detroit: Gale Research, 1993.

Prescott, Stephanie. "Julia Alvarez: Dominican American Storyteller." *Faces* 15, no. 6 (February, 1999): 30-32.

—Angela Athy

Rudolfo A. Anaya

BORN: Pastura, New Mexico; October 30, 1937

Anaya became one of the foremost Chicano novelists of the twentieth century.

TRADITIONS: Mexican American

PRINCIPAL WORKS: *Bless Me, Ultima,* 1972; *Heart of Aztlán,* 1976; *Tortuga,* 1979; *The Silence of the Llano,* 1982; *Alburquerque,* 1992; *Zia Summer,* 1995; *Jalamanta,* 1996; *Rio Grande Fall,* 1996

Rudolfo Anaya began writing during his days as a student at the University of New Mexico. His poetry and early novels dealt with major questions about his existence, beliefs, and identity. Anaya ended that phase of his life by burning all of the manuscripts of his work.

After college he took a teaching job and got married. He found his wife to be a great source of encouragement and an excellent editor and companion. Anaya began writing *Bless Me, Ultima* in the 1960's. He struggled with the work until in one of his creative moments Ultima appeared to him. She became the strongest character of the novel as well as the spiritual mentor for the novelist and the protagonist. Ultima led the way to a successful work. Anaya's next task was to get his novel published. After dozens of rejection letters from major publishers, Anaya

Rudolfo A. Anaya (Michael Mouchette)

turned to Quinto Sol Publications, a Chicano small press in Berkeley, California. The publishers not only accepted the work for publication but also recognized Anaya with the Quinto Sol Award for writing the best Chicano novel of 1972.

Bless Me, Ultima represents the first novel of a trilogy. The other two are *Heart of Aztlán* and *Tortuga*. *Heart of Aztlán* came as a result of Anaya's travels in Mexico during the 1960's, which raised the question of the relationship between the pre-Columbian Aztec world, called Aztlán, and Chicano destiny. *Tortuga* was inspired by a diving accident at an irrigation ditch during Anaya's high school days. The accident left Anaya disabled; the protagonist in the novel also experiences such events. The quality of the first three works enshrined Anaya as the foremost Chicano novelist of his time. His numerous other excellent works have confirmed this high regard. The essence of his literary production reflects the search for the meaning of existence as it is expressed in Chicano community life.

Anaya's works blend realistic description of daily life with the hidden magic of humanity; his work may be categorized as having the qualities of Magical Realism, which mingles, in a straightforward narrative tone, the mystical and magical with the everyday. Most of his developed characters reflect this duality.

Bless Me, Ultima
TYPE OF WORK: Novel
FIRST PUBLISHED: 1972

Bless Me, Ultima is Anaya's first novel of a trilogy that also includes *Heart of Aztlán* (1976) and *Tortuga* (1979). It is a psychological and magical portrait of a quest for identity by a child. In this classic work, Antonio, the protagonist, is subjected to contradicting influences that he must master in order to mature. These influences include symbolic characters and places, the most powerful of which are Ultima, a *curandera* who evokes the timeless past of a pre-Columbian world, and a golden carp, which swims the river waters of the supernatural and offers a redeeming future.

Antonio is born in Pasturas, a very small village on the Eastern New Mexican plain. Later, the family moves across the river to the small town of Guadalupe, where Antonio spends his childhood. His father belongs to the Márez family and is a cattleman; Antonio's mother is of the Luna family, whose background is farming. They represent the initial manifestation of the divided world into which Antonio is born. Division is a challenge he must resolve in order to find himself. Antonio's father wants him to become a horseman of the plain. Antonio's mother wants him to become a priest to a farming community, which is in the highest tradition of the Luna family.

The parents' wishes are symptoms of a deeper spiritual challenge facing

Antonio involving his Catholic beliefs and those associated with the magical world of a pre-Columbian past. Ultima, the *curandera* and a creature of both worlds, helps guide Antonio through the ordeal of understanding and dealing with these challenges.

Ultima is a magical character who touches the core of Antonio's being. She supervised his birth. Later she comes to stay with the family in Guadalupe when Antonio is seven. On several occasions, Antonio is a witness to her power.

Antonio's adventure takes him beyond the divided world of the farmer and the horseman and beyond the Catholic ritual and its depictions of good and evil. With Ultima's help, he is able to bridge these opposites and channel them into a new cosmic vision of nature, represented by the river, which stands in the middle of his two worlds, and by the golden carp, which points to a new spiritual covenant.

The novel ends with the killing of Ultima's owl by one of her enemies. He discovered that the owl carried her spiritual presence. This killing also causes Ultima's death, but her work is done. Antonio can choose his destiny.

Heart of Aztlán
TYPE OF WORK: Novel
FIRST PUBLISHED: 1976

Heart of Aztlán is Anaya's second novel of a trilogy that includes *Bless Me, Ultima* (1972) and *Tortuga* (1979). It is a psychological portrait of a quest for Chicano identity and empowerment. It is the story of the Chávez family, who leave the country to search for a better life in the city only to discover that their destiny lies in a past thought abandoned and lost.

The story is carried by two major characters, Clemente Chávez, the father, and Jason, one of the sons. Jason depicts the adjustments the family has to make to everyday life in the city. Clemente undergoes a magical rebirth that brings a new awareness of destiny to the community and a new will to fight for their birthright.

The novel begins with the Chávez family selling the last of their land and leaving the small town of Guadalupe for a new life in Albuquerque. They go to live in Barelas, a barrio on the west side of the city that is full of other immigrants from the country.

The Chávezes soon learn, as the other people of the barrio already know, that their lives do not belong to them. They are controlled by industrial interests represented by the railroad and a union that has sold out the workers. They are controlled by politicians through Mannie García, "el super," who delivers the community vote.

In Barelas, Clemente also begins to lose the battle of maintaining control of the family, especially his daughters, who no longer believe in his insistence on the tradition of respect and obedience to the head of the family. The situation gets worse when Clemente loses his job in the railroad yard during a futile strike.

Clemente becomes a drunk and in his despair attempts to commit suicide. Crespín, a magical character who represents eternal wisdom, comes to his assistance and points the way to a new life. With Crespín's help, Clemente solves the riddle of a magical power stone in the possession of "la India," a sorceress who symbolically guards the entryway to the heart of Aztlán, the source of empowerment for the Chicano.

Clemente's rebirth takes the form of a journey to the magical mountain lake that is at the center of Aztlán and Chicano being. Reborn, Clemente returns to his community to lead the movement for social and economic justice. It is a redeeming and unifying struggle for life and the destiny of a people.

The novel ends with Clemente physically taking a hammer to the Santa Fe water tower in the railroad yard, a symbol of industrial might, before coming home to lead a powerful march on his former employers.

Tortuga

TYPE OF WORK: Novel
FIRST PUBLISHED: 1979

Tortuga is Anaya's third novel of a trilogy that also includes *Bless Me, Ultima* (1972) and *Heart of Aztlán*. It is a tale of a journey to self-realization and supernatural awareness. In the story, Benjie Chávez, the protagonist, undergoes the ordeal of symbolic rebirth in order to take the place of Crespín, the keeper of Chicano wisdom who, upon his death, leaves that task to the protagonist.

At the end of *Heart of Aztlán*, Benjie is wounded by his brother Jason's rival. Benjie falls from a rail yard water tower and is paralyzed. He is transported to a hospital in the South for rehabilitation. His entry into the hospital is also symbolically an entry into a world of supernatural transformation.

The hospital sits at the foot of Tortuga Mountain, from which flow mineral springs with healing waters. Benjie is also given the name Tortuga (which means "turtle") after he is fitted with a body cast that makes him look like a turtle. What follows is a painful ordeal. The protagonist is subjected to demanding therapy and is exposed to every kind of suffering and deformity that can possibly afflict children. Not even this, however, prepares him for the visit to the "vegetable" ward, where rotting children—who cannot move or even breathe without the help of an iron lung—are kept alive.

It is in the vegetable ward that Tortuga meets Salomón, a vegetable, but one with supernatural insight into the human condition. Salomón enters Tortuga's psyche and guides him on the path to spiritual renewal. Salomón compares Tortuga's challenge with the terrible ordeal newly born turtles undergo as they dash to the sea. Most of them do not make it, as other creatures lie in wait to devour them. Tortuga must survive the path of the turtles' dash in order to arrive at his destiny, which is called "the path of the sun."

Another part of Tortuga's ordeal includes a moment when Danny, another important character, pushes him into a swimming pool, where he nearly drowns, surviving only because other people rush to his aid. Tortuga symbolically survives the turtle dash to the sea. The vegetables are not so lucky. One night Danny succeeds in turning off the power to their ward. With the iron lungs turned off, they all die.

The end of the novel and Tortuga's rehabilitation also bring the news that Crespín, the magical helper of Tortuga's home neighborhood, has died. The news of Crespín's death arrives along with his blue guitar, a symbol of universal knowledge, which is now in Benjie's care.

SUGGESTED READINGS

Dick, Bruce, and Silvio Sirias, eds. *Conversations with Rudolfo Anaya.* Jackson: University of Mississippi Press, 1998.

González-T., César A., ed. *Rudolfo A. Anaya: Focus on Criticism.* La Jolla, Calif.: Lalo Press, 1990.

Miguélez, Armando. "Anaya's *Tortuga.*" *Denver Quarterly* 16, no. 3 (1981): 120-121.

Restivo, Angelo. Review of *Tortuga,* by Rudolfo A. Anaya. *Fiction International* 12 (1980): 283-284.

Tatum, Charles M. *Chicano Literature.* Boston: Twayne, 1982.

Trejo, Arnulfo D. "*Bless Me, Ultima:* A Novel." *Arizona Quarterly* 29 (1973): 95-96.

Vasallo, Paul, ed. *The Magic of Words: Rudolfo Anaya and His Writings.* Albuquerque: University of New Mexico Press, 1982.

—David Conde

Maya Angelou
(Marguerite Johnson)

BORN: St. Louis, Missouri; April 4, 1928

Through poems and autobiographical narratives, Angelou describes her life as an African American, single mother, professional, and feminist.

TRADITIONS: African American

PRINCIPAL WORKS: *I Know Why the Caged Bird Sings*, 1970; *Just Give Me a Cool Drink of Water 'fore I Diiie*, 1971; *Gather Together in My Name*, 1974; *Oh Pray My Wings Are Gonna Fit Me Well*, 1975; *Singin' and Swingin' and Gettin' Merry Like Christmas*, 1976; *And Still I Rise*, 1978; *The Heart of a Woman*, 1981; *Shaker, Why Don't You Sing?*, 1983; *All God's Children Need Traveling Shoes*, 1986; *Wouldn't Take Nothing for My Journey Now*, 1993; *Even the Stars Look Lonesome*, 1997

Before her first autobiographical work, *I Know Why the Caged Bird Sings*, was published, Maya Angelou had a richly varied, difficult life. Her work has made her one of the most important African American female voices in the twentieth century. All of her writing is steeped in recollection of African American slavery and oppression. It also includes frank discussion of the physical and psychological pain of child abuse, the sexual anxieties of adolescence, unmarried motherhood, drug abuse, unhappy marriage, and divorce.

In *Gather Together in My Name*, Angelou struggles as a single mother to raise her son, while earning a living as Creole cook, army enlistee, madam, and prostitute. In *Singin' and Swingin' and Gettin' Merry Like Christmas*, she becomes a singer and an exotic dancer in San Francisco before joining the traveling cast of a George Gershwin musical on a twenty-two-nation tour. In *The Heart of a Woman*, she describes her later work as northern coordinator of Martin Luther King, Jr.'s Southern Christian Leadership Conference. In *All God's Children Need Traveling Shoes*, her frustrations with American racism and yearnings for her African roots lead her to a four-year stay in Ghana.

In her writings Angelou describes racism, prejudice, oppression, and other social ills. She comes to know males as pimps, drug pushers, occasional lovers, traditional and untraditional husbands, and Muslim polygamists. Angelou responds to these experiences with an increasing sense of what it means to be an African American woman in the twentieth century. In *Wouldn't Take Nothing for My Journey Now*, Angelou offers her philosophy of life based upon tolerance and respect for diversity.

All God's Children Need Traveling Shoes
TYPE OF WORK: Autobiography
FIRST PUBLISHED: 1986

All God's Children Need Traveling Shoes belongs to a series of autobiographical narratives tracing Angelou's personal search for identity as an African American woman. In this powerful tale, Angelou describes her emotional journey to find identity and ancestral roots in West Africa. Angelou reveals her excitement as she emigrates to Ghana in 1962 and attempts to redefine herself as African, not American. Her loyalty to Ghana's founding president, Kwame Nkrumah, reflects hope in Africa's and her own independence. She learns the Fanti language, toys with thoughts of marrying a prosperous Malian Muslim, communes with Ghanaians in small towns and rural areas, and identifies with her enslaved forebears. Monuments such as Cape Coast Castle, where captured slaves were imprisoned before sailing to America, stand on African soil as vivid reminders of an African American slave past.

In Ghana Angelou hopes to escape the lingering pains of American slavery and racism. Gradually, however, she feels displaced and uncomfortable in her African environment. Cultural differences and competition for employment result in unpleasant encounters between Ghanians and African Americans. Despite such frustrations, Angelou's network of fellow African American emigrants offers mutual support and continuing hope in the African experience. A visit by Malcolm X provides much-needed encouragement, but his presence is also a reminder of ties with the United States. Angelou and her African American friends express their solidarity with the American Civil Rights movement by demonstrating at the United States embassy in Ghana.

As she sorts through her ambivalent feelings about Africa, Angelou also rethinks her role as mother. At the beginning of *All God's Children Need Traveling Shoes*, Angelou's son Guy almost dies in an automobile accident. Later in the narrative he develops a relationship with an older woman and struggles to gain admittance to the University of Ghana. In dealing with all these events, Angelou learns to balance her maternal feelings with her son's need for independence and self-expression. Finally recognizing the powerful ties binding her to American soil, Angelou concludes her narrative with a joyful journey home from Ghana and a renewed sense of identity as an African American.

I Know Why the Caged Bird Sings
TYPE OF WORK: Autobiography
FIRST PUBLISHED: 1970

Angelou begins her autobiographical *I Know Why the Caged Bird Sings* with reflections about growing up black and female during the Great Depression in the small, segregated town of Stamps, Arkansas.

Maya Angelou (AP/Wide World Photos)

Following their parents' divorce, Angelou, then three years old, moved to Stamps with her brother Bailey to live with their paternal grandmother and uncle Willie. Their home was the general store, which served as the secular center of the African American community in Stamps. Angelou's memories of this store include weary farmworkers, the euphoria of Joe Louis's successful prizefight, and a terrifying nocturnal Ku Klux Klan hunt.

Angelou also recollects lively African American church services, unpleasant interracial encounters, and childhood sexual experimentation. An avid love of reading led the young Angelou to African American writers, including the poet Paul Laurence Dunbar, from whose verse Angelou borrows the title for her narrative.

Singing is heard in Angelou's memories of her segregated Arkansas school. At their grade-school graduation ceremony, Angelou and her classmates counter the racism of a condescending white politician with a defiant singing of James Weldon Johnson's "Lift Every Voice and Sing." For Angelou this song becomes a celebration of the resistance of African Americans to the white establishment and a key to her identity as an African American poet.

Angelou spends portions of the narrative with her mother in St. Louis and in California. She has a wild visit to Mexico with her father and is even a homeless runaway for a time. As a girl in St. Louis, Angelou is sexually abused by her mother's boyfriend. Following his trial and mysterious death, Angelou suffers a period of trauma and muteness. Later, an adolescent Angelou struggles with her sexual identity, fears that she is a lesbian, and eventually initiates an unsatisfactory heterosexual encounter, from which she becomes pregnant.

Angelou matures into a self-assured and proud young woman. During World War II, she overcomes racial barriers to become one of the first African American female streetcar conductors in San Francisco. Surviving the uncertainties of an unwanted pregnancy, Angelou optimistically faces her future as an unwed mother and as an African American woman.

Poetry

FIRST PUBLISHED: *Just Give Me a Cool Drink of Water 'fore I Diiie*, 1971; *Oh Pray My Wings Are Gonna Fit Me Well*, 1975; *And Still I Rise*, 1978; *Shaker, Why Don't You Sing?*, 1983; *The Complete Collected Poems of Maya Angelou*, 1994

Maya Angelou's poetry complements the search for self-identity as an African American woman described in her series of autobiographical narratives beginning with *I Know Why the Caged Bird Sings*. The caged bird image, which she borrows from a poem by African American poet Paul Laurence Dunbar, recurs in her work and expresses the collective yearning of African Americans for freedom as well as Angelou's search for individuality and independence.

In her poetry Angelou often focuses on the oppression of African Americans, including some that the media love to demonize: welfare mothers, prostitutes, and drug pushers. She describes the female African American experience with particular power in "Our Grandmothers," which begins with a slave mother dreading the approaching sale of her children. Angelou also proudly celebrates the accomplishments of African Americans such as Martin Luther King, Jr., and Malcolm X.

Angelou's childhood in Stamps, Arkansas, merges with the Southern slave experience of her African American ancestors in poems about Arkansas,

Georgia, Virginia, and the Southern slave plantation. Frequently, Angelou uses the vocabulary and slang of African American English. She also broadens her focus and speaks of urban African Americans and comfortable working white liberals.

Some of these themes are found in "On the Pulse of Morning," written for the inauguration of Bill Clinton as president of the United States in 1993. Using geographic references to Arkansas, to the Mississippi and Potomac Rivers, and to the many peoples of the United States, Angelou affirms the diversity and brotherhood of humanity and a dawn of equality in American history.

Another important theme for Angelou is Africa. Angelou lived in Ghana for the four years described in *All God's Children Need Traveling Shoes*. For Angelou, Africa's pyramids and history are a source of pride; its black inhabitants are a criterion of beauty.

Finally, in her poems Angelou reflects on love and her own erotic feelings. Her search for physical and emotional satisfaction in her relationships is sometimes satisfying and sometimes frustrating. Always, however, the poet Angelou defines herself as a woman and an African American.

SUGGESTED READINGS

Courtney-Clarke, Margaret. *Maya Angelou: The Poetry of Living.* New York: Clarkson Potter, 1999.

Elliot, Jeffrey M., ed. *Conversations with Maya Angelou.* Jackson: University Press of Mississippi, 1989.

Kallen, Stuart A. *Maya Angelou: Woman of Words, Deeds, and Dreams.* Edina, Minn.: Abdo and Daughters, 1993.

King, Sarah E. *Maya Angelou: Greeting the Morning.* Brookfield, Conn.: Millbrook, 1994.

Lisandrelli, Elaine Slivinski. *Maya Angelou: More Than a Poet.* Springfield, N.J.: Enslow, 1996.

McPherson, Dolly A. *Order out of Chaos.* London: Virago, 1990.

Pettit, Jayne. *Maya Angelou: Journey of the Heart.* New York: Lodestar Books, 1996.

Shapiro, Miles. *Maya Angelou.* Philadelphia: Chelsea House, 2000.

Shuker, Nancy. *Maya Angelou.* Morristown, N.J.: Silver Burdett, 1990.

Spain, Valerie. *Meet Maya Angelou.* New York: Random House, 1994.

Walker, Pierre A. "Racial Protest, Identity, Words and Form in Maya Angelou's *I Know Why the Caged Bird Sings.*" *College Literature* 22 (1995): 91-108.

—Thomas J. Sienkewicz

Mary Antin

BORN: Polotzk, Russia; June 13, 1881
DIED: Suffern, New York; May 17, 1949

Antin's The Promised Land *is the classic Jewish American immigrant autobiography.*

TRADITIONS: Jewish
PRINCIPAL WORKS: *From Plotzk to Boston*, 1899; *The Promised Land*, 1912; *They Who Knock at the Gates: A Complete Gospel of Immigration*, 1914; *Selected Letters of Mary Antin*, 1999

Mary Antin was born in Polotzk in what was then czarist Russia. Antin's place of birth and her Jewishness determined what her identity would have been had her family stayed in Polotzk. Had they stayed, she would have been an Orthodox Jewish wife of a Jewish man, the mother of Jewish children, and a woman with only enough education to enable her to read the Psalms in Hebrew. As a Jew, she could not live beyond the pale of settlement in Russia and could never become assimilated into Russian society. As a young child, she felt stifled by this identity.

In *The Promised Land* she compares her moving at age thirteen to America, where she felt she had freedom to choose her own identity, to the Hebrews' escape from bondage in Egypt. In America, she received a free education in Boston public schools. She had access to public libraries. She had access to settlement houses, like Hale House (in which she later worked), where she experienced American culture. She had a freedom of which she could hardly dream in Europe. The woman who in Polotzk would never have become more than barely literate chose for herself in the New World the identity of a writer and social worker. At fifteen, she published her first poem in the *Boston Herald*. At eighteen, she published her first autobiographical volume, *From Plotzk to Boston*, which resulted in her being hailed as a child prodigy. Eventually, she reworked the material from this book into her masterpiece, *The Promised Land*.

After being graduated from Girl's Latin School in Boston, Antin went to the Teachers' College of Columbia University in New York City and then to Barnard College, where she met and married Amadeus W. Grabau, a geologist, Columbia professor, and Gentile. She felt that her marriage cemented her chosen identity as a fully assimilated American. Although her husband eventually left her and settled in China, she never lost her faith in the possibilities of total assimilation into American society. She felt that since she had become fully assimilated, so could all other Jewish immigrants to the country she spoke of without irony as the promised land.

The Promised Land

TYPE OF WORK: Autobiography
FIRST PUBLISHED: 1912

The Promised Land is Antin's mature autobiography. In it, she tells the story of what she considers her escape from bondage in Eastern Europe and her finding of freedom in America. Early in the book, she compares herself to a treadmill horse who can only go round and round in the same circle. She sees herself in Polotzk in what was then Russia as imprisoned by her religion (Jews were allowed to live only in certain places in Czarist Russia and to work only at certain trades) and her sex (among Orthodox Jews in Eastern Europe, women were not permitted education beyond learning to read the Psalms in Hebrew).

After her father suffered a long illness and as a result failed in business, he went to America. His family followed him to Boston, where Mary grew up. In America, she felt that she had all the freedom she lacked in the Old World. She could get free secular education. The public schools of Boston, she felt, opened new intellectual vistas for her. She also had access to public libraries and settlement houses that provided her with cultural activities. Thus, she felt she had "a kingdom in the slums."

She responded to America's possibilities by doing extremely well in school and by publishing her first poem when she was fifteen. Her father proudly bought copies of the newspaper in which it appeared and distributed it to friends and neighbors, bragging about his daughter the writer.

She became a member of the Natural History Club of Boston, and through it, learned about the lives of its members who, she felt, represented what was best about America, a country in which she felt she was a welcomed participant. Visiting many of the members in their homes, she became convinced that she had true equality in America.

In her book, Antin says that if she could accomplish so much, so can all immigrants. She admits that her father, because of an inability to master the English language and because of bad luck, did not prosper in the New World, but she still remains optimistic about America and about the possibilities of total assimilation for America's immigrant population. Whereas the Old World represents, for her, lack of freedom and a predetermined identity, she sees the New World as representing freedom and the ability to choose her own identity.

SUGGESTED READINGS

Antin, Mary. *Selected Letters of Mary Antin.* Syracuse, N.Y.: Syracuse University Press, 1999.

Guttmann, Allen. *The Jewish Writer in America: Assimilation and the Crisis of Identity.* New York: Oxford University Press, 1971.

Liptzin, Sol. *The Jew in American Literature.* New York: Bloch, 1966.

Tuerk, Richard. "At Home in the Land of Columbus: Americanization in European-American Immigrant Autobiography." In *Multicultural Autobiography: American Lives,* edited by James Robert Payne. Knoxville: University of Tennessee Press, 1992.

————. "Jewish-American Literature." In *Ethnic Perspectives in American Literature: Selected Essays on the European Contribution,* edited by Robert J. DiPietro and Edward Ifkovic. New York: Modern Language Association of America, 1983.

—*Richard Tuerk*

Reinaldo Arenas

BORN: Holguín, Oriente, Cuba; July 16, 1943
DIED: New York, New York; December 7, 1990

Arenas's novels reflect his rural upbringing and his fight against Cuban revolutionary institutions that condemned him because of his homosexuality.

TRADITIONS: Caribbean, Cuban American

PRINCIPAL WORKS: *Celestino antes del alba,* 1967 (revised as *Cantando en el pozo,* 1982; *Singing from the Well,* 1987); *El mundo alucinante,* 1969 (*Hallucinations: Being an Account of the Life and Adventures of Friar Servando Teresa de Mier,* 1971); *El palacio de las blanquísimas mofetas,* 1975 (*The Palace of the White Skunks,* 1990); *El portero,* 1989 (*The Doorman,* 1991); *El color del verano,* 1991 (*The Color of Summer,* 2000)

Reinaldo Arenas overcame a poor rural upbringing to become a renowned novelist and short-story writer. He belongs to a generation of young writers who received literary training in official programs to promote literacy among the Cuban poor. Such training, however, also involved heavy indoctrination by political organizations that promoted only revolutionary readings. Although his career depended upon his incorporation into such a political agenda, Arenas refused to take an ideological stand. His decision caused him prosecution by legal authorities, imprisonment, and exile.

A superb storyteller, Arenas, in his first novel, *Singing from the Well,* presents young peasant characters who find themselves in an existentialist quest. Surrounded by a bleak rural environment, these protagonists fight the absolute poverty that keeps them from achieving their dreams. They also must confront their homosexual feelings, which force them to become outcasts. Although the subject of homosexuality is not an essential theme of the novel–the subject is merely hinted–Arenas's novel received a cold reception from Cuban critics.

Hallucinations brought Arenas's first confrontations with revolutionary critics and political authorities. Dissatisfied with the Castro regime, Arenas in the novel equates the Cuban Revolution to the oppressive forces of the Spanish Inquisition by drawing parallels between the persecutory practices of the two institutions. He also published the novel abroad without governmental consent, a crime punishable by law. That violation caused him to lose job opportunities and made him the target of multiple attempts at indoctrination, which included his imprisonment in a forced labor camp in 1970.

In spite of constant threats, Arenas continued writing antirevolutionary works that were smuggled out of the country by friends and published abroad in French translations. The theme of these works is constant: denunciation of Castro's oppressive political practices, most significantly the forced labor camps. The novels also decry the systematic persecution of homosexuals by military police and the relocation of homosexuals in labor camps.

After an incarceration of almost three years (1973-1976), Arenas made several attempts to escape from Cuba illegally. He finally succeeded in 1980, when he entered the United States by means of the Mariel boat lift. In the United States he continued his strong opposition to the Castro regime and re-edited the literary work he had written in Cuba. In addition, he intensified his interest in homosexual characters who, like his early young characters, find themselves in confrontation with the oppressive societies that punish them because of their sexual orientation. His open treatment of homosexuality makes him a forerunner of writers on that subject in Latin American literature.

Arturo, the Most Brilliant Star

TYPE OF WORK: Novel
FIRST PUBLISHED: *Arturo, la estrella más brillante*, 1984 (English translation, 1989)

Arenas's commitment to resisting and denouncing Cuba's indoctrination practices is evident in his short novel *Arturo, the Most Brilliant Star*. This work is also significant in that Arenas links his political views on the Cuban Revolution with his increasing interest in gay characters. The plot was inspired by a series of police raids against homosexuals in Havana in the early 1960's. The process was simple: The police picked up thousands of men, usually young men, and denounced them as homosexuals on the grounds of their wearing certain pieces of clothing commonly considered to be the garb of gay men. Those arrested had to work and undergo ideological training in labor camps.

Arturo is one of the thousands of gay men forced into a work camp. He becomes a fictional eyewitness of the rampant use of violence as a form of punishment. The novel's descriptions of the violence coincide with eyewitness accounts by gay men who have made similar declarations after their exile from Cuba.

Arturo faces the fact that a labor camp foments homosexual activity between the prisoners and the guards. A dreary and claustrophobic existence prompts some men to do female impersonations. If caught, those impersonators become a target of police brutality. Arturo, a social outcast, suffers rejection by his fellow prisoners because initially he does not take part in the female impersonations. Partly as the result of verbal and physical abuse, he joins the group at last and becomes the camp's best female impersonator. His transformation, especially his fast control of the female impersonator's jargon, reminds the reader of the revolutionary jargon forced upon the prisoners, which at first they resist learning and later mimic to ironic perfection.

Arturo's imagination forces him to understand his loneliness in the camp. In order to escape from the camp, he strives to create his own world, one that is truly fantastic and one of which he is king. The mental process is draining, and he has to work under sordid conditions that threaten his concentration, but he is successful in his attempt, and his world grows and extends outside the camp. The final touch is the construction of his own castle, in which he discovers a handsome man waiting for him on the other side of the walls. In his pursuit of his admirer Arturo does not recognize that his imaginary walls are the off-limits fences of the camp. When he is ordered to stop, he continues to walk out of the camp, and he is shot dead by a military officer.

Arenas's novel represents the beginning of a literary trend in Latin America that presents homosexuals as significant characters. It also focuses on the sexual practices of homosexual men, something that was a literary taboo.

The Pentagonía

TYPE OF WORK: Novels
FIRST PUBLISHED: *Celestino antes del alba,* 1967 (*Singing from the Well,* 1987); *El palacio de las blanquísimas mofetas,* 1975 (*The Palace of the White Skunks,* 1990); *Otra vez el mar,* 1982 (*Farewell to the Sea,* 1986); *El asalto,* 1990 (*The Assault,* 1994); *El color del verano,* 1991 (*The Color of Summer,* 2000)

The Pentagonía documents life in Cuba from the early 1950's onward. Although the novels deal with a variety of themes and with diverse characters, one subject stands out as a common denominator: homosexuality. Many characters face sexual oppression by Cuban society and must fight for their incorporation into productive social roles.

Arenas's novels document the lives of various male characters from their childhood to adulthood, including their handling of their homosexuality. *Singing from the Well* opens the set by presenting children oppressed by poverty; these children also face the sexual dynamics of a highly chauvinistic society. The nameless characters are representative of Cuban homosexual youth and return as more mature characters in subsequent novels, which can be read as sequels.

The Palace of the White Skunks takes Arenas's coming-of-age themes one step further by removing an unhappy young man from his restrictive society. Inspired by claims of social equality, Fortunato joins Castro's guerrilla forces in the fight against the Cuban dictator. His dreams are shattered, however, by the strong antihomosexual attitude of men in the military forces. As a result of his being homosexual, Fortunato is labeled weak and imperfect, certainly not the model of the revolutionary man.

Farewell to the Sea abandons young characters to explore the life of a married man, who appears to be living a full life. Héctor is married and a proud father. He expresses total commitment to revolutionary ideology, for which the state has awarded him a free trip to a beach resort. There he meets a young man, with whom he has romantic encounters. When his friend is found dead in a remote area of the beach, Héctor decides to abandon his vacation. The reader comes to understand that Héctor is a homosexual man who despises the revolution, who has experienced homosexual life, but who is forced to live as a prorevolutionary heterosexual in order to survive.

Arenas wrote the last two novels while fighting AIDS-related illnesses. With *The Color of Summer* he makes his most direct attacks against revolutionary persecution of homosexuals. Characters have to lead lives of pretense in order to avoid the economic disaster that follows revelation of homosexuality. *The Assault* focuses on revolutionary censorship, showing how homosexuals are forced to turn against their own relatives. Physical violence abounds in Arenas's novels, reflecting on a violent revolutionary society.

SUGGESTED READINGS

Schwartz, Kessel. "Homosexuality and the Fiction of Reinaldo Arenas." *Journal of Evolutionary Psychology* 5, nos. 1-2 (1984): 12-20.

Soto, Francisco. *Reinaldo Arenas.* New York: Twayne, 1998.

———. *Reinaldo Arenas: "The Pentagonía."* Gainesville: University Press of Florida, 1994.

—Rafael Ocasio

Jimmy Santiago Baca

BORN: Sante Fe, New Mexico; January 2, 1952

Baca's poetry expresses the experience of a "detribalized Apache," reared in a Chicano barrio, who finds his values in family, the land, and a complex cultural heritage.

TRADITIONS: American Indian, Mexican American
PRINCIPAL WORKS: *Immigrants in Our Own Land*, 1979; *Swords of Darkness*, 1981; *What's Happening*, 1982; *Poems Taken from My Yard*, 1986; *Martín; &, Meditations on the South Valley*, 1986; *Black Mesa Poems*, 1989; *Working in the Dark: Reflections of a Poet of the Barrio*, 1992; *Set This Book on Fire*, 1999

Jimmy Santiago Baca began to write poetry as an almost illiterate *vato loco* (crazy guy, gangster) serving a five-year term in a federal prison. He was twenty years old, the son of Damacio Baca, of Apache and Yaqui lineage, and Cecilia Padilla, a Latino woman, who left him with his grandparents when he was two. Baca stayed with them for three years, then went into a boys' home, then into detention centers and the streets of Albuquerque's barrio at thirteen. Although he "confirmed" his identity as a Chicano by leafing through a stolen picture book of Chicano history at seventeen, he felt himself "disintegrating" in prison. Speaking of his father, but alluding to his own situation when he was incarcerated, Baca observed: "He was everything that was bad in America. He was brown, he spoke Spanish, was from a Native American background, had no education."

As a gesture of rebellion, Baca took a guard's textbook and found that "sounds created music in me and happiness" as he slowly enunciated the lines of a poem by William Wordsworth. This led to a zealous effort at self-education, encouraged by the recollection of older men in detention centers who "made barrio life come alive . . . with their own Chicano language." Progressing to the point where he was writing letters for fellow prisoners, he placed a few poems in a local magazine, *New Kauri*, and achieved his first major publication with *Immigrants in Our Own Land*, a book whose title refers to the condition of inmates in a dehumanizing system and to his own feelings of estrangement in American society. This was a turning point for Baca, who realized that he could reclaim the community he was separated from and sing "the freedom song of our Chicano dream" now that poetry "had lifted me to my feet."

With this foundation to build on, Baca started a family in the early 1980's, restored an adobe dwelling in Albuquerque's South Valley, and wrote *Martín;*

43

&, Meditations on the South Valley because "the entire Southwest needed a long poem that could describe what has happened here in the last twenty years." Continuing to combine personal history and communal life, Baca followed this book with *Black Mesa Poems*, which links the landscape of the South Valley to people he knows and admires. Writing with confidence and an easy facility in Spanish and English, Baca uses vernacular speech, poetic form, ancient Mexican lore, and contemporary popular culture.

Black Mesa Poems

TYPE OF WORK: Poetry
FIRST PUBLISHED: 1989

Set in the desert of New Mexico, Baca's *Black Mesa Poems* explores the poet's continuing search for connections with his family, home, and cultural heritage. In vivid detail and striking imagery, the loosely connected poems catalog the poet's complex relationships with his past and the home he makes of Black Mesa.

Baca's intricate relationship to the land includes his knowledge of its history. He is keenly aware of the changes the land has gone through and the changes the people of that land have experienced. He writes of his personal sense of connection with arroyos and cottonwoods and of the conflicts between the earlier inhabitants of Black Mesa and the changes brought by progress. Dispossessed migrant workers are portrayed as the price of Anglo progress, and the arid land that once nourished strong cattle now offers only "sluggish pampered globs" from feedlots. Even the once sacred places have been unceremoniously "crusted with housing tracts." His people have been separated from their ancestral land, yet Baca celebrates his identification

Jimmy Santiago Baca (Lawrence Benton)

with the old adobe buildings and Aztec warriors in the face of modern Anglo society.

Despite nostalgia, Baca eludes naïve sentimentality by attaching himself to the land. His sense of self and identity with his race is rooted in the physical landscape of Black Mesa. He evokes a strong connection with the history of his people through rituals, including drum ceremonies that "mate heart with earth." Sketches evoke a rich sense of community life in the barrio. The poet presents himself in terms of his own troubled history, but he knows that the conflict between the "peaceful" man and the "destructive" one of his past is linked to the modern smothering of noisy jet fighters and invading pampered artists looking to his land for a "primitive place."

Memories and images of snapshotlike detail combine in these poems to create a portrait of a man defining himself in relation to his personal and cultural history. The poet knows he is "the end result of Conquistadores, Black Moors, American Indians, and Europeans," and he also notes the continuing invasion of land developers. Poems about his children combine memories of his troubled past with Olmec kings and tribal ancestors. The history of his ancestors' relationship with the land informs his complex and evolving sense of identity. Throughout the *Black Mesa Poems*, Baca's personal history becomes rooted in Black Mesa.

Martín; &, Meditations on the South Valley
TYPE OF WORK: Poetry
FIRST PUBLISHED: 1986

Told in the semiautobiographical voice of Martín, the two long poems "Martín" and "Meditations on the South Valley" offer the moving account of a young Chicano's difficult quest for self-definition amid the realities of the barrio and his dysfunctional family. Abandoned by his parents at a young age, Martín spends time with his Indio grandparents and in an orphanage before striking out on his own at the age of six. His early knowledge of his grandparents' heritage gives him the first indication that his quest for identity will involve the recovery of a sense of family and a strong connection with the earth.

As Martín grows older and is shuttled from the orphanage to his bourgeois uncle's home, he realizes that his life is of the barrio and the land and not the sterile world of the rich suburbs. Martín's quest eventually leads him on a journey throughout the United States in which he searches for himself amid the horrors of addiction and the troubled memories of his childhood. Realizing that he must restore his connection with his family and home, he returns to the South Valley by way of Aztec ruins, where he ritualistically establishes his connection with his Mother Earth and his Native American ancestry. "Martín" ends with the birth of his son and Martín's promise to never leave him. The cycle of abandonment and abuse seems to have ended, and Martín is on his way to becoming the good man he so strongly desires to be.

"Meditations on the South Valley" continues the story of Martín, reinforcing his newfound sense of identity. The poem begins with the burning of his house and the loss of ten years of writing. In the process of rebuilding his life, Martín and his family must live in the Heights, an antiseptic tract housing development that serves to reinforce his identification with the land of the South Valley. Told in brief sketches, the insights in "Meditations on the South Valley" encourage Martín to nurture the growing connections with his new family and his promise to his young son. The poem ends with the construction of his new home from the ruins of an abandoned flophouse in the South Valley. Martín's friends come together to construct the house, and, metaphorically, Martín and his life as a good Chicano man are reborn from the garbage piles and ashes of the house they reconstruct.

Working in the Dark
TYPE OF WORK: Essays and poetry
FIRST PUBLISHED: 1992

Baca's collection *Working in the Dark: Reflections of a Poet of the Barrio* is a blunt and honest gathering of essays, journal entries, and poetry that describe some of the more poignant incidents in a long journey that Baca has made from a "troubled and impoverished Chicano family" to a position of prominence as a widely admired poet. Baca's subject as a writer is the life and history of Albuquerque's South Valley. Baca passionately explores the crucial episodes in a process of self-growth and self-discovery beginning with his most desperate moments as an empty, powerless, inarticulate young man, through an expanding series of revelations about life and language in prison, and ending with his eventual construction of a self based on his relationships to the land, his family, and his identity as a "detribalized Apache" and Chicano artist.

The heart of the book is the fourth section, "Chicanismo: Destiny and Destinations." After covering his discovery in prison of the redemptive powers of language, and his sense of a loss of Chicano culture in an Anglo world, Baca recalls the one positive feature of his youth: the three years he spent in the home of his grandparents before he was five. This memory kept a dim vision alive through the years when Baca began to realize that "none of what I did was who I was." In the first part of the "Chicanismo" section, Baca delivers a systematic critique of the methods used by a dominant Anglo culture to stereotype, demean, and distort Chicano life. Drawing on his prison experience and on his troubles in school and in various temporary jobs, Baca describes how he felt doubly imprisoned as an immigrant in his own land and as one under the control of unknowing authorities.

As part of a plan to reclaim his cultural heritage, Baca reaches back into history to show how valuable and vital Chicano culture has been. In a satirical commentary on the Columbus quincentennial, which Baca debunks with a punning title "De Quiencentennial?" (whose quincentennial is it, anyway?), Baca introduces some of the positive, admirable facets of the life of the South Valley near Albuquerque. One of the strongest features of the life of *la raza* (the race) has been an oral tradition that, as Baca points out, has defied attempts to suppress or extinguish its vitality, "Our language, which I have inherited, is a symphony of rebellion against invaders." In the last section of the book, "Gleanings from a Poet's Journal," Baca demonstrates this linguistic power as he explains how he wrote in the dark when Chicanos could not find access to print, how the barrio is like an "uncut diamond" for the artist to shape, and how Baca responds to queries about his "Indian-ness."

SUGGESTED READINGS

Baca, Jimmy Santiago. "'Poetry Is What We Speak to Each Other': An Interview with Jimmy Santiago Baca." Interview by John Keene. *Callaloo* 17, no. 1 (Winter, 1994): 33.

Coppola, Vincent. "The Moon in Jimmy Baca." *Esquire* (June, 1993): 48-56.

Levertov, Denise. Introduction to *Martín; &, Meditations on the South Valley*, by Jimmy Santiago Baca. New York: New Directions, 1987.

Olivares, Julian. "Two Contemporary Chicano Verse Chronicles." *The Americas Review* 16 (Fall-Winter, 1988): 214-231.

Rector, Liam. "The Documentary of What Is." *Hudson Review* 41 (Summer, 1989): 393-400.

—Leon Lewis/William Vaughn

James Baldwin

BORN: New York, New York; August 2, 1924
DIED: St. Paul de Vence, France; November 30, 1987

*Baldwin's experiences as an African American gay man became the
source for essays and fiction that were often angry but always honest.*

TRADITIONS: African American
PRINCIPAL WORKS: *Go Tell It on the Mountain,* 1953; *Notes of a Native Son,* 1955;
Giovanni's Room, 1956; *The Fire Next Time,* 1963; *Going to Meet the Man,* 1965

At nineteen, James Baldwin left Harlem, the black section of New York City.
He traveled across Europe and the United States, living for years in France,
where he died at age sixty-three. More than any other place, Harlem shaped
Baldwin's identity. He never completely left the ghetto behind.

Baldwin returned often to Harlem to visit family. Much of his writing
features the stores and streets of Harlem, in such essays as "The Harlem
Ghetto" and "Notes of a Native Son," in stories such as "Sonny's Blues" and
"The Rockpile," and in such novels as *Go Tell It on the Mountain.*

Baldwin claimed to love and hate Harlem, a place of old buildings, empty
lots, fire escapes, and tired grass. Harlem was also rich with churches and
corner stores, with railroad tracks and the Harlem River. Such scenes molded
Baldwin's worldview. Baldwin's identity was also shaped by his sexuality. He
was admittedly gay, though he never embraced that term or what he called
the gay world. He considered it limiting to separate gay and straight worlds.
People were people, according to him. Baldwin's second novel, *Giovanni's
Room,* deals with gay themes; writing and publishing such a work in the 1950's
was a considerable act of courage. Baldwin explores similar themes in *Another
Country* (1962). Baldwin said that he wrote *Giovanni's Room* to understand his
own sexuality, that the book was something he had to finish before he could
write anything else.

Baldwin's thoughts and writings were shaped most powerfully, however,
by his identity as an African American. He experienced racism early, yet still
excelled in school and at writing for school newspapers. As a young adult he
endured segregation. Only by moving to France in his twenties did Baldwin
gain the emotional distance to understand what being black in the United
States meant. He participated in the Civil Rights movement, taking part in
demonstrations and writing about that struggle. Baldwin uses his gay and
African American identities to explore universal themes of loneliness, alienation, and affection.

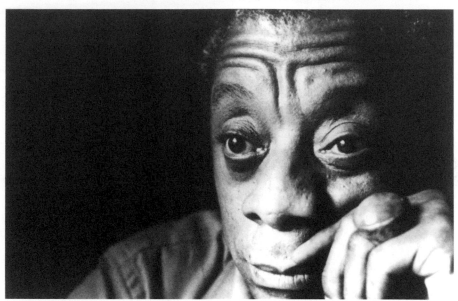

James Baldwin (Library of Congress)

Giovanni's Room

TYPE OF WORK: Novel
FIRST PUBLISHED: 1956

Giovanni's Room was Baldwin's second novel, after *Go Tell It on the Mountain* (1953). It was a risky book for Baldwin because it openly explored male homosexuality at a time when few writers discussed gay themes. It almost went unpublished. Knopf had taken Baldwin's first novel, but rejected *Giovanni's Room* and may even have suggested that Baldwin burn the manuscript to protect his reputation. Other rejections followed before Dial Press accepted the book for publication.

Baldwin, who was gay, had touched on homosexual love in "The Outing" (1951) and toward the end of *Go Tell It on the Mountain*, but *Giovanni's Room* was a frank portrayal of a gay man's feelings and torments. The book involves white rather than black characters, which added to the book's commercial and critical risk. *Giovanni's Room* focuses on David, an American expatriate living in Paris, France. Other characters include Hella, an American woman and David's lover, and Giovanni, an Italian who becomes David's gay partner. The story is narrated in first person by David.

Part 1 begins with Hella having left for America and Giovanni about to be executed. The rest is told primarily in flashbacks. In the flashbacks, David comes to Paris after a homosexual affair and attaches himself to Hella. He asks her to marry him, and she goes to Spain to think about it. During Hella's absence, David meets Giovanni, who works in a bar owned by a gay man. David and Giovanni are immediately drawn together and become lovers. David moves into Giovanni's room and the two are happy for a time. David cannot fully accept his gay identity, however, and reminds himself that Hella will return. In part 2, Giovanni and David's relationship sours, mainly because David begins to despise his own feelings and to resent Giovanni's affection. The tension increases when Giovanni loses his job.

Hella comes back and David returns to her without even telling Giovanni. He pretends to be purely heterosexual, and finally breaks off his relationship with Giovanni, who is devastated emotionally. David and Hella plan to get married, but then hear that Giovanni has murdered the owner of the bar where he once worked. Giovanni is sentenced to death. David stays with Hella during Giovanni's trial, but finally gives in to his feelings and goes to the gay quarter. Hella sees him with a man and realizes David will never love her fully. She leaves for America, and David is left to think of Giovanni and to feel empty. David can neither accept his nature nor escape it.

Notes of a Native Son
TYPE OF WORK: Essays
FIRST PUBLISHED: 1955

Baldwin is a fine novelist, as such works as *Go Tell It on the Mountain* (1953) and *Giovanni's Room* (1956) prove. Many readers consider his nonfiction to be even finer than his fiction. His essays, which may be found in collections such as *Notes of a Native Son* (1955) and *Nobody Knows My Name: More Notes of a Native Son* (1972), are passionate and often scathing.

His personal feelings and experiences are freely expressed in his essays. His anger at black-white relations in America, his ambivalence toward his father, and his thoughts on such writers as Truman Capote, Norman Mailer, and William Faulkner are displayed openly. He is honest, and made enemies for it. On the other hand, he has many readers' respect for saying what he thinks.

Notes of a Native Son was Baldwin's first nonfiction collection, and it contains his "Autobiographical Notes" and three sections totaling ten essays. In "Autobiographical Notes," Baldwin sketches his early career—his Harlem birth, his childhood interest in writing, his journey to France. "Autobiographical Notes" and various essays describe the difficult process of Baldwin's establishment of his identity. Part 1 of *Notes of a Native Son* includes three essays. "Everybody's Protest Novel" examines *Uncle Tom's Cabin: Or, Life Among the Lowly* (1852), which Baldwin considers self-righteous and so sentimental as to be dishonest. "Many Thousands Gone" examines Richard Wright's *Native Son* (1940), which Baldwin describes as badly flawed. "*Carmen Jones:* The Dark Is Light Enough" is another biting review, of the Hollywood motion picture musical *Carmen Jones* (1955). Baldwin says that the film lacks imagination and is condescending to blacks. Part 2 contains three essays. "The Harlem Ghetto" is one of the most powerful, digging into the physical and emotional turmoil of Harlem, including problems between blacks and Jews. "Journey to Atlanta" looks at an African American singing group's first trip to the South. It is a humorous, cynical, look at the treatment that the group, which included two of Baldwin's brothers, received. "Notes of a Native Son" examines Baldwin's anger and despair after his father's death.

Part 3 contains four essays. "Encounter on the Seine: Black Meets Brown" and "A Question of Identity" are about the feelings and attitudes of Americans in Paris in the 1940's and 1950's. "Equal in Paris" is Baldwin's account of being arrested and jailed, temporarily, in a case involving some stolen sheets that he did not steal. Baldwin describes the insight he had while in the hands of the French police: that they, in dealing with him, were not engaging in the racist cat-and-mouse game used by police in the United States. Finally, "Stranger in the Village" discusses Baldwin's time in a Swiss village and the astonished curiosity of people who had never seen a black person before. In all these essays, Baldwin explores his world and himself.

SUGGESTED READINGS

Campbell, James. *Talking at the Gates: A Life of James Baldwin.* New York: Viking Press, 1991.

Goldstein, Richard. "Go the Way Your Blood Beats." In *James Baldwin: The Legacy*, edited by Quincy Troupe. New York: Simon & Schuster, 1989.

Kenan, Randall. *James Baldwin.* New York: Chelsea House, 1994.

Leeming, David. *James Baldwin.* New York: Alfred A. Knopf, 1994.

McBride, Dwight A., ed. *James Baldwin Now.* New York: New York University Press, 1999.

Miller, D. Quentin. *Re-viewing James Baldwin: Things Not Seen.* Philadelphia: Temple University Press, 2000.

Rosset, Lisa. *James Baldwin.* New York: Chelsea House, 1989.

Weatherby, W. J. *James Baldwin: Artist on Fire.* New York: Donald I. Fine, 1989.

—Charles A. Gramlich

Toni Cade Bambara

BORN: New York, New York; March 25, 1939
DIED: Philadelphia, Pennsylvania; December 9, 1995

Bambara saw herself as a literary combatant who wrote to affirm the selfhood of blacks.

TRADITIONS: African American

PRINCIPAL WORKS: *Gorilla, My Love*, 1972; *The Sea Birds Are Still Alive: Collected Stories*, 1977; *The Salt Eaters*, 1980; *Those Bones Are Not My Child*, 1999

Given the name Miltona Mirkin Cade at birth, Toni Cade acquired the name Bambara in 1970 after she discovered it as part of a signature on a sketchbook she found in her great-grandmother's trunk. Bambara spent her formative years in New York and Jersey City, New Jersey, attending public and private schools in the areas. Although she maintained that her early short stories are not autobiographical, the protagonists in many of these pieces are young women who recall Bambara's inquisitiveness as a youngster.

Bambara attended Queens College, New York, and received a bachelor of arts degree in 1959. Earlier that year she had published her first short story, and she also received the John Golden award for fiction from Queens College. Bambara then entered the City College of New York, where she studied modern American fiction, but before completing her studies for the master's degree, she traveled to Italy and studied in Milan, eventually returning to her studies and earning the master's in 1963.

From 1959 to 1973, Bambara saw herself as an activist. She held positions as social worker, teacher, and counselor. In her various roles, Bambara saw herself as working for the betterment of the community. During the 1960's, Rutgers State University developed a strong fine arts undergraduate program. Many talented black artists joined the faculty to practice their crafts and to teach. Bambara was one of those talented faculty members. She taught, wrote, and participated in a program for raising the consciousness of minority women.

Like many artists during the 1960's, Bambara became involved in the black liberation struggle. She realized that all blacks needed to be liberated, but she felt that black women were forgotten in the struggle. She was of the opinion that neither the white nor the black male was capable of understanding what it means to be a black female. White and black males created images of women, she argued, that "are still derived from their needs." Bambara saw a kinship with white women, but admitted: "I don't know that our priorities are the same." Believing that only the black woman is capable

Toni Cade Bambara (Joyce Middler)

of explaining herself, Bambara edited *The Black Woman: An Anthology* (1970).

In 1973, Bambara visited Cuba, and in 1975 she traveled to Vietnam. Her travels led her to believe that globally, women were oppressed. Her experiences found expression in *The Sea Birds Are Still Alive*. In the late 1970's,

Bambara moved to the South to teach at Spellman College. During this period she wrote *The Salt Eaters,* which focuses on mental and physical well-being. With her daughter, Bambara moved to Pennsylvania in the 1980's, where she continued her activism and her writing until her death.

Gorilla, My Love
TYPE OF WORK: Short fiction
FIRST PUBLISHED: 1972

Published in 1972, *Gorilla, My Love* is a collection of short stories written between 1959 and 1971. The book is an upbeat, positive work that redefines the black experience in America. It affirms the fact that inner-city children can grow into strong, healthy adults. It indicates clearly that black men are not always the weak, predatory element in the family but can be a strong, protective force. It intimates that African Americans are not the socially alienated, dysfunctional people that the mainstream society sometimes suggests. Instead, the stories project an image of a people who love themselves, who understand themselves, and who need no validation.

The fifteen short stories that compose the text are set in urban areas, and the narrative voices are usually streetwise, preadolescent girls who are extremely aware of their environment. The titular story, "Gorilla, My Love" is centered in the misunderstanding between a child and an adult. Jefferson Vale announces that he is getting married, but he has promised his preadolescent niece, Hazel, to marry her. Hazel sees her "Hunca" Bubba as a "lyin dawg." Although her uncle and her grandfather attempt to console her, Hazel believes adults "mess over kids, just cause they little and can't take em to court."

All of the stories are informative and entertaining. A story that typifies the anthology is "Playin with Ponjob," which details how a white social worker, Miss Violet, underestimates the influence of a local thug and is forced to leave the community. "Talkin Bout Sunny" explores the effects of the mainstream on the black male by pointing out how pressures from the larger community cause Sunny to kill his wife. "The Lesson" points out the disparity between the rich and the poor by telling of children window-shopping on Fifth Avenue. "Blues Ain't No Mockin Bird" details how one man protects his family from prying photographers employed by the welfare system.

What is significant in "Playin with Ponjob" is that Bambara does not depict Ponjob as being predatory. He is male, "jammed-up by the white man's nightmare." To the community, he is "the only kind of leader we can think of." In "Talkin Bout Sunny" Bambara indicates that the larger community is partly responsible for Sunny's actions, but she also indicates that the community of Sunny's friends is also responsible because they know of his distemper, but do nothing. "The Lesson" teaches children that what one wealthy person spends on one toy can feed eight of them for a year. "Blues Ain't No Mockin Bird" indicates that the patriarch of an extended family can protect his own. The collection depicts African Americans as a strong, progressive people.

The Salt Eaters
TYPE OF WORK: Novel
FIRST PUBLISHED: 1980

The Salt Eaters opens with Velma Henry sitting on a stool in the South West Community Infirmary of Claybourne, Georgia, being healed by Minnie Ransom. Claybourne is a beehive of progressive activity. The Academy of the Seven Arts, run by James "Obie" Henry, Velma's husband, is the center of intellectual and social activities. Velma, performing the duties of seven employees, keeps the institution running. Overwhelmed by the infighting at the academy, her domestic problems with Obie, and her refusal to accept her spiritual powers, Velma has attempted suicide, and Minnie is laboring to "center" Velma, to make Velma whole.

The novel includes a spiritual plane where mortals interact with other life forms. Minnie Ransom operates on both planes. She is sitting opposite Velma while surrounded by her twelve disciples, the Master's Mind. Sometimes she reaches out and touches Velma physically. Other times she does "not touch [Velma] flesh on flesh, but touch[es] mind on mind from across the room or from across town." While Minnie is having these telepathic tête-à-têtes with Velma, she also confers at times with a spirit guide who helps her with the healing. When "centering" Velma becomes difficult, Minnie makes telepathic trips to the Chapel of the Mind to recharge her psychic energies.

The healing, which should take minutes, takes two hours–the time span of the novel. Velma, like Minnie, takes telepathic trips, during which she bumps into other characters, human and spiritual. These characters, filtered through Velma's subconscious, are for the most part what people the novel.

Bambara skillfully combines the European American traditional mode of storytelling with African and African American concepts and traditions. The Academy of the Seven Arts is concerned with empirical knowledge, but the institution is also concerned with teaching folk art and folk traditions. The medical center accommodates physicians who practice modern medicine, but the center also makes use of the skills of Minnie Ransom. The spring celebration is a ritual celebrated by human beings, but in Claybourne the quick and the dead celebrate this rite.

Bambara's concepts of the new age, guiding spirits, out-of-body experiences, and telepathic visions were not, at first, taken seriously. Reality is not, however, measured only by empirical evidence. Near-death experiences, guardian angels, and intergalactic travel are part of popular understanding. As the concept of reality expands, the significance of *The Salt Eaters* deepens.

SUGGESTED READINGS

Bell, Bernard W. *The Afro-American Novel and Its Tradition.* Amherst: University of Massachusetts Press, 1987.

Bell, Roseann, et al. *Sturdy Black Brides: Vision of Black Women in Literature.* Garden City, N.J.: Anchor Press, 1979.

Collins, Janelle. "Generating Power: Fission, Fusion, and Post-Modern Politics in Bambara's *The Salt Eaters*." *MELUS* 21, no. 2 (Summer, 1996): 35-47.

Evans, Marre, ed. *Black Women Writers (1950-1980): A Critical Evaluation.* Garden City, N.J.: Anchor Press, 1984.

Hargrave, Nancy D. "Youth in Bambara's *Gorilla, My Love*." In *Women Writers of the Contemporary South,* edited by Peggy Whitman Prenshow. Jackson: University of Mississippi Press, 1984.

Tate, Claudia. *Black Women Writers at Work.* New York: Continuum, 1983.

Wilentz, Gay. *Healing Narratives: Women Writers Curing Cultural Dis-ease.* New Brunswick, N.J.: Rutgers University Press, 2000.

—*Ralph Reckley, Sr.*

Amiri Baraka
(LeRoi Jones)

BORN: Newark, New Jersey; October 7, 1934

Baraka's poetry, drama, and music criticism make him one of the most influential African American writers of his generation.

TRADITIONS: African American

PRINCIPAL WORKS: *Blues People: Negro Music in White America*, 1963; *Dutchman*, pr., pb. 1964; *The Slave*, pr., pb. 1964; *The System of Dante's Hell*, 1965; *Home: Social Essays*, 1966; *Selected Poetry of Amiri Baraka/LeRoi Jones*, 1979; *Daggers and Javelins: Essays 1974-1979*, 1984; *The Autobiography of LeRoi Jones/Amiri Baraka*, 1984; *The LeRoi Jones/Amiri Baraka Reader*, 1991 (edited by William J. Harris); *Transbluesency: Selected Poems of Amiri Baraka/LeRoi Jones (1961-1995)*, 1995; *New Poems (1984-1995)*, 1997

Introspective yet concerned with public, political issues, Amiri Baraka's works frequently focus on his personal attempt to define an African American identity. Born into a close-knit family that had migrated from the South, Baraka was a bright student. In adolescence Baraka became aware of differences between African American middle-class and working-class lives and viewpoints. He recalls the identity crisis that grew out of his developing class awareness in such works as "Letter to E. Franklin Frazier," his novel *The System of Dante's Hell*, and short stories collected in *Tales* (1967). His interest in jazz and blues also began in adolescence and was reinforced by the mentorship of poet Sterling A. Brown, one of Baraka's professors at Howard University.

After an enlistment in the Air Force, Baraka settled in New York's Greenwich Village in 1957 and began publishing *Yugen*, a poetry magazine that became one of the important journals of the Beat generation. After the success of his play *Dutchman* and his recognition as an important critic for his study *Blues People: Negro Music in White America*, the assassination of Malcolm X was a shocking event that caused Baraka to reject his previous faith in the possibilities of a racially integrated society. In 1965, he embraced a Black Nationalist political viewpoint and helped establish the Black Arts Repertory Theatre/School in Harlem, which became the center of a nationwide Black Arts movement. This movement attempted to produce literature, music, and visual art addressed to the masses of African Americans. The Black Arts movement aimed at expressing a unique ethnic worldview and what Baraka

Amiri Baraka (AP/Wide World Photos)

called "a Black value system." His works of this period often depict a hostile white society and question whether middle-class aspirations and individualism endangered the progress of African Americans as a group. He saw the collective improvisation of jazz as a model for the arts and for political activism.

Turning to Marxism in 1974, Baraka extended these ideas. Dedicating his work to revolutionary action, Baraka suggested that the situation of African Americans paralleled that of colonized Third World peoples in Africa and Asia. Teaching at the State University of New York and other colleges, Baraka produced highly original poems, plays, and essays that continued to address controversial issues and to reach a wide international readership. His experiments with literary form—particularly the use of African American vernacular speech—also have influenced many younger American writers.

Blues People
TYPE OF WORK: Essay
FIRST PUBLISHED: 1963

The first full-length analytical and historical study of jazz and blues written by an African American, *Blues People: Negro Music in White America* presents a highly original thesis suggesting that music can be used as a gauge to measure the cultural assimilation of Africans in North America from the early eighteenth century to the twentieth century. Broad in scope and insightfully opinionated, *Blues People* caused controversy among musicologists and other critics. Intending his remarks as negative criticism, Ralph Ellison was accurate in noting that Baraka is "attracted to the blues for what he believes they tell us of the sociology of Negro American identity and attitude."

Baraka contends that although slavery destroyed many formal artistic traditions, African American music represents certain African survivals. Most important, African American music represents an African approach to culture. As such, the music sustains the African worldview and records the historical experience of an oppressed people.

Baraka also argues that while Africans adapted their culture to the English language and to European musical instruments and song forms, they also maintained an ethnic viewpoint that is preserved and transmitted by their music. Stylistic changes in the music mirror historical changes in the attitudes and social conditions of African Americans. The chapter "Swing—From Verb to Noun" compares the contributions of African American and white jazz musicians in the 1920's and 1930's, demonstrating how some artists developed and extended an ethnic folk music tradition while others added what they learned from that tradition to the vocabulary of a more commercialized American popular music. Baraka's view that music is capable of expressing and maintaining a group identity leads to his assertion that even in later decades, increasingly dominated by the recording and broadcasting industry, African American artists continued to be the primary contributors and innovators. A classic work of its kind, *Blues People* offers an interesting view of how cultural products reflect and perhaps determine other social developments.

Daggers and Javelins

TYPE OF WORK: Essays and lectures
FIRST PUBLISHED: 1984

The essays and lectures collected in *Daggers and Javelins: Essays, 1974-1979* represent Baraka's vigorous attempt to identify an African American revolutionary tradition that could parallel anticolonial struggles in Third World countries of Africa, Asia, and South America. Baraka applies a Marxist analysis to African American literature in these essays.

Having become disappointed with the progress of the Black Power movement and its emphasis on grassroots electoral politics, Baraka came to Marxism with the zeal of a new convert. "The essays of the earliest part of this period," he writes, "are overwhelmingly political in the most overt sense." While some of the essays in *Daggers and Javelins* address jazz, film, and writers of the Harlem Renaissance, all of them do so with the purpose of assessing what Baraka calls their potential to contribute to a revolutionary struggle.

In "The Revolutionary Tradition in Afro-American Literature," Baraka distinguishes between the authentic folk and vernacular expression of African American masses and the poetry and prose produced by middle-class writers in imitation of prevailing literary standards. Considering the slave narratives of Frederick Douglass and others as the beginnings of a genuine African American literature, he criticizes works that promote individualism or are merely "a distraction, an ornament." Similarly, "Afro-American Literature and Class Struggle" and other essays consider how the economic structure of society affects the production and the appreciation of art. "Notes on the

History of African/Afro-American Culture" interprets the theoretical writings of Karl Marx and Friedrich Engels and draws parallels between colonized African societies and the suppression of African American artistic expression by the American cultural mainstream.

Broadening his scope in essays on African and Caribbean authors, Baraka suggests that figures such as the Kenyan novelist Ngugi wa Thiong'o and the poet Aimé Césaire from Martinique can provide models for how African American artists can escape being co-opted into an elite that supports the status quo and, instead, produce art that offers a "cathartic revelation of reality" useful in promoting social change.

Dutchman
TYPE OF WORK: Drama
FIRST PRODUCED: 1964; first published, 1964

A powerful one-act drama, *Dutchman* brought immediate and lasting attention to Baraka. The play is a searing two-character confrontation that begins playfully but builds rapidly in suspense and symbolic resonance. Set on a New York subway train, *Dutchman* opens with a well-dressed, intellectual, young African American man named Clay absorbed in reading a magazine. He is interrupted by Lula—a flirtatious, beautiful white woman a bit older than he. As Lula suggestively slices and eats an apple, she and Clay tease each other with bantering talk that becomes more and more personal. She reveals little about herself, but Lula is clearly in control of the conversation and the situation as she perceptively and provokingly challenges Clay's middle-class self image. Lula is, in fact, a bit cruel. "What right do you have to be wearing a three-button suit and striped tie?" she asks. "Your grandfather was a slave, he didn't go to Harvard." Aware of his insecurities, Lula dares Clay to pretend "that you are free of your own history."

Clay's insecurities about his race, social status, and masculine prowess—slowly revealed as his answers shift from machismo to defensiveness—become the targets for Lula's increasingly direct taunts. Eventually, Lula's attempt to force Clay to see in himself the negative stereotypes of the black male—as either oversexed stud or cringing Uncle Tom—goad him into an eloquently bitter tirade. Black music and African American culture, he tells her, are actually repressions of a justified rage that has kept African American people sane in the face of centuries of oppression. Clay seems as desperate to prove this to himself as he is to convince Lula. He does not seem to know whether the rage or the repression has taken the greater toll on African American sanity. The scene escalates in dramatic force until Lula unexpectedly stabs Clay to death.

Baraka has said that *Dutchman* "is about how difficult it is to become a man in the United States." Nevertheless, the ancient symbolism of apple and temptation, and the myth of the ghostly pirate ship, *The Flying Dutchman,* used in Richard Wagner's opera and other literary works, are carefully suggested in Baraka's play and amplify the dimensions of racial conflict.

Selected Poetry of Amiri Baraka/ LeRoi Jones

TYPE OF WORK: Poetry
FIRST PUBLISHED: 1979

Perhaps the most influential African American poet of the last half of the twentieth century, Baraka helped define the Beat generation and served as a guide for the Black Arts movement of the 1960's. Baraka's work is simultaneously introspective and public; his combination of unrhymed open forms, African American vernacular speech, and allusions to American popular culture produces poems that express Baraka's personal background while addressing political issues. Baraka's poetry draws upon the poetic techniques of William Carlos Williams and Charles Olson, and upon traditional oratory, ranging from the African American church to streetcorner rapping.

Baraka has divided his work into three periods: his association with the Beats (1957-1963), a militant Black Nationalist period (1965-1974), and, after 1975, an adherence to Marxism and Third World anticolonial politics. These periods are marked by changes in the poet's ideology but not in his poetic style. Early poems such as "Hymn to Lanie Poo"—focusing on tension between middle-class and poor black people—and "Notes for a Speech" consider whether or not African Americans have a genuine ethnic identity and culture of their own as opposed to a segregated existence that only mirrors white America. This theme receives more attention in poems of the 1960's such as "Poem for Willie Best" and "Poem for HalfWhite College Students" which indict Hollywood stereotypes. Another collection, *Transbluesency: Selected Poems (1961-1995),* represents much of Baraka's work after 1979.

Poems of the Black Nationalist period address questions of the poet's personal and racial identity. The poems of this period suggest that poetry itself is a means of creating individual and communal identity. In "Numbers, Letters" Baraka writes: "I can't be anything I'm not/ Except these words pretend/ to life not yet explained." Explicitly political poems, such as "The Nation Is Like Ourselves," propose that each person's efforts or failings collectively amount to a community's character. After 1975, poems such as "In the Tradition" argue—with some consistency with Baraka's earlier views— that although Marxism is the means to political progress, only an art of the people that insists on showing that "the universal/ is the entire collection/ of particulars" will prepare people to work toward a better future. "In the Tradition" and a later series titled "Why's" present musicians and political leaders as equally powerful cultural activists, reinforcing Baraka's idea that poetry is a force for change.

SUGGESTED READINGS

Anadolu-Okur, Nigun. *Contemporary African American Theater: Afrocentricity in the Works of Larry Neal, Amiri Baraka, and Charles Fuller.* New York: Garland, 1997.

Brown, Lloyd W. *Amiri Baraka.* Boston: Twayne, 1980.

Ellison, Ralph. *The Poetry and Poetics of Amiri Baraka: The Jazz Aesthetic.* Columbia: University of Missouri Press, 1985.

————. *Shadow and Act.* New York: Vintage Books, 1972.

Fox, Robert Eliot. *Conscientious Sorcerers: The Black Postmodernist Fiction of LeRoi Jones/Amiri Baraka, Ishmael Reed, and Samuel R. Delany.* Westport, Conn.: Greenwood Press, 1987.

Neal, Larry. *Visions of a Liberated Future: Black Arts Movement Writings.* New York: Thunder's Mouth Press, 1989.

Nielsen, Aldon L. *Writing Between the Lines: Race and Intertextuality.* Athens: University of Georgia Press, 1994.

Reilly, Charlie, ed. *Conversations with Amiri Baraka.* Jackson: University Press of Mississippi, 1994.

Sollors, Werner. *Amiri Baraka/LeRoi Jones: The Quest for a "Populist Modernism."* New York: Columbia University Press, 1978.

Tate, Greg. "Growing Up in Public: Amiri Baraka Changes His Mind." *Flyboy in the Buttermilk: Essays on Contemporary America.* New York: Simon & Schuster, 1992.

Woodard, K. Komozi. *A Nation Within a Nation: Amiri Baraka (LeRoi Jones) and Black Power Politics.* Chapel Hill: University of North Carolina Press, 1999.

—*Lorenzo Thomas*

Saul Bellow

BORN: Lachine, Quebec, Canada; June 10, 1915

Bellow was perhaps the first Jewish writer in America to reject the categorization of his work as being Jewish American literature; he became a major American novelist.

TRADITIONS: Jewish

PRINCIPAL WORKS: *Dangling Man,* 1944; *The Victim,* 1947; *The Adventures of Augie March,* 1953; *Seize the Day,* 1956; *Henderson the Rain King,* 1959; *Herzog,* 1964; *Mr. Sammler's Planet,* 1970; *Humboldt's Gift,* 1975; *The Dean's December,* 1982; *More Die of Heartbreak,* 1987; *Ravelstein,* 2000

Saul Bellow grew up in the polyglot slums of Montreal and Chicago. He was saved from a bleak existence by his love of learning. He acquired a knowledge of Yiddish, Hebrew, and French, in addition to Russian and English. His Russian immigrant parents were orthodox Jews; Bellow's exposure to other cultures led him to reject a purely Jewish identity. He discovered the work of Mark Twain, Edgar Allan Poe, Theodore Dreiser, and Sherwood Anderson, all leaders in shaping Americans' consciousness of their national identity.

After being graduated from Northwestern University, Bellow obtained a scholarship to pursue graduate study in anthropology at the University of Wisconsin but found his real interest lay in creative writing. He considered his first two novels, *Dangling Man* and *The Victim,* "apprentice work." Not until the publication of *The Adventures of Augie March* did he achieve recognition as a major new voice in American fiction. He had forged a spontaneous, exuberant personal style which was a poetic synthesis of lower-class vernacular, Yiddishisms, profuse neologisms, the language of polite society, and the jargon of academia.

Bellow thought too much had been made of persecution and exclusion. He pointed to the exciting opportunities for growth available to all Americans. He insisted on being not a Jew addressing other Jews, but an American addressing other Americans. Creative writing for him was an adventure in self-discovery. He called his breakthrough novel *The Adventures of Augie March* because he considered life an adventure in spite of hardships, disappointments, and failure.

Among his numerous honors, Bellow received National Book Awards for *The Adventures of Augie March* in 1954, *Herzog* in 1964, and *Mr. Sammler's Planet* in 1970. His crowning achievement was the Nobel Prize in Literature in 1976. Most of his fiction concerns a search for self-realization in a confusing, often hostile world. Bellow's heroes rarely know what they want but know what they do not want: they are chronically dissatisfied with the complacency, inertia, and materialism around them.

Bellow was also inspirational as a teacher. He is most closely identified with the University of Chicago. The fact that Bellow was married and divorced four times reflects the quixotic spirit seen in Augie March, Eugene Henderson, and other autobiographical creations.

Bellow will be best remembered for his example to writers attempting to discover and declare their identities, often as members of disadvantaged minorities. Bellow expressed—and was shaped by—the adventurous, iconoclastic, and fiercely democratic spirit of twentieth century America.

The Adventures of Augie March
TYPE OF WORK: Novel
FIRST PUBLISHED: 1953

The Adventures of Augie March is an autobiographical *Bildungsroman* covering a Jewish American's struggle to find himself, through trial and error, from the 1920's through the 1940's. Bellow's hero-narrator Augie March is bewildered by the freedom and opportunities available to Jews in America after centuries of persecution and segregation in other lands.

Augie is a resilient but not a strongly motivated character. Not knowing what he wants, he allows himself to be misguided by a succession of domineering personalities, beginning with the family's tyrannical boarder, Mrs. Lausch, a refugee from Czarist Russia, who tries to make him an Old World gentleman.

Augie and his older brother Simon have to go to work while still children to supplement the meager family income. Both quickly become hardened by the streets of Chicago. Criminal acquaintances involve Augie in felonies that nearly get him sent to prison. Augie, however, has a love for education and self-improvement because they offer hope of finding self-realization and escape from the ghetto. The combination of slang and erudite diction Augie uses in telling his story is an outstanding feature of the novel.

Simon is another domineering personality who tries to run Augie's life. Ruthless, money-hungry Simon cannot understand his younger brother's indifference to materialism and despises his bookworm mentality. They have a dynamic love-hate relationship throughout the novel.

Simon marries into a wealthy family and becomes a millionaire, but Augie sees that his unhappy brother is suicidal. Augie wants more from life than money and a loveless marriage. He tries shoplifting, union organizing, smuggling illegal immigrants, managing a punch-drunk boxer, and other fiascos. He experiences many changes of fortune. He plunges into love affairs with women who try to redirect his life. The most formidable is a huntress who collects poisonous snakes and trains an eagle to catch giant iguanas in Mexico.

When World War II comes, Augie joins the Merchant Marine and barely survives after his ship is torpedoed. After the war, he and his wife move to Europe, where he grows rich trading in black-market merchandise. At novel's end he has still not found himself. Augie finds that he has settled for a comfortable but shallow existence, but he realizes that other people have no better understanding of who they are or what they want than he does himself.

During the 1950's and 1960's *The Adventures of Augie March* was popular with young readers because they identified with a protagonist who rejected traditional values and sought self-realization in a world seemingly doomed to atomic annihilation.

SUGGESTED READINGS

Bigler, Walter. *Figures of Madness in Saul Bellow's Longer Fiction.* Bern, Switzerland: Peter Lang, 1998.

Dutton, Robert R. *Saul Bellow.* New York: Twayne, 1982.

Gerson, Steven M. "The New American Adam in *The Adventures of Augie March.*" *Modern Fiction Studies* 25 (Spring, 1979): 117-128.

Harper, George Lloyd. "Saul Bellow." In *Writers at Work: The Paris Review Interviews,* edited by George Plimpton. New York: Penguin, 1977.

Hyland, Peter. *Saul Bellow.* New York: St. Martin's Press, 1992.

Kiernan, Robert F. *Saul Bellow.* New York: Continuum, 1989.

Miller, Ruth. *Saul Bellow: A Biography of the Imagination.* New York: St. Martin's Press, 1991.

—Bill Delaney

Arna Wendell Bontemps

Born: Alexandria, Louisiana; October 13, 1902
Died: Nashville, Tennessee; June 4, 1973

Bontemps, recognized as a scholar and historian of the Harlem Renaissance, is considered one of the most significant African American writers.

Traditions: African American
Principal works: *God Send Sundays*, 1931; *Black Thunder*, 1936; *Great Slave Narratives*, 1969 (editor)

Arna Bontemps, at age twenty-one, accepted a teaching position in New York City at the beginning of the Harlem Renaissance. Through his poetry, novels, short stories, and essays, he became one of that movement's defining writers. Bontemps, whose father was a bricklayer and whose mother, a schoolteacher, instilled in him a love of books, was born in Louisiana, but, because of white threats against his family, was reared and educated in California, where he was graduated from Pacific Union College in 1923.

The Bontemps family settled in the Watts section of Los Angeles in 1905. At the time they were the only African American family in the neighborhood. When Bontemps was twelve years old, his mother died, and he was sent to live with relatives in the California countryside. There, by becoming his Uncle Buddy's "companion and confidant in the corn rows," Bontemps gained access to a living embodiment of Southern black folk culture. According to Bontemps, Uncle Buddy was an "old derelict" who drank alcohol and loved "dialect stories, preacher stories, ghost stories, slave and master stories. He half-believed in signs and charms and mumbo-jumbo, and he believed whole-heartedly in ghosts." Concerned at Uncle Buddy's influence, Bontemps's father sent his son to a white boarding school, admonishing him, "Now don't go up there acting colored." Fifty years later, the rebuke still rankled: Recalling his father's advice in 1965, Bontemps exclaimed, "How dare anyone, parent, schoolteacher, or merely literary critic, tell me not to act colored?" Pride in color and heritage stamps all Bontemps's works.

The African American experience is at the heart of all Bontemps's work. His novel *God Send Sundays*, which he and Countée Cullen adapted for Broadway in 1946, is based loosely on the life of Uncle Buddy. The work offers a glimpse of the Southern racing circuit through the eyes of a black jockey in the late 1800's. Another novel, *Black Thunder*, is based on Gabriel Prosser's slave rebellion. Bontemps edited an anthology, *Great Slave Narratives*, and *The Book of Negro Folklore* in 1958. With Langston Hughes, Bontemps edited *The Poetry of the Negro 1746-1949* (1963). Bontemps was a central figure in the rediscovery and dissemination of African American literature.

Bontemps was a librarian at Fisk University from 1943 to 1965. Although he left to teach at the University of Illinois and then at Yale during the late 1960's, he returned to Fisk in 1971 and remained there until his death in 1973.

Black Thunder
TYPE OF WORK: Novel
FIRST PUBLISHED: 1936

Black Thunder, Bontemps's defining novel, is a fictionalized account of the early nineteenth century Gabriel Insurrection, in Virginia. The novel, which chronicles the Gabriel Prosser-led rebellion against the slave owners of Henrico County, was generally lauded by critics as one of the most significant black American works of fiction. Richard Wright praised the work for dealing forthrightly with the historical and revolutionary traditions of African Americans.

Gabriel Prosser, a slave convinced that anything "equal to a grey squirrel wants to be free," urges the other slaves to revolt against their owners. The rebellion is hastened when a brutal slaveowner whips a slave, Bundy, to death. Even though the rebellion ultimately fails, Gabriel Prosser nonetheless emerges as a potent hero. The "power of black folk" credo is central to *Black Thunder*. Bontemps's treatment of Bundy's funeral is

Arna Wendell Bontemps (Library of Congress)

faithful in detail to the customs of the time. Bontemps's use of signs and portents pushes the story to its heroic ending. Stunning characterizations of Pharaoh, Drucilla, Ben, and Gabriel become multileveled, believably universal personalities through Bontemps's skillful use of folk material. Elements of magic appear in *Black Thunder* just as they appear in folktales and beliefs as recorded by collectors.

Bundy's spirit returns to haunt Pharaoh, the slave who betrays the rebellion and whose death is foreshadowed. Use of charms and countercharms is rampant, conjure-poisoning looms at all times, and rebellious slaves debate omens in the stars. The tapestry that Bontemps weaves shows the intricate beliefs of slaves to be colorful and compelling. Bontemps's narrative techniques have origins in black folklore about death, ghosts, and spirits.

Black Thunder's strength, largely, is in its depiction of an alternate worldview, which, while retaining the power to sanctify or punish, is painfully adapting to a new land and people. Critics note that Bontemps situates his story in the politics of the times: Readers see blame for slave unrest placed at the feet of Thomas Jefferson during John Quincy Adams's bitter reelection campaign. Bontemps depicts the Virginia legislature debate considering sectional segregation of blacks, slaves and free, and chronicles the press. *Black Thunder* was written during the 1930's; some critics believe it reflects the mood of the Depression.

Great Slave Narratives
TYPE OF WORK: Autobiographies
FIRST PUBLISHED: 1969

Great Slave Narratives, Bontemps's 1960's revival of a once-popular American literary genre, is a compilation of three book-length narratives written by former slaves. During much of the nineteenth century, slave narratives were best-sellers for American publishers. The reintroduction of this literary form was inspired by the Black Power movement of the 1960's and 1970's and the resurgent interest in black culture and the African American experience. Readers were again curious about how it felt to be black and a slave; they wanted to know how the world looked through the eyes of one who had achieved a measure of freedom by effort and suffering. Who, readers wanted to know, were the people who had passed through the ordeal, and how had they expressed their thoughts and feelings?

Bontemps chose for this book three outstanding examples of the genre. The first, *The Interesting Narrative of the Life of Olaudah Equiano, or Gustavus Vassa, the African* (1789), by Olaudah Equiano, who was given the name Gustavus Vassa, gained wide attention, and is particularly interesting for the author's vivid recall of his African background. In 1794, it went into its eighth edition, with many more to follow in America and Europe.

The second book, *The Fugitive Blacksmith; Or, Events in the History of James W. C. Pennington, Pastor of a Presbyterian Church, New York, Formerly a Slave in the State of Maryland, United States* (1850), is the colorful tale of a full-blooded African who was honored with the degree of Doctor of Divinity by the University of Heidelberg, Germany. Yale University denied him admission as a regular student but did not interfere when he stood outside the doors of classrooms in order to hear professors lecture. Pennington also was the first black to write a history of his people in America: *A Text Book of the Origin and History of the Colored People* (1841).

The final narrative in the trilogy, *Running a Thousand Miles for Freedom: Or, The Escape of William and Ellen Craft from Slavery* (1860), an exciting story of a courageous slave couple's escape, is perhaps the high point in the development of the slave narrative genre. Apparently no two slaves in their flight from subjugation to freedom ever thrilled the world so much as did this handsome young couple. Not everyone was pleased, however. President James Polk was so infuriated by their success that he threatened to use the Fugitive Slave Law and the military in their recapture. By then the Crafts were in England.

Bontemps, in his introduction to *Great Slave Narratives*, explained the importance of this "half-forgotten history," placing it in the context of American literature: "Hindsight," he wrote, "may yet disclose the extent to which this writing, this impulse, has been influential on subsequent American writing, if not indeed on America's view of itself. . . . The standard literary sources and the classics of modern fiction pale in comparison as a source of strength."

SUGGESTED READINGS

Aptheker, Herbert. *A Documentary History of the Negro People.* Secaucus, N.J.: Citadel Press, 1973.

Bader, Barbara. "History Changes Color: A Story in Three Parts." *The Horn Book Magazine* 73 (January/February, 1997): 91-98.

Baker, Houston A., Jr. *Black Literature in America.* New York: McGraw-Hill, 1971.

Blackett, R. J. M. *Building an Antislavery Wall.* Baton Rouge: Louisiana State University Press, 1983.

Blockson, Charles L. *The Underground Railroad: First Person Narratives of Escapes to Freedom in the North.* New York: Prentice Hall, 1987.

Bontemps, Arna. *Arna Bontemps-Langston Hughes Letters, 1925-1967.* Selected and edited by Charles H. Nichols. New York: Paragon House, 1990.

———. Introduction to *Black Thunder.* Beacon Press: Boston, 1968.

Davis, Arthur P. *From the Dark Tower: Afro-American Writers, 1900-1960.* Washington, D.C.: Howard University Press, 1974.

Jones, Kirkland C. *Renaissance Man from Louisiana: A Biography of Arna Wendell Bontemps.* Westport, Conn.: Greenwood Press, 1992.

Sundquist, Eric J. *The Hammers of Creation: Folk Culture in Modern African-American Fiction.* Athens: University of Georgia Press, 1992.

Weil, Dorothy. "Folklore Motifs in Arna Bontemps' *Black Thunder.*" *Southern Folklore Quarterly* 35 (March, 1971): 1-14.

—Barbara Day

Cecilia Manguerra Brainard

BORN: Cebu, Philippines; November 21, 1947

Brainard has reminded American readers of how Filipinos earned their independence.

TRADITIONS: Filipino American

PRINCIPAL WORKS: *Woman with Horns and Other Stories,* 1987; *Philippine Woman in America,* 1991; *Song of Yvonne,* 1991 (published in the United States as *When the Rainbow Goddess Wept,* 1994); *Fiction by Filipinos in America,* 1993; *Acapulco at Sunset and Other Stories,* 1995; *Contemporary Fiction by Filipinos in America,* 1997 (editor)

Born one year after the Philippines gained its independence, Cecilia Manguerra Brainard was surrounded from the start with a sense of her country's having been born at almost the same time as herself. After centuries of Spanish colonialism, more than four decades of American control, and four years of Japanese occupation, finally, in 1946, Filipinos were free to determine their own future. The Americans had helped prepare for this moment through elective models and had fought side by side with Filipinos during the war, and the Americans were vital to the difficult postwar reconstruction, but Brainard grew up well aware of her fellow Filipinos' own proud contributions toward establishment of an independent Philippines. The street on which she lived in Cebu was called Guerrillero Street in honor of her father, a guerrilla and then a civil engineer involved in rebuilding shattered Philippine cities. Many of the anecdotes in her first novel, *Song of Yvonne,* came from tales of war remembered by her family.

As a result, even when Brainard left home for graduate studies at the University of California at Los Angeles in the late 1960's, she brought with her an identity as a Filipina. She married a former member of the Peace Corps, Lauren Brainard, who had served on Leyte, an island close to Cebu. In California, she worked on documentary film scripts and public relations from 1969 to 1981. Then she began the newspaper columns later collected in *Philippine Woman in America,* which describe the enrichment and frustration felt by Philippine Americans who are straddling two cultures. Conscious of her own Americanization and anxious to provide her three sons with cultural choices, she formed Philippine American Women Writers and Artists, an organization intent on publishing remembered legends and scenes from the contributors' childhoods. Brainard's organization was intended to provide a continuum of presence from varied pasts to a shared future. Such dedication to the "memory of a people" is in the ancient Philippine tradition of the female *babaylan*, or priestess.

Woman with Horns and Other Stories
TYPE OF WORK: Short fiction
FIRST PUBLISHED: 1987

The stories in this collection by Brainard derive from the author's attempt to compensate for the fact that Filipino culture, for hundreds of years, was considered too primitive to be significant in the eyes of nations such as Spain, the United States, and Japan. The author's nationalism (reinforced by nostalgia after her emigration to California) is reinforced by her placing many of the tales in Ubec—the reverse spelling of Cebu, the Philippine island of the author's birth. The fact that invading forces so often destroyed or neglected native records provided the final impulse for Brainard to depend on her imagination for invention of details wherever history has been forced to remain silent. Her stories also show her division of allegiance between her native land and her adopted country.

An example of Brainard's creative approach to history is found in the story "1521." The failure of Ferdinand Magellan to complete his circumnavigation of the world is usually explained by his coming between two hostile Filipino chiefs. Yet "1521" suggests that Lapu-Lapu may have killed Magellan in revenge for the death of Lapu-Lapu's infant son at Spanish hands. "Alba," however, shows more tolerance when, in 1763, during the English occupation of Manila, Doña Saturnina gives birth to a fair-skinned son. The son is accepted by her husband. Similarly, in "The Black Man in the Forest" old guerrilla general Gregorio kills an African American soldier but will not let his body be cannibalized despite near-starvation brought on by the Philippine-American War. The title story recounts how, in 1903, an American public health director finds renewed interest in life, after the death of his wife, with Agustina, a seductive Filipina widow. The effects of war are remarked in "Miracle at Santo Niño Church," in which Tecla suffers nightmares about the Japanese who bayoneted her family. "The Blue-Green Chiffon Dress" uses the period of the Vietnam War as occasion for a brief encounter between Gemma and a soldier heading back to combat. "The Discovery" describes a Filipina's torn loyalties between her American husband and a former Filipino lover who, like her homeland, seems ravaged by time and violent circumstance.

The collection does not observe the historical sequence. For the modern Filipino, perhaps, all past time is being experienced for the first time by a people whose history has been withheld from them. In any given period, however, Filipino resilience has proved to outweigh victimization. Melodrama in the stories' circumstances repeatedly gives way to quietude and certitude.

SUGGESTED READINGS

Casper, Leonard. "Four Filipina Writers." *Amerasia Journal*, Winter, 1998, 143.
_____. *Sunsurfers Seen from Afar: Critical Essays, 1991-1996.* Metro Manila, Philippines: Anvil, 1996.
Zapanta Manlapaz, Edna. *Songs of Ourselves.* Metro Manila, Philippines: Anvil, 1994.

—Leonard Casper

Gwendolyn Brooks

BORN: Topeka, Kansas; June 7, 1917

The first black author to win the Pulitzer Prize in poetry, Brooks affirms the power of ordinary people.

TRADITIONS: African American
PRINCIPAL WORKS: *A Street in Bronzeville*, 1945; *Annie Allen*, 1949; *Maud Martha*, 1953; *The Bean Eaters*, 1960; *In the Mecca*, 1968; *Riot*, 1969; *Family Pictures*, 1970; *Report from Part One: An Autobiography*, 1972; *Beckonings*, 1975; *To Disembark*, 1981; *The Near-Johannesburg Boy and Other Poems*, 1986; *Blacks*, 1987; *Gottschalk and the Grand Tarantelle*, 1988; *Winnie*, 1988; *Children Coming Home*, 1991; *Report from Part Two*, 1996

Gwendolyn Brooks, the child of loving parents who valued learning, was encouraged to write. Her father provided a desk and bookshelves; her mother took her to meet the writers Langston Hughes and James Weldon Johnson. After being graduated from Wilson Junior College, she was married to Henry Lowington Blakely, also a writer, in 1939.

From Langston Hughes she received encouragement to write about the everyday aspects of black life. She wrote about relatives she knew or stories she heard growing up. Her early poetry also reflects her dreams for romance. The Pulitzer Prize-winning *Annie Allen* traces the growth of a young woman from childhood to maturity. Brooks is not, however, a romantic poet. Her work exhibits a realistic and unsentimental understanding of what it means to be a black woman in twentieth century America. The strength of her poetry lies in its illumination and criticism of a society that does not respect and reward those who are good. The forms of her work often contain a similar criticism of the literary world: *Annie Allen*, for example, is a parody of a traditional epic poem.

Brooks's novel *Maud Martha* compassionately explores a woman's search for identity and her resulting spiritual growth. Many African American themes are illumined: The light skin versus dark skin motif is one. Much in the novel is taken from Brooks's life. Her autobiography, *Report from Part One*, is a creative composite of experiences, memories, photographs, and interviews. It is less a literary chronology than it is a storytelling experience in the oral tradition.

In the late 1960's, Brooks began working closely with young black writers whose concerns for the poor and oppressed mirrored her own. Her poetry of this period, *Riot* and *Family Pictures*, exhibits a strong voice, an increased use of black speech patterns, and a larger focus on black consciousness. She celebrated her achievement of selfhood with a decision to publish her work with African American publishers. Throughout her career Brooks has looked to the men, women, and children in her black community for inspiration. Through them and for them she has made a difference.

Poetry

FIRST PUBLISHED: *A Street in Bronzeville*, 1945; *Annie Allen*, 1949; *The Bean Eaters*, 1960; *Selected Poems*, 1963; *In the Mecca*, 1968; *Riot*, 1969; *Family Pictures*, 1970; *Aloneness*, 1971; *Beckonings*, 1975; *Primer for Blacks*, 1980; *To Disembark*, 1981; *The Near-Johannesburg Boy*, 1986; *Blacks*, 1987; *Gottschalk and the Grand Tarantelle*, 1988; *Winnie*, 1988

Gwendolyn Brooks, who began her career in 1945 with the publication of her first book, *A Street in Bronzeville*, was first inspired by encouraging parents, her own wisdom, and a personal dedication to words. The Civil Rights movement of the late 1960's, which fostered cultural renewal in black America, expanded her consciousness, nourished her growth, and sustained her lifelong love and appreciation for blackness. It is not unusual to hear Brooks speak of the period before 1967 as a time when she had "sturdy" artistic ideas, and the period after 1967 as a time when she felt "sure."

Her first two books of poetry, *A Street in Bronzeville* and *Annie Allen*, and others written in the 1950's and 1960's appear to conform to tradition in their use of the sonnet form and of slant rhyme. There is, however, nothing traditional about one 1945 sonnet's subject: abortion. In many ways, *A Street in Bronzeville* is untraditional, innovative, and courageous, although written with a sturdy respect for tradition. *Annie Allen*, for which Brooks was awarded a Pulitzer Prize

Gwendolyn Brooks (Jill Krementz)

in poetry—the first awarded to an African American—uses narrative verse to trace the growth of a semiautobiographical character from girlhood to womanhood. Brooks drew upon personal experiences and social issues as subjects for many early poems. In 1960, she published *The Bean Eaters*, a collection containing two well-known poems: "We Real Cool," about seven pool players at the Golden Shovel, and "The Chicago *Defender* Sends a Man to Little Rock," written after the 1957 murder of Emmett Till. Her early career also includes publication of *Bronzeville Girls and Boys* (1956), a children's book, and *Selected Poems.*

Although her poetry remained grounded in the joy, frustration, injustice, and reality of black life, Brooks's involvement with young writers in the late 1960's and her poetry workshops for the Blackstone Rangers, a Chicago gang, produced a new voice. Earlier structured forms gave way to free verse. Vocabulary flowed more freely into black vernacular. In *In the Mecca*, a book-length poem about Chicago's old Mecca Building, a mother's search for her child ultimately becomes a metaphor for the individual search for self in an inhumane society: "The Lord was their shepherd./ Yet did they want."

Her sure years produced another identity-affirming change in Brooks's career: the decision to publish with black publishers. *Riot, Family Pictures*, and *Beckonings* chronicle social unrest and anger. Although discouraged by the lack of societal change, Brooks continually praises the indefatigable black spirit. Little Lincoln West in "The Life of Lincoln West" finds comfort in knowing he is "the real thing" in spite of society's abuse. In "To Black Women" from *To Disembark*, she calls upon her black sisters in the diaspora to create flowers, to prevail despite "tramplings of monarchs and other men." Later books, such as *The Near-Johannesburg Boy* and *Winnie*, reflect the wider black community. Whether writing about leaders in Africa or children in Chicago, Brooks is conscious of the fact that her people are black people. To them she appeals for understanding.

A Street in Bronzeville

TYPE OF WORK: Poetry
FIRST PUBLISHED: 1945

A Street in Bronzeville, Brooks's first poetry collection, poignantly reflects the reality of oppression in the lives of urban blacks. The poems portraying ordinary yet unforgettable individuals—from the flamboyant Satin Legs Smith to the sad hunchback girl who yearns for a pain-free life—launched Brooks's successful career. The poetic walk through Bronzeville begins with "the old-marrieds," whose longtime exposure to crowded conditions has eliminated loving communication from their lives.

The long-married couple is followed closely by poems exploring how life in a "kitchenette building" thwarts aspirations. Brooks wonders how dreams can endure in a fight with fried potatoes and garbage ripening in the hall. With honesty and love she portrays resilient characters: Pearl May Lee, whose man has been falsely accused of raping a white woman; Mame, the queen of the blues, who has no family and endures the slaps and pinches of rude men in the club where she sings; Moe Belle Jackson, whose husband "whipped her good last night"; and poor baby Percy, who was burned to death by his brother Brucie. Alongside this unblinking look at life's pain, Brooks now and then gently conveys humorous moments, such as the woman at the hairdresser's who wants an upsweep to "show them girls," and the domestic worker who thinks her employer is a fool.

Alienation in city life is a theme Brooks explores unflinchingly. Matthew Cole seems to be a pleasant man, but in the dirtiness of his room, with fat roaches strolling up the wall, he never smiles. Maud, in the poem "Sadie and Maud," tries to escape Bronzeville by going to college, but finds herself living alone, a thin brown mouse in an old house.

Composed of twelve poems, the last section of the book, "Gay Chaps at the Bar," is dedicated to Brooks's brother, Staff Sergeant Raymond Brooks, and other soldiers who returned from the war trembling and crying. The second poem, "still do I keep my look, my identity," affirms a soldier's individuality even as he dons a government-issue uniform and goes off to meet death on some distant hill. Each body has its pose, "the old personal art, the look."

Ultimately, the critique of America plays itself out in a critique of traditional literary form. Brooks parodies the sonnet in content and form. She uses slant rhyme for the entire collection because she thinks life in Bronzeville is "an off-rhyme situation."

SUGGESTED READINGS

Bloom, Harold. ed. *Gwendolyn Brooks.* Philadelphia: Chelsea House, 2000.

Evans, Mari. *Black Women Writers.* Garden City, N.Y.: Doubleday, 1984.

Kent, George E. *A Life of Gwendolyn Brooks.* Lexington: University Press of Kentucky, 1990.

Melhem, D. H. *Gwendolyn Brooks: Poetry and the Heroic Voice.* Lexington: University Press of Kentucky, 1987.

Mootry, Maria K., and Gary Smith. *A Life Distilled: Gwendolyn Brooks, Her Poetry and Fiction.* Chicago: University of Illinois Press, 1987.

Park, You-me, and Gayle Wald. "Native Daughters in the Promised Land: Gender, Race, and the Question of Separate Spheres." *American Literature* 70, no. 3 (September, 1998): 607.

−Carol F. Bender

Claude Brown

BORN: New York, New York; February 23, 1937

Brown's autobiography, Manchild in the Promised Land, *is considered one of the best and most realistic descriptions of coming of age in a black urban ghetto.*

TRADITIONS: African American

PRINCIPAL WORKS: *Manchild in the Promised Land,* 1965; *The Children of Ham,* 1976

By the time he was thirteen years old, Claude Brown had been hit by a bus, whipped with chains, thrown into a river, and shot in the stomach. Spending more time on the streets of Harlem than in school, Brown was an accomplished thief by the age of ten, when he became a member of the Forty Thieves, a branch of the infamous Buccaneers gang. In a desperate attempt to save their son from his early downward spiral into the penal system, the Browns sent Claude to live with his grandparents for a year. The sojourn seemed to have had little effect on him, because soon after his return to Harlem he was sent to the Wiltwyck School for emotionally disturbed boys.

Brown's early life was a seemingly endless series of events leading to one form or another of incarceration. All told, Brown was sent to reform school three times, and in between those times he ran con games and sold hard drugs. He avoided heroin addiction only because the one time he tried the drug he nearly died. Avoiding drug dependency may have been the key factor in his ability to escape the fate of early death or lengthy incarceration that met so many of his peers. Sensing that he would perish if he remained in Harlem, Brown moved to Greenwich Village at seventeen and began to attend night school.

As he began to understand that living in the ghetto did not mean a certain destiny of crime, misery, and poverty, he no longer believed that living in Harlem would inevitably ruin his life. While selling cosmetics he devoted many hours daily to playing the piano, and eventually enrolled in and was graduated from Howard University. During Brown's first year at Howard, he was urged to write about Harlem for a magazine by Ernest Papanek, who had been the school psychologist at Wiltwyck School. As Brown reflected on his life he began to understand what a difficult feat it is to survive the ghetto, and his writing describes the reasons for the general despair found there. The magazine article led to an offer from a publisher for Brown to write what eventually became *Manchild in the Promised Land.*

Manchild in the Promised Land

TYPE OF WORK: Autobiography
FIRST PUBLISHED: 1965

Brown's classic autobiography *Manchild in the Promised Land* is a quintessentially American story of hardship and disadvantage overcome through determination and hard work, but with a critical difference. It became a best-seller when it was published in 1965 because of its startlingly realistic portrayal of growing up in Harlem. Without sermonizing or sentimentalizing, Brown manages to evoke a vivid sense of the day-to-day experience of the ghetto, which startled many readers and became required reading, along with *The Autobiography of Malcolm X* (1965), for many civil rights activists.

Manchild in the Promised Land describes Brown's resistance to a life path that seemed predetermined by the color of his skin and the place he was born. In the tradition of the slave narrative of the nineteenth century, Brown sets about to establish his personhood to a wide audience, many of whom would write him off as a hopeless case. The book opens with the scene of Brown being shot in the stomach at the age of thirteen after he and his gang are caught stealing bed sheets off a laundry line. What follows is the storyline most would expect of a ghetto child—low achievement in school, little parental supervision, and a sense of hopelessness about the future. There are crime, violence, and drugs lurking in every corner of Harlem, and young Sonny (Claude) falls prey to many temptations.

In spite of spending most of his early years committing various petty crimes, playing hooky from school, living in reform schools, and being the victim of assorted beatings and shootings, Brown manages to elude the destiny of so many of his boyhood friends—early death or successively longer incarcerations. Sensing that he would perish, literally or figuratively, if he remained on the path that seemed destined for him, he leaves Harlem for a few years and begins to chart a different outcome for his life, which includes night school, playing the piano, graduating from Howard University, and beginning law school.

Although Brown offers no formula for escaping the devastation that so often plagues ghetto life, he shows by example that it is possible to succeed in constructing, even in the ghetto, a positive identity.

SUGGESTED READINGS

Baker, Houston A., Jr. "The Environment as Enemy in a Black Autobiography: *Manchild in the Promised Land.*" *Phylon* 32 (Spring-Summer, 1971): 53-59.

Brown, Claude. "Manchild in Harlem." *The New York Times Magazine*, September 16, 1984, 36-77.

Hamalian, Leo. "Claude Brown, Writer." *Artist and Influence* 14 (March 19, 1995): 80-92.

Hartshorne, Thomas L. "Horatio Alger in Harlem: *Manchild in the Promised Land.*" *Journal of American Studies* 24, no. 2 (August, 1990): 243-251.

—*Christy Rishoi*

William Wells Brown

BORN: Lexington, Kentucky; c. 1814
DIED: Chelsea, Massachusetts; November 6, 1884

A former slave and an outspoken critic of slavery, Brown wrote Clotel, *which
is the first known novel written by an African American.*

TRADITIONS: African American
PRINCIPAL WORKS: *Narrative of William W. Brown, a Fugitive Slave, Written by
Himself,* 1847; *Clotel: Or, The President's Daughter, a Narrative of Slave Life in
the United States,* 1853; *The Black Man: His Antecedents, His Genius, and His
Achievements,* 1863

The Southern laws that made slave literacy illegal were on the books for a
reason. William Wells Brown, a former slave, employed his talents as a writer
to argue for African American freedom. In the pre-Civil War years, his
eloquence as an orator made him an important figure in the abolitionist
crusade, and recognition of his literary activities led to appreciation of his
pioneering uses of fiction to critique slavery.

Brown's speeches were often incisive and militant. He showed little admiration for those patriots (such as Thomas Jefferson) who, Brown pointed out,
owned and fathered slaves even as they founded a new nation dedicated to
liberty and equality. He questioned the respect that is generally accorded to
the Declaration of Independence and to the Revolutionary War by revealing
how these icons of American history failed to confront African enslavement.
At an antislavery meeting in 1847 he said that if the United States "is the
'cradle of liberty,' they have rocked the child to death."

Opponents of abolition often founded their arguments on racist assumptions. Brown's detractors made much of the fact that Brown's father was a
white man (probably his master's brother), and implied that his achievements
stemmed from the "white blood" of his father. For example, when Brown
traveled to Europe to gain overseas support for abolitionism, an English
journalist sneered that Brown was "far removed from the black race . . . his
distinct enunciation evidently showed that a white man 'spoke' within."

Brown never sought to deny his racial heritage. In later versions of *Clotel*
published in 1860 and 1864, Brown recast his mulatto hero as a black rebel.
As he makes clear in *Narrative of William W. Brown, a Fugitive Slave, Written by
Himself,* his works were motivated by a deep commitment to the plight of the
three million American slaves, a number that included his own family.
Brown's literary efforts undertaken in behalf of his enslaved brethren were
no doubt supported by his earlier role in secreting fugitive slaves to Canada.

William Wells Brown (Associated Publishers, Inc.)

These fugitives, as Brown had himself, often fled slavery at the price of severing familial ties. He dramatized the strain that slavery places upon family connections in *Clotel,* the first known African American novel. Creating a historical fiction from the well-known fact that Jefferson had a slave mistress, Brown details the outrage of the auction block, the struggle for autonomy, and the tragic ends of slave women who could trace their bloodlines to the author of the Declaration of Independence. The mixed heritage of his heroines—white and black, free and enslaved—points to the contradictions of a nation that idealized liberty even as it practiced slavery.

The Narrative of William W. Brown, a Fugitive Slave
TYPE OF WORK: Autobiography
FIRST PUBLISHED: 1847

In his slave narrative, Brown assailed the prevailing notion of his time that slaves lacked legal or historical selfhood. His autobiography asserts that he has an autonomous identity. *The Narrative of William W. Brown, a Fugitive Slave, Written by Himself,* like many of the stories written by former slaves, does more than chronicle a journey from bondage to freedom. The work also reveals the ways in which the former slave author writes a sense of self, denied by the South's "peculiar institution," into existence.

So great was slavery's disregard of black personhood that William, as a boy on a Kentucky plantation, is forced to change his name when his master's nephew, also named William, comes to live as part of the white household. Brown never forgets this insult. He writes of his flight across the Mason-Dixon line: "So I was not only hunting for my liberty, but also hunting for a name." He finds a name by accepting as his surname that of an Ohio Quaker, Wells Brown, who gives him food and shelter during his escape. He also insists on retaining his first name, showing that his conception of freedom includes the ability to define, shape, and control one's own identity.

Brown is careful to record that his achievement of an unfettered identity is not without its tragic consequences. His personal freedom is undercut by reminders that his mother and siblings remain enslaved. When an escape undertaken in 1833 with his mother fails, his mother is sent to the Deep South, and Brown temporarily gives up his plans of liberty. His repeated sorrowful musings about his mother and sister suggest that Brown's freedom and self-definition are processes infused not only with hope and triumph but also with alienation and loss. His statement that "the fact that I was a freeman . . . made me feel that I was not myself" registers his ambivalence at forever leaving his family in order to find liberty.

Although his purpose is at times weakened by a tragic family history that includes memories of his sister's sale and visions of his mother performing hard labor on a cotton plantation, his understanding of national history lends resolve and determination to his quest. His thoughts of "democratic whips" and "republican chains" work to expose the severe contradictions that haunt the United States and reinforce his decision to risk becoming a fugitive once again in an attempt to reach Canada. In this way, Brown's personal narrative functions as national criticism. His narrative is an American autobiography and an unflinching examination of America.

SUGGESTED READINGS

Andrews, William L. *To Tell a Free Story: The First Century of Afro-American Autobiography, 1760-1865.* Champaign: University of Illinois Press, 1986.

Cassady, Marsh. "William W. Brown." *American History* 30 (January/February, 1996): 16-18.

Davis, Charles T., and Henry Louis Gates, Jr. *The Slave's Narrative.* New York: Oxford University Press, 1985.

Ernest, John. *Resistance and Reformation in Nineteenth-Century African-American Literature: Brown, Wilson, Jacobs, Delany, Douglass, and Harper.* Jackson: University Press of Mississippi, 1995.

Farrison, William Edward. *William Wells Brown: Author and Reformer.* Chicago: University of Chicago Press, 1969.

Yellin, Jean Fagan. *The Intricate Knot: Black Figures in American Literature, 1776-1863.* New York: New York University Press, 1972.

—Russ Castronovo

Carlos Bulosan

BORN: Binalonan, Pangasinan, Luzon, Philippines; November 2, 1911
DIED: Seattle, Washington; September 11, 1956

Bulosan provides the best introduction to the lives of Filipino immigrant workers in America.

TRADITIONS: Filipino American
PRINCIPAL WORKS: *Letter from America,* 1942; *The Voice of Bataan,* 1943; *The Laughter of My Father,* 1944; *America Is in the Heart,* 1946

Carlos Bulosan never forgot his background as a Filipino farmer's son. He expressed the pride he had in this background as well as the severe social situations which small farmers as well as other hired workers faced in their day-to-day attempts to earn a livelihood. A turning point in Bulosan's life, which fixed in his memory and conscience the small farmers' and hired workers' need for a voice, came when Bulosan's father lost the family's small farm and entered the world of serfdom—slavery—in his native Philippines.

Bulosan learned one important lesson from his father: Bulosan saw his father retain his personal identity by confronting his daily tasks and hardships with laughter and cunning. His father showed how one is able to speak as loudly against injustices through satire and laughter as through political diatribe. Bulosan recounts many stories of his father in the numerous pieces which appeared in leading American publications.

In search of a better life, Bulosan worked his way to America, landing in Seattle on July 22, 1930, and found himself on the streets with others looking for work during the Depression. The good life escaped Bulosan because jobs were few and because of the extreme jingoism rampant in America at the time. Although Bulosan never intended to lose his identity as a Filipino, those with whom he came into contact constantly berated him for being an outsider and a Filipino.

Bulosan began to take whatever job he could find, always being relegated to secondary positions because of his ethnicity. As hard as he tried to fit into the American Dream of a better life, he was denied entrance. Bulosan chronicles his father's difficult life in America as an unwanted outsider in his autobiographical novel, *America Is in the Heart.* Bulosan's dream of a life better than that of his father was never realized. He soon learned that he, too, was a slave to those controlling the jobs. This no doubt contributed to Bulosan's strong support and activity in the many workers' movements that arose during his life. Bulosan's hard life also, no doubt, contributed to his early death.

America Is in the Heart
TYPE OF WORK: Autobiography and novel
FIRST PUBLISHED: 1943

In this poignant tale of immigrant dreams and racial discrimination, Bulosan depicts growing up in the Philippines, voyaging to the United States, and enduring years of hardship and despair as an itinerant laborer and union organizer on the West Coast.

Bulosan gives his readers the uncomfortable perspective of harsh discrimination because of racial and economic status. The actual form of the book, however, is difficult to characterize. Unlike a novel, it contains real-life situations, but neither is it autobiography, in the strictest sense. Though narrated in the first person by a character named Carlos Bulosan, the book is neither really nor exclusively an account of his life. For example, unlike the book's narrator, the real Bulosan was not as impoverished. Bulosan states that the events in the book are a composite: They happened either to him or to someone he knew or heard about. The book, then, is a conglomerate portrait of Filipino-American life in the early twentieth century, but Bulosan presents the events as personal history so that the reader is more likely to take what he says to be truth. The use of the first-person narrative voice conveys immediacy and energy, arousing sympathy in a way that a third-person narrative would not.

This is an "everyperson" story, an immigrant myth. As such, it is very episodic in nature, depicting brief or extended encounters first with one character who was influential to Bulosan and then moving on to another character. The voice of Bulosan is constant throughout the novel, and two of his brothers emerge periodically throughout, although no other long-term relationships are described.

The book shows Bulosan growing up in a small *barrio*, or village, in the central Philippines, working in the fields with his father, selling salted fish with his mother, and attending school as he was able. At seventeen, he emigrates to the United States, landing in Seattle and being sold for five dollars to a labor contractor. He moves from one manual job to another up and down the Washington and California coasts, depending on which crops are ready to harvest. He becomes a union organizer and experiences abuse and cruelty at the hands of white leaders and townspeople. His hospitalization for two years because of tuberculosis enables him to read an average of a book a day and to write newsletters that promote the union cause.

America Is in the Heart is a coming-of-age story from an immigrant's point of view. The first third of the book shows Bulosan's youth within the circle of his impoverished but loving family. In the beginning of the second third of the book, Bulosan is optimistic and naïve as he lands on the shores of Seattle at seventeen. Although he is soon duped, sold for hire, and abused, his disillusion never breaks his spiritual faith in the United States or his desire to forge ahead in his own intellectual development and for the welfare of all

Filipino workers. He is forced by "oldtimers," the more seasoned Filipino laborers, into losing his virginity with a Mexican prostitute; his maturity cannot be complete without this sexual awakening. The final third of the book depicts the fruits of his adult labor: the formation of fledgling labor unions and the beginnings of a grass-roots network that will begin to hold white owners and managers accountable for humane working and living conditions for their immigrant itinerant laborers.

SUGGESTED READINGS

Evangelista, Susan, ed. *Carlos Bulosan and His Poetry: A Biography and Anthology.* Seattle: University of Washington Press, 1985.

Lee, Rachel C. *The Americas of Asian American Literature: Gendered Fictions of Nation and Transnation.* Princeton, N.J.: Princeton University Press, 1999.

San Juan, E., Jr. *Carlos Bulosan and the Imagination of the Class Struggle.* New York: Oriole Editions, 1976.

_____, ed. *Introduction to Modern Pilipino Literature.* New York: Twayne, 1974.

—Tom Frazier/Jill B. Gidmark

Abraham Cahan

Born: Podberezy, Lithuania; July 6, 1860
Died: New York, New York; August 31, 1951

As a novelist and a journalist, Cahan was a voice for his fellow Jewish immigrants.

Traditions: Jewish
Principal works: *Yekl: A Tale of the New York Ghetto,* 1896; *The Imported Bridegroom and Other Stories of the New York Ghetto,* 1898; *The White Terror and the Red: A Novel of Revolutionary Russia,* 1905; *The Rise of David Levinsky,* 1917

As a young man in Russia, Abraham Cahan experienced many different identities: pious Jew, Russian intellectual, Nihilist. By his early twenties, in response to prevalent anti-Semitism and recent pogroms, Cahan had become a full-fledged revolutionary socialist, dedicated to the overthrow of the czar and hunted by the Russian government. Hoping to create in America a prototype communist colony in which Jew and gentile were equal, Cahan immigrated to New York in 1882.

Upon his arrival, Cahan modulated his outspoken socialism and embarked on a distinguished career as a Yiddish-language journalist, English teacher, and novelist. As editor for the Yiddish-language *Jewish Daily Forward,* Cahan transformed the paper from a dry mouthpiece for socialist propaganda into a vital community voice, still socialist in its leanings but dedicated to improving the lives of its audience.

One of the early realists, Cahan is appreciated for his frank portrayals of immigrant life. *Yekl: A Tale of the New York Ghetto,* Cahan's first novel in English, follows the rocky road toward Americanization of Yekl Podkovnik, a Russian Jewish immigrant desperately trying to assimilate. Faced with two choices for a wife, Yekl chooses the more assimilated Mamie over his Old World spouse, Gitl, but for all his efforts to become "a Yankee," Yekl's tale ends on a melancholy note, demonstrating that he is unable to break out of his immigrant identity simply by changing his clothes, his language, and his wife.

Cahan's sense of the loss and confusion faced by immigrants to America is also evident in *The Rise of David Levinsky.* This masterful novel tells the rags-to-riches story of a clothier who, despite his wealth and success, is lonely and forlorn, distant from his Russian Jewish beginnings, and alienated from American culture. Following the publication of *Yekl,* Cahan was ushered into the national spotlight by William Dean Howells, who had encouraged many other regional and ethnic writers. Cahan's career in mainstream English-language publishing, however, was short-lived. After *The Rise of David Levinsky* Cahan wrote no more fiction in English, choosing instead to act as a mentor for other writers and to pour his energies into the *Jewish Daily Forward.*

The Rise of David Levinsky
TYPE OF WORK: Novel
FIRST PUBLISHED: 1917

In 1913, in response to a request from the popular *McClure's* magazine for articles describing the success of Eastern European immigrants in the U.S. garment trade, Cahan wrote several short stories instead. Subsequently published as a novel, these pieces of fiction permitted Cahan to explore problematic aspects of the process of Americanization, produce vignettes of immigrant Jewish life, and describe the development of a major American industry.

Cahan uses the life of David Levinsky to explore three interrelated themes. From the opening paragraph, in which Levinsky asserts that although he is a millionaire he is not a happy man, Cahan examines the ambiguous meaning of success and the personal and psychological cost of achieving material gains. Success distances Levinsky from his friends—the companions who came to America with him and those who helped him during his early and difficult years in the New World. His great wealth overawes them, making them uncomfortable in his presence. In turn, Levinsky can never be certain whether people associate with him out of friendship or because they hope to get some of his money. His business success is accomplished through methods that are unethical when they are not illegal, in violation of the values he learned as a child. Appealing to the Social Darwinist creed of "survival of the fittest" to justify his actions, Levinsky is too insecure psychologically to be certain he is, in fact, truly one of "the fittest."

A second major theme is the development of the American ready-to-wear clothing industry and the surprisingly rapid rise to prominence within that industry of recent Russian Jewish immigrants. Levinsky's success illustrates how this occurred, but the contradictions between his methods and his inherited values make the meaning of success ambiguous.

The third theme, the process of adaptation to American life by Russian Jewish immigrants of Levinsky's generation, takes up large segments of the novel. Levinsky experiences the teeming Lower East Side, with its peddlers and markets, its storefront synagogues of recent immigrants, their poverty-stricken homes, and their vigorous intellectual life. As he rises in wealth, Levinsky describes the overfurnished homes of the wealthy, their religious compromises, and the lavish resort hotels that also serve as marriage marts. The novel contains a social history of Jewish immigrants in the years before World War I, as they adapt to a new American reality.

In fulfilling the commission from *McClure's,* Cahan used his fictional manufacturer to show how, in the late 1880's and early 1890's, Russian Jews replaced German Jews at the head of the cloak-and-suit trade. Levinsky, always short of cash during his early years, learned to use unethical subterfuges to postpone payment of his bills. He could undercut major firms on prices because the Orthodox East European Jewish tailors he hired were willing to work longer hours for lower wages in return for not having to work on Saturday. Concentrating his clothing line on a few successful designs, frequently illegally copied from those of established manufacturers, Levinsky achieved an economy of operation that permitted him to sell stylish goods at low prices, a process that made fashionable clothes readily available to the majority of American women.

When Cahan turned his *McClure's* short stories into a longer work, with far greater depth of characterization and scope of social observation, he created the first major novel portraying the Jewish experience in America. In effect, he also created a new literary genre within which there have been many followers. Such acclaimed writers as Bernard Malamud, Philip Roth, and Saul Bellow have continued to explore themes first articulated by Cahan.

SUGGESTED READINGS

Chametzky, Jules. *From the Ghetto: The Fiction of Abraham Cahan.* Amherst: University of Massachusetts Press, 1977.

Girgus, Sam B. *The New Covenant: Jewish Writers and the American Idea.* Chapel Hill: University of North Carolina Press, 1984.

Marovitz, Sanford E. *Abraham Cahan.* New York: Twayne, 1996.

_____. "The Lonely New Americans of Abraham Cahan." *American Quarterly* 20 (Summer, 1968): 196-210.

Sanders, Ronald. *The Downtown Jews: Portraits of an Immigrant Generation.* New York: Harper & Row, 1969.

Walden, Daniel, ed. *The Changing Mosaic: From Cahan to Malamud, Roth, and Ozick.* Albany: State University of New York Press, 1993.

—Anne Fleischmann/Milton Berman

Bebe Moore Campbell

BORN: Philadelphia, Pennsylvania; 1950

Campbell offers telling portraits of people of many backgrounds.

TRADITIONS: African American

PRINCIPAL WORKS: *Sweet Summer: Growing Up with and Without My Dad*, 1989; *Your Blues Ain't Like Mine*, 1992; *Brothers and Sisters*, 1994; *Singing in the Comeback Choir*, 1998

As a child, Bebe Moore Campbell spent her school years in Philadelphia with her mother and her summers in North Carolina with her father. She writes of this divided life in *Sweet Summer: Growing Up with and Without My Dad*, drawing sharp contrasts between the two worlds. She credits both parents with shaping her into a writer.

Her mother, an avid storyteller, designated Sundays as church day and library day. Having learned the value of stories and writing, Campbell composed stories for her father, cliffhangers designed to elicit his immediate response. By the third grade, she knew that she wanted to be a writer; however, not until her mother gave her a book written by an African American did she feel affirmed in that ambition. The knowledge that African Americans wrote books gave her the permission she needed to pursue her dream.

Her first novel, *Your Blues Ain't Like Mine*, was inspired by the 1955 murder of Emmett Till, an African American teenager from Chicago who was killed in Mississippi after speaking to a white woman. Till's death was widely discussed in the African American community, and Campbell grew up feeling that she had known him. Since his murderers were never brought to justice, she sought in *Your Blues Ain't Like Mine* to create a fictional world in which the justice that society withheld exists. The novel showcases her ability to portray many diverse characters.

Her second novel, *Brothers and Sisters*, is set around another event affecting the African American community. Rodney King, an African American motorist, was beaten by police officers in Los Angeles in 1992. The beating was captured on videotape, but the policemen were found not guilty in their first trial, resulting in riots. Delving into the aftermath of this event, *Brothers and Sisters* explores the way in which race affects the relationship between an African American woman and a white woman.

Although Campbell's works reflect her experiences as a woman, she feels that she has been oppressed more for her color than for her gender. Her writings are primarily shaped by her identity as an African American, but her diverse characters reveal more of the commonalities that exist between people than the differences.

Your Blues Ain't Like Mine

TYPE OF WORK: Novel
FIRST PUBLISHED: 1992

Your Blues Ain't Like Mine, Campbell's first novel, chronicles the aftermath of the murder of Armstrong Todd, an event which reverberates in the lives of two families, one black and one white. The novel opens in 1955 in Hopewell, Mississippi, where Armstrong, a fifteen-year-old African American, has come from Chicago to spend the summer with his grandmother. Unused to the ways of the South, he is not aware of the consequences that await him for speaking to Lily Cox, a white woman. When Armstrong is killed by Lily's husband Floyd, family members of the murderer and the victim are forced to examine their lives in relation to this act.

Over time Lily comes to realize that Armstrong's death was prompted more by Floyd's desire to please his father than to protect her. This growing awareness causes her to question her passive allegiance to her husband, a role which she had been taught that women should assume. This shift is furthered by her daughter Doreen, who is not afraid to stand up to her father, a man from whom she feels her mother needed more protection than from Armstrong.

In Chicago, Todd's parents, Delotha and Wydell, must deal with their feelings of guilt and failure which their son's death produces. Delotha's identity is bound up in her obsession to produce another male child to take Armstrong's place, a son whom she must protect from white people. Yet her resolve is pitted against Wydell's reluctance to be a father again, born of his fear of failing yet another child. Eventually, another son, W. T., is born to them, a boy threatening to be lost not to whites but to the streets of Chicago. When Wydell takes his son to Hopewell, another aspect of the interwoven identities of the two families surfaces.

When the novel opens, Lily Cox is listening to the singing of African Americans as they work the cotton fields. She says that the music makes her feel "strong and hopeful," as if she were being healed. When the novel closes, Wydell shows his son where he and others worked the fields, explaining to him that the workers battled the harshness of their lives with song. The songs recalled by Wydell form the backdrop of Lily's life. Both acknowledge song as a source of healing for broken souls. Campbell has said that the title of her novel reflects some irony. In some ways all blues are the same, since human pain is human pain.

SUGGESTED READINGS

Campbell, Bebe Moore. "Bebe Moore Campbell: Her Memoir of 'A Special Childhood' Celebrates the Different Styles of Her Upbringing in a Divided Black Family." Interview by Lisa See. *Publishers Weekly*, June 30, 1989, 82-84.

Edgerton, Clyde. Review of *Your Blues Ain't Like Mine*, by Bebe Moore Campbell. *The New York Times Book Review*, September 20, 1992, 7, 17.

Groban, Betsy. Review of *Singing in the Comeback Choir*, by Bebe Moore Campbell. *The New York Times Book Review*, April 12, 1998, 17.

Time. Review of *Your Blues Ain't Like Mine*, by Bebe Moore Campbell. November 9, 1992, 89.

–Jacquelyn Benton

Denise Elia Chávez

BORN: Las Cruces, New Mexico; August 15, 1948

Chávez's poetry, fiction, and numerous plays show Mexican American women searching for personal identity and space in a complex cultural environment.

TRADITIONS: Mexican American
PRINCIPAL WORKS: *The Last of the Menu Girls*, 1986; *Face of an Angel*, 1990

Denise Chávez was born in the desert Southwest, and she writes about the Native Americans, Mexican Americans, Anglo-Americans, and others who provide the region's rich cultural tapestry. Her works consistently focus on the strength and endurance of ordinary working-class Latino women.

Chávez had twelve years of Catholic schooling and started writing diaries and skits while still in elementary school. She received her bachelor of arts degree in theater from New Mexico State University in 1971, her master of fine arts in theater from Trinity University in San Antonio, Texas, in 1974, and her master of arts in creative writing from the University of New Mexico in 1984. During her school years she worked in a variety of jobs—in a hospital, in an art gallery, and in public relations. She also wrote poetry, fiction, and drama, always with emphasis on the lives of women. She taught at Northern New Mexico Community College, the University of Houston, Artist-in-the-Schools programs, and writers' workshops.

Chávez has written numerous plays and literary pieces, which she often performed or directed, including a national tour with her one-woman performance piece. Her plays have been produced throughout the United States and Europe. Her plays (mostly unpublished), written in English and Spanish, include *Novitiates* (1971), *The Flying Tortilla Man* (1975), *Rainy Day Waterloo* (1976), *The Third Door* (1978), *Sí, hay posada* (1980), *The Green Madonna* (1982), *La morenita* (1983), *El más pequeño de mis hijos* (1983), *Plague-Time* (1984), *Novena Narrativas* (1986), and *Language of Vision* (1987).

The Last of the Menu Girls, interrelated stories about a young Chicana, and the novel *Face of an Angel* have established Chávez's high reputation as a fiction writer. Both works address critical questions of personal and cultural identity with extraordinary wit and compassion. Chávez has a striking ability to create a sense of individual voice for her characters, and she makes that voice resonate for readers who may or may not be familiar with the places and people about whom she writes.

Face of an Angel

TYPE OF WORK: Novel
FIRST PUBLISHED: 1994

Face of an Angel specifically addresses the quest for identity of Soveida Dosa-mantes, a hardworking waitress at El Farol Mexican Restaurant in southern New Mexico. The rich cast of characters around Soveida provides detailed portraits of the lives of Mexican, American, and Mexican American working-class men and women in the Southwest. The work describes these characters' various struggles to know themselves and to be accepted in a multicultural setting. The novel speaks compellingly of the importance of the individual self and the social attitudes that allow the individual freedom to function.

Soveida, who narrates most of the novel, has grown up in Agua Oscura, a fictional small town in the desert Southwest. Soveida explores the boundaries of her life through her interactions with her mother Dolores, her grandmother Mama Lupita, her cousin Mara, and a wide cast of other townspeople. As Chávez brings this population of memorable characters to life, their actions and motivations are shown to be reflections of social attitudes about race, ethnicity, gender, and class. It is difficult for them to break through these received attitudes to wholeness and acceptance of others. Soveida, for exam-ple, seems destined to repeat the same mistakes other women in her family made in their choice of partners, and she becomes involved with a number of lazy and hurtful men, including her two husbands.

Soveida eventually writes a handbook for waitresses, called "The Book of Service," based on her thirty years of work at El Farol. The advice she gives about service reflects her ideas about her life and her connections with other people, and it shows her growing sense of pride in herself as a Chicana. She has learned to question and reject the limited roles assigned to Mexican American women in a male-dominated society, and instead she develops a philosophy that encompasses individual strength and endurance combined with a genuine respect for others, as shown through service.

Soveida's philosophy is reinforced by the novel's unrestrained, irreverent, and hilarious scenes, by the effective use of colloquial bilingual speech, and by the in-depth exploration of such universal issues as poverty, personal relationships, illness, and death. Chávez's characters are all individuals with distinctive voices, and she draws them together in ways that show the possibilities of changing social prejudices. Her major themes focus on the rights and responsibilities of the individual and on the need for an evolving social consciousness.

The Last of the Menu Girls

TYPE OF WORK: Short fiction
FIRST PUBLISHED: 1986

Chávez's *The Last of the Menu Girls* is a collection of seven interrelated stories about Rocío Esquibel, a young Mexican American woman in southern New Mexico who seeks to understand herself, her family, and her community. Rocío's development from girl to woman gives unity to the collage of stories. As Rocío observes those around her she provides a portrait of a culturally diverse community and a clear insight into the human condition.

The title story introduces Rocío at age seventeen beginning her first job as an aide in a hospital in her home town. It is the summer of 1966. One of her tasks is to take menus to patients and get their requests for meals. Rocío studies the patients with great attention. She sees them as individuals with differing needs, and her heart reaches out to them so fully that she suspects she is too emotional for the job. Her emotional investment, however, helps Rocío understand others and makes her better able to understand herself. By the end of the summer Rocío has been promoted to other duties in the hospital, and the system has changed; she is literally the last of the menu girls. Her compassion for others continues to serve her well as a way of understanding herself and her relationship to the world.

In the other stories Rocío increasingly looks to the past, to her personal history and to that of her Mexican American culture. She also tries to envision the future, to create the woman she hopes to be. By the end of the stories Rocío has found her mission. As her mother says, it would take a lifetime to write even the story of their home; there are stories all around. Rocío dedicates herself to writing the lives of the ordinary people she knows, people who often cannot speak for themselves. In the process of telling their stories, Rocío will speak for herself and for her culture.

Chávez's talents as a playwright and a poet give a distinctive quality to her fiction. She captures the small gestures and the precise voice of her characters and shows, rather than tells, their actions. Her work is filled with humor and the hope of the heart that makes her characters enduring.

SUGGESTED READINGS

Balassi, William, John F. Crawford, and Annie O. Eysturoy, eds. *This Is About Vision: Interviews with Southwestern Writers.* Albuquerque: University of New Mexico Press, 1990.

Farah, Cynthia. *Literature and Landscape: Writers of the Southwest.* El Paso: Texas Western Press, 1988.

Herrera-Sobek, María, and Helena Maria Viramontes, eds. *Chicana Creativity and Criticism: Charting New Frontiers in American Literature.* Houston, Tex.: Arte Público Press, 1988.

Reed, Ishmael. *Hispanic American Literature.* New York: HarperCollins, 1995.
Salas, Abel M. "The Word Game." *Hispanic* 9 (October, 1996): 18-20.

—Lois A. Marchino

Frank Chin

BORN: Berkeley, California; February 25, 1940

Author of the first Asian American play produced on the New York stage, Chin is among the first few writers to present the experiences of Chinese Americans.

TRADITIONS: Chinese American

PRINCIPAL WORKS: *The Chickencoop Chinaman*, pr. 1972, pb. 1981; *Aiiieeeee! An Anthology of Asian-American Writers*, 1974, revised 1983 (with others); *The Year of the Dragon*, pr. 1974, pb. 1981; *The Chinaman Pacific and Frisco R. R. Co.*, 1988; *Donald Duk*, 1991; *The Big Aiiieeeee! An Anthology of Chinese American and Japanese American Literature*, 1991 (with others); *Gunga Din Highway*, 1994; *Bulletproof Buddhists and Other Essays*, 1998

A fifth-generation Chinese American, Frank Chin has been witness to a most dramatic chapter in the history of his people. The chapter started with the 1943 repeal of the racially discriminatory Chinese Exclusion Act of 1882. Chin has lived in a social and cultural environment that tends to distort the image of his people and to ignore their history. Chin sees it as his mission to restore their image and remember the heroism, the pioneering spirit, and the sufferings of his people by writing about them from a Chinese American perspective. His plays and novels are informed by his knowledge of the history of Chinese Americans, his understanding of their cultural heritage, and his vision of their future.

Chin believes that the history of Chinese Americans constitutes a heroic and vital part of the history of the American West. In the 1970's, his sense of history was accompanied by a pessimistic prediction. Chin was aware that legislative racism had turned the Chinese American community into a bachelor society in the past and that euphemized discrimination was luring many young Chinese Americans toward assimilation. Hence, he declared in an essay, "Yellow Seattle," that Chinese America was doomed to extinction. This kind of pessimism permeates the two plays that he wrote in the 1970's: *The Chickencoop Chinaman* and *The Year of the Dragon*. Pervading these works is an atmosphere of gloom, decay, and death, with bitter young people full of self-contempt renouncing their racial identity and with their families and communities falling apart. The apparent revival of Chinatown and the growth of the Chinese community in the 1980's seem to have helped change Chin's view. Such a change is discerned in *Donald Duk*, in which an atmosphere of renewal and jubilant celebration prevail. In the play, a family and a commu-

nity conscientiously and successfully pass on their heritage from one generation to another in San Francisco's Chinatown.

Frank Chin (Corky Lee)

The Chickencoop Chinaman

TYPE OF WORK: Drama
FIRST PRODUCED: 1972; first published, 1981

The Chickencoop Chinaman is a subtle depiction of the experiences of a Chinese
American writer who loses and then regains his racial identity and cultural
heritage. Laced with historical allusions to legislative and euphemized discrimination against Chinese Americans, the play centers on a visit the writer,
Tam Lum, makes to Pittsburgh to collect materials for a documentary film
about a famous black boxer. The events that take place during his visit make
him realize that what he should do is pursue the lonely mission of telling
stories to the unassimilated children of the Chinese railroad builders and gold
miners.

The play begins with Tam telling an airline hostess that he was born to be
a writer for "the Chinamans sons of Chinamans." As the ensuing scenes show,
he has never had a chance to write about the heroism of his people. When a
boy, he used to sit in the kitchen, listening to his grandmother's stories of the
Chinese railroaders, but he heard no such stories on the radio. In his
desperate search for a hero of his own race, he imagined that the Lone Ranger

with his mask was a Chinese American in disguise. To his dismay, the Ranger turned out to be a decrepit white racist who ordered Tam to go back to Chinatown to preserve his culture.

Ironically, there was no Chinatown to which Tam could return to preserve his culture, for the old people there were trying to forget their history in order to survive. They urged him to destroy the past and get assimilated. Thus, he turned his back on his father, eradicated his memory of the railroaders, and married a white woman. A few years later, he found himself incompetent as a writer, deserted by his wife, and forgotten by his children. In order to keep himself busy and give his children a gift, he decided to make a film about a black former boxer and his father, Mr. Popcorn, who lived in Pittsburgh.

In Pittsburgh, Tam discovers that the boxer has invented a father. Mr. Popcorn adamantly refuses to play a fake father in a documentary film and chastises Tam for betraying his real father. Tam's plan for the film collapses; however, he learns that he must be true to his own identity and fulfill his destiny. The play ends with Tam standing in a kitchen, asking a group of children to turn off the radio and listen to the stories that his grandmother used to tell him about the Chinese railroaders in the Old West.

Donald Duk
TYPE OF WORK: Novel
FIRST PUBLISHED: 1991

Donald Duk is a psychologically realistic depiction of a fifth-generation Chinese American boy who, by learning his family history and his cultural heritage, frees himself from the trauma caused by the racial stereotyping of his people. Set in San Francisco's Chinatown during a New Year's celebration, the novel delineates the initiation of its protagonist, Donald Duk, in a manner that interweaves history, legend, surrealistic dreams, and psychological realism.

Donald is troubled more by his racial identity than by his funny name. Repeatedly he has heard people at school and in the media say that his people are traditionally timid and passive, introverted and nonassertive; therefore, they are alien to American heroism and pioneering spirit. He is thus filled with self-contempt and tormented by everything Chinese. With the Chinese New Year approaching, he becomes more and more depressed and withdrawn, for the New Year will provide another opportunity for his schoolteachers to repeat in class the same thing that everybody else says about his people.

The New Year during which Donald completes the first twelve-year cycle of his life (there are twelve years in the Chinese zodiac) is the right time for the elders in his family and in the community to tell him what everybody has chosen not to say about his people. From these elders he learns that his people came from a land that had produced its own Robin Hoods, and that Chinese railroaders, his great-great grandfather among them, blasted their way through Nevada, lived in tunnels carved in deep frozen snow for two winters, set a world record in track-laying, and went on strike for back pay and Chinese foremen for Chinese gangs. He is so fascinated with these railroaders' heroism and pioneering spirit that scenes of their toil and struggle appear one after another in his dreams.

Through careful library research, Donald determines that his dreams are actually flashbacks to the real events that have been excluded in history books by the majority culture. With his newly gained understanding of the cultural heritage of his people, he is eager to go back to school to challenge the stereotype of his people with his story about their courage and assertiveness.

The Year of the Dragon

TYPE OF WORK: Drama
FIRST PRODUCED: 1974; first published, 1981

The Year of the Dragon is an anguished depiction of a Chinese American man and his family, in conflict between the younger generation's urge toward assimilation and the older generation's obsession with tradition. Set in the late 1960's in San Francisco's Chinatown, the play represents Frank Chin's artistic expression of his view that historically Chinese America is doomed. The play begins with Fred Eng, a tour guide in Chinatown, welcoming a group of tourists and wishing them happiness in the Year of the Dragon. He speaks like Charlie Chan but he wants to drop his phony accent and just be himself. Fred cannot be just himself; he knows that tourists expect a Chinese American to speak like Charlie Chan.

Fred wanted to be a writer and went to college, but his ailing father, Wing Eng, called him back to Chinatown to take over the father's travel agency and care for Fred's mother, Hyacinth, and two younger siblings, Mattie and Johnny. The ensuing scenes show that Wing has gathered his family, including his first wife from China, so that he can die as a Chinese would like to, surrounded by a happy family and assured that Fred will stay in Chinatown to care for his two mothers. Wing's family is by no means happy. His first wife, who has just arrived from China and whose expected presence causes resentment from others, seems to feel out of place in her husband's home. Hyacinth frequently escapes to the bathroom to sing her lullaby. Mattie, who has "married out white" like many other Chinese Americans, cannot stand her father's home. She urges the family to "forget Chinatown and be just people." Johnny is a juvenile delinquent still on probation, and Fred is torn between his obligation to his father as a son and his sense of himself as an individual. He plans to stay in Chinatown for a while but have everyone else leave for Boston after his father dies. He urges Johnny to marry a white girl.

Wing vehemently rejects Fred's plan, insisting that Fred and his two mothers should stay in Chinatown. He dies amid a violent argument with his son while the festive sounds are floating into the house. At the end of the play, Fred appears like "a shrunken Charlie Chan," welcoming tourists to Chinatown.

SUGGESTED READINGS

Chen, Jack. *The Chinese of America.* San Francisco: Harper & Row, 1980.

Davis, Robert Murray. "Frank Chin: Iconoclastic Icon." *Redneck Review of Literature* 23 (Fall, 1992): 75-78.

McDonald, Dorothy Ritsuk. "An Introduction to Frank Chin's *The Chickencoop Chinaman* and *The Year of the Dragon.*" In *Three American Literatures: Essays in Chicano, Native American, and Asian American Literature for Teachers of American Literature,* edited by Houston A. Baker, Jr. New York: Modern Language Association of America, 1982.

Moran, Edward. "Frank Chin." *Current Biography* 60 (March, 1999): 17-20.

Samarth, Manini. "Affirmations: Speaking the Self into Being." *Parnassus: Poetry in Review* 17, no. 1 (1992): 88-101.

Sechi, Joanne Harumi. "Being Japanese-American Doesn't Mean 'Made in Japan.'" In *The Third Woman: Minority Women Writers of the United States,* edited by Dexter Fisher. Boston: Houghton Mifflin, 1989.

—Chenliang Sheng

Louis H. Chu

BORN: Toishan, Kwangtung Province, China; October 1, 1915
DIED: New York, New York; 1970

*Chu is acknowledged as the first Chinese American novelist to depict
Chinatown life realistically.*

TRADITIONS: Chinese American
PRINCIPAL WORK: *Eat a Bowl of Tea,* 1961

Born in China, Louis Chu emigrated to America when he was nine years old.
Thus Asia and America played significant roles in his formative experience.
In *Eat a Bowl of Tea,* Chu's only published novel, he writes knowledgeably
and feelingly about life in a rural community of South China as well as about
life in New York's urban Chinatown. Chu's life and career in the United States
followed a pattern of education and employment that many immigrants
would envy. After completing high school in New Jersey, Chu attended
Upsala College, earning his degree in 1937. He then attended New York
University, obtaining an M.A. in 1940. Two years of graduate study at the
New School for Social Research in New York rounded off his formal education. During World War II, Chu served in the Signal Corps of the U.S. Army.
In 1940, he married Pong Fay, who had been born and raised in China; they
brought up four children in Hollis, New York, a Queens suburb, where they
made a Chinese-speaking home.

Things Chinese American were very much a part of Chu's career. From
1951 to 1961, he was a disc jockey for radio station WHOM in New York City
(he was the only Chinese American disc jockey in the city). His radio show,
called *Chinese Festival,* could be heard four evenings a week. In 1961, Chu
went to work for the city's Department of Welfare and became the director of
a center in New York's Chinatown. He was also an entrepreneur, being the
owner of the Acme Company, and played an active role in the Chinatown
community, holding the post of executive secretary of the Soo Yuen Benevo-
lent Association for more than a decade.

Chu's experience and observation provided ample grist for the mill of his
novel, *Eat a Bowl of Tea,* whose protagonist wrestles with issues of traditional
Confucian filial duty, marital infidelity, and his identity as a Chinese in
America during the 1940's.

Eat a Bowl of Tea

TYPE OF WORK: Novel
FIRST PUBLISHED: 1961

Widely acclaimed by Asian American writers and critics, Chu's *Eat a Bowl of Tea* is the first Chinese American novel that realistically depicts New York's Chinatown bachelor society in the United States shortly after World War II. The novel focuses on the struggles of a young Chinese American who attempts to define his identity.

As the novel opens, it is revealed that the protagonist, Wang Ben Loy, a bridegroom of two months, has become impotent. Ben Loy is a Chinese American in his twenties, a filial son, obedient to his Confucian father, Wah Gay, who left him in China for twenty-five years while establishing himself in America.

Wah Gay, owner of a gambling establishment in Chinatown, sends for Ben Loy, who works as a waiter, joins the U.S. Army, then returns to waiting tables at a Chinese restaurant. Ben Loy alleviates his frustrations by regularly patronizing prostitutes; unfortunately, he contracts several venereal diseases. In 1948, Ben Loy fulfills his filial duty by marrying Mei Oi, a China-born daughter of Wah Gay's longtime friend.

Neglected by her husband, Mei Oi becomes pregnant by Ah Song, a notorious Chinatown philanderer. Chu appears sympathetic with women by implying that husbands must share blame for the infidelity of their wives when sexual and emotional needs are unsatisfied.

Mei Oi passes off the expected child as Ben Loy's, but when Ah Song is sighted sneaking from her apartment, Chinatown buzzes with gossip. Feeling disgraced, Wah Gay ambushes Ah Song after a tryst at Mei Oi's apartment and slices off his left ear. Justice is served when the unofficial Chinatown judicial system condemns Ah Song to five years' ostracism. Having lost face, Wah Gay exiles himself.

Ben Loy and Mei Oi go west to San Francisco, where Mei Oi has a baby whom Ben Loy accepts. They look forward to having others after Ben Loy's impotence is cured by a Chinese herbalist, who makes him "eat a bowl of tea" of medicinal herbs. Most important, Ben Loy breaks from the patriarchal control of his traditionalist Confucian father and becomes the arbiter of his Asian American identity.

SUGGESTED READINGS

Chua, Cheng Lok. "Golden Mountain: Chinese Versions of the American Dream in Lin Yutang, Louis Chu, and Maxine Hong Kingston." *Ethnic Groups* 4 (1982): 33-59.

Hsiao, Ruth. "Facing the Incurable: Patriarchy in *Eat a Bowl of Tea.*" In *Reading the Literatures of Asian America,* edited by Shirley Geok-lin Lim and Amy Ling. Philadelphia: Temple University Press, 1992.

Kim, Elaine H. *Asian American Literature: An Introduction to the Writings and Their Social Context.* Philadelphia: Temple University Press, 1982.

Ling, Jinqi. "Reading for Historical Specificities: Gender Negotiations in Louis Chu's *Eat a Bowl of Tea.*" *MELUS* 20, no. 1 (1995): 35-51.

—C. L. Chua and Janet Fujimoto

Sandra Cisneros

BORN: Chicago, Illinois; December 20, 1954

Cisneros's work introduced a powerful and zestful Latina voice to American literature.

TRADITIONS: Mexican American
PRINCIPAL WORKS: *The House on Mango Street,* 1984; *My Wicked, Wicked Ways,* 1987; *Woman Hollering Creek and Other Stories,* 1991; *Loose Woman,* 1994

Sandra Cisneros had a library card before she could read. Her mother insisted that Sandra and her six brothers know books, although the family was too poor to buy them. Her father was Mexican, her mother American-born. Cisneros spoke Spanish with her father and English outside the home and always identified herself as American. Her family moved frequently, and as a result she was shy, turning inward and to books. Not a distinguished student in schools where little was expected of Chicanas, she read voraciously, and she began to write when she was ten. After being graduated from Loyola University in Chicago, she enrolled at the University of Iowa Writers' Workshop, where she completed her master of fine arts in 1978.

At the writers' workshop she experienced an identity crisis that led to her finding her voice. She found this voice in her childhood and in the stories that became *The House on Mango Street.* This book is based on memories of her life after her family settled into their first house, a time important to her identity, because she then began to observe critically the kinds of feminine identity her culture

Sandra Cisneros (Rubén Guzmàn)

offered. Cisneros found a voice by creating the voice of Esperanza (hope).

The success of *The House on Mango Street* led to Cisneros's teaching writing, to international lectures, and to awards and grants, including a writing grant from the National Endowment for the Arts. In most of her work, a woman's struggle for self-determination is a central theme. Obstacles include confining Mexican American traditions of feminine identity and the racism and sexism that confront a Chicana in a white-dominated society. Although Cisneros takes this struggle seriously and some of her pieces are deeply bitter, the overall tone of her work is exuberant, as reflected in the longest poem title in *Loose Woman:* "I Am So Depressed I Feel Like Jumping in the River Behind My House but Won't Because I'm Thirty-Eight and Not Eighteen."

The House on Mango Street

TYPE OF WORK: Novella
FIRST PUBLISHED: 1984

The House on Mango Street speaks in an adolescent Chicana's voice of coming-of-age in a poor Chicago neighborhood in the mid-twentieth century. Cisneros's first book of fiction received immediate acclaim, becoming a widely studied text in schools and universities.

The novella consists of sketches, each exploring some aspect of the experiences of the narrator, Esperanza Cordero, after her family moves into a house of their own. These sketches are drawn from Cisneros's own life; her family moved into a Puerto Rican neighborhood on Chicago's north side during her twelfth year. Cisneros discovered this voice and subject in resistance against the pressure to conform to what she felt was, at the University of Iowa Writers' Workshop, a "terrible East-coast pretentiousness." She realized that growing up Chicana in Chicago set her apart from most other writers. Esperanza's story also is one of resistance, especially against the expectations for women in her culture. She and her family have dreamed of having an even grander home, but she discovers strongly ambivalent feelings about home once they have one. On one hand, it is a place to be and to become. On the other, it is a sort of prison, especially for women.

In "The Family of Little Feet," Esperanza and two girlfriends get high-heeled shoes and wander playfully into the neighborhood, imagining themselves adults. At first, when men notice them and women seem jealous, they enjoy the attention, but when a drunk demands a kiss from Esperanza in exchange for a dollar, she and her friends flee and get rid of the shoes. Every other specifically feminine artifact and feature becomes a potential trap: hips, cooking, dresses, physical beauty, and most of all houses. Repeatedly, wives and daughters are locked in houses, where they serve men.

Finally, Esperanza dreams of a house of her own, one that is not her husband's or her father's but hers. At the end of the novella, Esperanza begins the story again, revealing that her book has become her house on Mango Street, the home in her heart that her best female mentors have told her to find. By writing, she gets hold of it, and in this way she can have a home and still resist becoming a man's property.

Woman Hollering Creek and Other Stories
TYPE OF WORK: Short fiction
FIRST PUBLISHED: 1991

Woman Hollering Creek and Other Stories is a widely admired collection of short stories. Most of the stories are set in Texas, some in Mexico. Most deal with the pressures upon Chicanas to conform to traditional ideas of femininity.

The title story is about Cleo, a naïve Mexican girl who marries a Mexican American. She soon finds herself pregnant with her second child, isolated in a foreign land where she cannot even speak with most people. Her frustrated husband beats her, destroying the dreams of happiness in marriage she learned from Mexican soap operas. When she flees, she gets help from a woman who hollers joyfully as they cross the Woman Hollering Creek bridge, teaching Cleo a new meaning for the creek's name and another way to be a woman.

Two stories explore the problem of being "the other woman": "Never Marry a Mexican" and "Eyes of Zapata." This role may seem to be a form of rebellion against conventional women's roles, but a mistress's role can be as restrictive as a wife's, and the price of what freedom it offers proves high. The narrator of "Bien Pretty" more successfully breaks free of traditional forms, living an artist's life, taking lovers as she is inclined, learning that she can be in control, even after losing lovers. She becomes determined to change the image of women in love she sees in soap operas; she wants to re-create them as people who make things happen.

Cisneros described writing this collection as a community project. She met friends at a San Antonio diner on weekends, drew on the unbelievable things they discussed, and then shared her drafts while revising them. This approach accounts in part for the variety of voices and forms. Two especially witty pieces are "Little Miracles, Kept Promises" and "Los Boxers." The first consists of notes left at saints' shrines, many requests for divine intervention in amusing problems. The final long note recounts the writer's discovery that the Virgin Mary is a multifaceted goddess who has helped her begin to escape the restrictive traditional woman's role. "Los Boxers" is the monologue of a widower who has learned to do his own laundry; he explains to a young mother the economies he has discovered by applying masculine intelligence to "woman's work." Using many voices, this collection explores themes of gender and identity in twentieth century Latino and general American culture.

SUGGESTED READINGS

Carter, Nancy C. "Claiming the Bittersweet Matrix: Alice Walker, Sandra Cisneros, and Adrienne Rich." *Critique* 35, no. 4 (Summer, 1994): 195-205.

Cisneros, Sandra. "A Deluge of Voices: Interview with Sandra Cisneros." Interview by Rosemary Bray. *The New York Times Book Review*, May 26, 1991, 6.

_____. "On the Solitary Fate of Being Mexican, Female, Wicked, and Thirty-Three: An Interview with Writer Sandra Cisneros." Interview by Pilar E. Rodríguez Aranda. *The Americas Review* 18, no. 1 (Spring, 1990): 64-80.

Hoffert, Barbara. "Sandra Cisneros: Giving Back to Libraries." *Library Journal* 117, no. 1 (January, 1992): 55.

Mirriam-Goldberg, Caryn. *Sandra Cisneros: Latina Writer and Activist.* Springfield, N.J.: Enslow, 1998.

Sagel, Jim. "Sandra Cisneros: Conveying the Riches of the Latin American Culture Is the Author's Literary Goal." *Publishers Weekly* 238, no. 15 (March 29, 1991): 74.

Tabor, Mary B. W. "A Solo Traveler in Two Worlds: At the Library with Sandra Cisneros." *The New York Times*, January 7, 1993, B2, C1.

—Terry Heller

Eldridge Cleaver

BORN: Wabbaseka, Arkansas; August 31, 1935
DIED: Pomona, California; May 1, 1998

Soul on Ice, an electrifying mixture of confessional writing and social commentary, is one of the major documents of the 1960's.

TRADITIONS: African American
PRINCIPAL WORKS: *Soul on Ice*, 1968; *Soul on Fire*, 1978

Eldridge Cleaver was born in the small village of Wabbaseka, Arkansas, near Little Rock. In 1946, he moved with his family to Rose Hill, a mainly Chicano neighborhood in the Los Angeles area. Cleaver was first arrested, for stealing bicycles, in 1947, and in 1949 he was sent to reform school, where he became a Roman Catholic. He explains in *Soul on Ice* that he chose the Catholic Church because "all the Negroes and Mexicans went there."

In 1954, Cleaver was sent to prison for selling marijuana. Four years later he was charged with attempted rape and assault with intent to kill and was sent to Folsom Prison, from which he was paroled in November, 1966. A year later, Cleaver married Kathleen Neal. The publication of *Soul on Ice* in

Eldridge Cleaver (Library of Congress)

February, 1968, marked Cleaver's appearance as a self-educated intellectual to be reckoned with. In the work he speaks fluently on issues that were sensitive among blacks and whites. He attacks writer James Baldwin for his alleged bowing to whites, condemns homosexuality as a "sickness," and reviles black women. *Soul on Ice* began a crucial year for Cleaver. On April 6, Cleaver was wounded in a shoot-out with the Oakland police that resulted in Bobby Hutton's death. As a result of this incident, Cleaver's parole was revoked. Faced with return to prison, Cleaver fled to Montreal and on to Havana.

Cleaver was kept under guard for seven months in Cuba before being sent in 1969 to Algiers, where his hatred for capitalism intensified. In 1970, he led a group of eleven on a trip to Pyongyang, North Korea, and on to Hanoi and Peking. When two groups of black Americans hijacked planes to Algiers, Algeria forced the Cleavers to move to Paris, where they obtained legal residence in 1974.

The two years he spent in Paris proved crucial to Cleaver; his thinking turned conservative, and in late 1975, he returned to the United States as an evangelical Christian. He was arrested but released in 1976 on $100,000 bail. His active career as an evangelist faltered in the 1980's.

Soul on Ice
TYPE OF WORK: Essays
FIRST PUBLISHED: 1968

The seventeen essays collected in *Soul on Ice* contribute to the long tradition of prison writing. In the first essay, "On Becoming," Cleaver recalls his earlier association in Soledad prison with angry young blacks who "cursed everything American." His reading of Thomas Paine, Voltaire, and the writings of Vladimir Ilich Lenin convinced Cleaver of the nearly universal confusion that ruled in the realm of political and social affairs. Cleaver became an iconoclast who took the writings of Russian anarchist Mikhail Bakunin and Russian revolutionary Sergey Nechayev (1847-1882) as his guide to political life.

Following his release from Soledad, Cleaver became obsessed with "The Ogre," or the white woman, cultivated an image of himself as an outlaw, and committed rape as an "insurrectionary act." Imprisonment at Folsom forced him to look at himself and to write to save himself. "I had to find out who I am and what I want to be, what type of man I should be, and what I could do to become the best of which I was capable." *Soul on Ice*, then, among other things, is a discovery of identity.

Three decades after their writing, most of the essays retain considerable power. "The White Race and Its Heroes," for example, offers penetrating insights into race relations in "schizophrenic" America, although its vision of a world revolution led by people of color turns out to have lacked prescience. "Lazarus, Come Forth" analyzes the significance of the black celebrity in a clear-eyed account of the Muhammad Ali boxing match with Floyd Patterson. "Notes on a Native Son" attacks James Baldwin for what Cleaver perceives as "the hatred for blacks permeating his writings" and for Baldwin's "flippant, schoolmarmish dismissal" of Norman Mailer's *The White Negro* (1957), which Cleaver found "prophetic and penetrating." Cleaver's contempt for Baldwin is complicated by Cleaver's judgment of homosexuality as a sickness and by Cleaver's charge that the homosexual Baldwin criticized Richard Wright because Baldwin despised Wright's masculinity.

Two of the more important themes in *Soul on Ice* are the identification of white oppression of blacks in the United States with white colonial capitalist exploitation of minorities everywhere, especially in Vietnam, and a rather mystical ethic of love and sexuality preached in "The Primeval Mitosis." "The Primeval Mitosis" analyzes the power relations between the sexes and the black and white races. *Soul on Ice* resists dismissal as a period piece. The book continues to impress with its energy and powers of intelligent observation.

SUGGESTED READINGS

Anderson, Jervis. "Race, Rage, and Eldridge Cleaver." *Commentary* 46 (December, 1968): 63-69.

Cleaver, Eldridge. "*Playboy* Interview: Eldridge Cleaver." Interview by Nat Hentoff. *Playboy*, December, 1968, 89-106.

Foner, Philip. *The Black Panthers Speak.* Philadelphia: Lippincott, 1970.

Forman, James. *The Making of Black Revolutionaries.* New York: Macmillan, 1972.

Kimball, Roger. "Emotions of Virtue." *New Criterion* 16 (June, 1998): 5.

Rout, Kathleen. *Eldridge Cleaver.* Boston: Twayne, 1991.

Schanche, Don A. *The Panther Paradox: A Liberal's Dilemma.* New York: David McKay, 1970.

Thomas, Tony. "Black Nationalism and Confused Marxists." *Black Scholar* 4 (September, 1972): 47-52.

—Frank Day

Lucille Clifton

BORN: Depew, New York; June 27, 1936

Clifton's unique strength in poetry is her understated complexity in celebrating all life as an African American woman.

TRADITIONS: African American

PRINCIPAL WORKS: *Good Times,* 1969; *Good News About the Earth: New Poems,* 1972; *An Ordinary Woman,* 1974; *Generations: A Memoir,* 1976; *Two-Headed Woman,* 1980; *Good Woman: Poems and a Memoir, 1969-1980,* 1987; *Next: New Poems,* 1987; *Quilting: Poems 1987-1990,* 1991; *The Book of Light: Poems,* 1993; *Blessing the Boats: New and Selected Poems, 1988-2000,* 2000

Lucille Clifton's parents had little education but were avid readers, and she grew to love books. Her father's stories steeped her in ancestral heritage, going back to Mammy Caroline, who was born in 1822 in Dahomey, Africa, seized as a child, and enslaved in the United States for much of her life. Caroline and other family members appear in *Generations: A Memoir* and in many of Clifton's poems.

Clifton's mother wrote and recited poetry. At age ten, Clifton became interested in writing, having learned from her mother that it is a means of self-expression. Being a writer never occurred to Clifton; she simply wrote. The first in her family to attend college, she had intellectual black friends, studied drama, and performed in plays—developing her voice and lyricism, and, in her writing, experimenting with sparse punctuation. In 1958, she married Fred Clifton, a philosophy professor. Continuing to write, Clifton did not attempt to have any poems published until her work was solicited. This happened when she was thirty-three, happily married, and with six children under the age of ten.

By then, Clifton had a wealth of education, experiences, and a growing family from which to draw for her writing. Her first published book of poetry, *Good Times,* focuses on difficulties in urban life. The book also honors strength and celebration in the face of adversity. In Clifton's second volume, she turns away from "white ways" to affirm "the Black." She celebrates her religious heritage and joins many contemporaries in celebrating racial heritage. With succeeding years and poetry volumes, Clifton's themes, subjects, and style have changed little.

Clifton has also achieved acclaim, and has been more prolific, in writing children's books. Some themes, ideas, and points of view found in her poetry are also found in her children's literature. In her children's books too, Clifton cultivates identity, values, and pride.

Poetry

PRINCIPAL WORKS: *Good Times*, 1969; *Good News About the Earth: New Poems*, 1972; *An Ordinary Woman*, 1974; *Two-Headed Woman*, 1980; *Good Woman: Poems and a Memoir, 1969-1980*, 1987; *Next: New Poems*, 1987; *Quilting: Poems 1987-1990*, 1991; *The Book of Light: Poems*, 1993

Hesitant to call herself a poet in spite of wide literary acclaim, Lucille Clifton has noted that poetry is her heart. She has unassumingly identified herself as a black woman, a wife, and mother who "makes poems." Her poems celebrate all of life—its daily realities, its mysteries, and, most significantly, its continuity. She has claimed that celebrating life is what she is about; her poems validate the claim.

Beginning with *Good Times*, Clifton has capitalized on what she knows best. Virtually all her poems fall into one or more of three broad areas of focus: family, African American experience, and female sensibility.

Clifton is a lyric poet whose work is unpretentious and has little rhyme. She continually achieves her goal of rendering big ideas in simple ways. Through short poems of simple language she relates brief portraits, encounters, or disturbances that are neatly presented in a few lines. Clifton seems more guided by consciousness or heart than form or structure. Her use of precise, evocative images is masterful, as evidenced in "miss rosie," which describes the title character as "a wet brown bag of a woman." In that poem, and many others, what Clifton does not say is part of the poem's power. Always significant are her use of spaces, few capital letters, and vernacular. In "homage to my hair," the poet changes from standard English to a black dialect with great effect; in "holy night," Mary speaks in a Caribbean dialect. Clifton's use of metaphor is frequent, compelling, and nowhere better than in "lucy and her girls," relating the power of family ties to natural phenomena. The contrast and tension Clifton achieves through frequent juxtaposition of concepts, as in "inner city," are laudatory. Many of her lines are memorable, as "my mouth is a cave of cries" in "chemotherapy." Only occasionally didactic, sometimes humorous, typically subtle or understated, Clifton's poetry has emotion, conviction, moral stance, Christian tenets, and hope. It has changed little through the years, except to sometimes reflect aging and all that that implies. Always, Clifton defines and affirms the African American experience, politically and aesthetically, with originality, voice, dignity, and pride. She has twice been nominated for the Pulitzer Prize in poetry.

SUGGESTED READINGS

Beckles, Frances N. *Twenty Black Women: A Profile of Contemporary Maryland Black Women*. Baltimore: Gateway Press, 1978.

Clifton, Lucille. *Generations: A Memoir*. New York: Random House, 1976.

Madhubuti, Haki. "Lucille Clifton: Warm Water, Greased Legs, and Dangerous Poetry." In *Black Women Writers, 1950-1980: A Critical Evaluation*, edited by Mari Evans. New York: Doubleday, 1984.

Salas, Susan, and Laura A. Wisner-Broyles, eds. *Poetry Criticism: Excerpts from Criticism of the Works of the Most Significant and Widely Studied Poets of World Literature*. Vol. 27. Detroit: Gale Research, 2000.

Sims, Rudine. "Profile: Lucille Clifton." *Language Arts* 59, no. 2 (February, 1982): 160-167.

—Sandra F. Bone

Countée Cullen

BORN: New York, New York; May 30, 1903
DIED: New York, New York; January 9, 1946

Cullen, one of the most prolific poets of the Harlem Renaissance,
combined English poetic styles with racial themes and identities.

TRADITIONS: African American

PRINCIPAL WORKS: *Color*, 1925; *The Ballad of the Brown Girl: An Old Ballad
Retold*, 1927; *Copper Sun*, 1927; *Caroling Dusk: An Anthology of Verse by Negro
Poets*, 1927 (editor); *The Black Christ and Other Poems*, 1929; *One Way to
Heaven*, 1932; *The Medea and Some Poems*, 1935; *The Lost Zoo (A Rhyme for the
Young, but Not Too Young)*, 1940; *On These I Stand: An Anthology of the Best
Poems of Countée Cullen*, 1947

Countée Cullen recognized early in his life that he wanted to use poetry to
express his belief that a poet's skin color should not dictate style and subject
matter in a poem. He began writing poetry while in high school. Cullen, a
Phi Beta Kappa honoree from New York University, had already published
Color by the time he entered graduate school at Harvard University. With a
master's in English and three additional books of poetry, Cullen was widely
known as the unofficial poet laureate of the Harlem Renaissance.

In his introduction to *Caroling Dusk: An Anthology of Verse by Negro Poets*,
Cullen set forth many of the ideas that shaped his identity as a poet and an
African American. He believed that poetry elevated any race and that African
American poets could benefit from using the rich traditions of English and
American verse. Cullen also chose not to include dialect poetry in his
anthology, viewing this style as out-of-date, restrictive, and best left to the
white poets who were still using it.

Cullen was not ashamed of his race, nor did he deliberately seek white
approval. He did feel that he should be receptive to many ideas to enhance
his poetry. Many of his poems, such as "Incident," "From the Dark Tower,"
and "Colors," protest racism and bigotry. However, in his collection *The Black
Christ and Other Poems*, themes of love and death prevail. Such themes show
the influence of the British Romantic poets John Keats and Percy Bysshe
Shelley. Keats especially was Cullen's artistic mentor. Cullen records his
response to having visited Keats's grave in "Endymion," a poem celebrating
the power of Keats's lyricism.

Cullen's use of genteel traditions and the black experience caused dilem-
mas and conflicts throughout his writing career. Critics praised Cullen for his
skillful use of the sonnet form, but they castigated him when he did not use

racial experiences as the primary source of his themes. However, even as he cautioned Harlem Renaissance poets about excessive use of racial themes, he published a novel about Harlem characters, *One Way to Heaven.*

From 1934 until his death, Cullen taught French and English at Frederick Douglass Junior High School, guiding students in the traditions that made him a celebrated poet.

On These I Stand
TYPE OF WORK: Poetry
FIRST PUBLISHED: 1947

On These I Stand: An Anthology of the Best Poems of Countée Cullen is a collection of the formerly published poems for which Cullen wanted to be remembered. Written during the 1920's and 1930's, these poems are from such works as *Color* (1925), *Copper Sun* (1927), *The Ballad of the Brown Girl* (1928), *The Black Christ and Other Poems* (1929), and *The Medea and Some Poems* (1935). Cullen also includes six new poems on subjects ranging from a tribute to John Brown ("A Negro Mother's Lullaby") to the evolution from birth to death ("Dear Friends and Gentle Hearts"). Cullen maintains the style of classical lyricists such as British poet John Keats in this collection, using rhymed couplets, ballads, or sonnet forms.

Color emphasizes racial themes and shows the influence of ideas associated with the Harlem Renaissance. There are religious overtones in some of the poems about the burden of racial oppression. The speaker recognizes a loss of faith but laments the racial prejudice against more religious blacks in "Pagan Prayer." Cullen's Simon the Cyrenian transcends his race by helping Christ bear the cross in "Simon the Cyrenian Speaks." The poem for which Cullen is widely known, "Yet Do I Marvel," questions the value of God's decision to give creative talent to a black person, whose talents are ignored.

Cullen joined other Harlem Renaissance writers in using African motifs. In "Heritage," one of the longer poems in *Color*, the speaker asks the question, What is Africa to me? An exotic and stereotyped image of Africa emerges, and the question is unanswered.

The selections from *Copper Sun* and *The Black Christ and Other Poems* show that gradually Cullen moved away from ideas about racial identity to those that preoccupy a Romantic mind influenced by Keats, Percy Bysshe Shelley, or Edna St. Vincent Millay. There are numerous poems on love, death, and the difficulties of the creative spirit in overcoming the burdens of the physical self.

"The Black Christ" is an extended narrative poem that demonstrates Cullen's love of the Romantic or transcendent, his interest in religious themes, and his concern about the plight of African Americans. The narrator, a black Southerner, witnesses the lynching of his brother, Jim. As Jim is enjoying a spring day with a white woman, a white man insults the woman and attacks Jim, who responds by killing him. Jim's lynching tests the narrator's faith in God. As the narrator berates his mother for her faith, Jim appears, resurrected, helping the narrator reclaim his faith. To complete *On These I Stand*, Cullen chose examples from *The Lost Zoo* (1940), his book of poems for children. "The Wakeupworld" and "The-Snake-That-Walked-Upon-His-Tail" instruct and delight. The collection *On These I Stand* attests Cullen's Romantic vision, his attraction to Harlem Renaissance themes, and his depiction of the African American experience.

SUGGESTED READINGS

Baker, Houston A. *Afro-American Poetics: Revisions of Harlem and the Black Aesthetic.* Madison: University of Wisconsin Press, 1988.

Davis, Arthur P. *From the Dark Tower: Afro-American Writers, 1900-1960.* Washington, D.C.: Howard University Press, 1974.

Huggins, Nathan. *Harlem Renaissance.* New York: Oxford University Press, 1971.

Lewis, David Levering. *When Harlem Was in Vogue.* New York: Alfred A. Knopf, 1981.

Onyeberechi, Sydney. *Critical Essays: Achebe, Baldwin, Cullen, Ngugi, and Tutuola.* Hyattsville, Md.: Rising Star, 1999.

Turner, Darwin T. *In a Minor Chord: Three Afro-American Writers and Their Search for Identity.* Carbondale: Southern Illinois University Press, 1971.

—Australia Tarver

Angela Y. Davis

BORN: Birmingham, Alabama; January 26, 1944

Davis's autobiographical work explores the development of the African American political consciousness in the late twentieth century.

TRADITIONS: African American

PRINCIPAL WORKS: *If They Come in the Morning: Voices of Resistance*, 1971 (with others); *Angela Davis: An Autobiography*, 1974; *Women, Race, and Class*, 1981; *Women, Culture, and Politics*, 1989; *Blues Legacies and Black Feminism: Gertrude "Ma" Rainey, Bessie Smith, and Billie Holiday*, 1998

Primarily known as a political activist, Angela Davis began writing as a result of her activities within the Black Liberation movement of the late 1960's and early 1970's. Her work consistently explores the destructive influences of racism, sexism, and economic inequality on the development of African Americans, women, and the poor. Davis felt the full impact of racism beginning with her childhood, having been born and raised in segregated Birmingham. The racial inequality that prevailed particularly in the American South did much to shape her consciousness as an African American. In her autobiography, for example, she expresses her determination as a child to "never harbor or express the desire to be white" in spite of the fact that most whites lived what in comparison to hers was a privileged life.

Davis attended Elizabeth Irwin High School in New York. She studied philosophy at Brandeis University, the Sorbonne in Paris, the University of Frankfurt, and the University of California at San Diego. In 1968, she officially joined the Communist Party, having concluded that "the emancipation of all oppressed groups" could be achieved through the emancipation of the proletariat.

As a result of her membership in the Communist Party, the Board of Regents of the University of California fired Davis from her teaching position at UCLA in 1969; she was reinstated after a trial. Charged with murder and kidnapping in connection with an escape attempt from a California courthouse, Davis was arrested and imprisoned in 1970 after spending several months on the run. She was tried and acquitted in 1972.

Davis's early writings center on the difficulties African Americans face in trying to establish a positive African American identity and political consciousness within a system that is racially oppressive. In *If They Come in the Morning: Voices of Resistance* and *Angela Davis: An Autobiography*, Davis presents a personal account of the ways the legal and penal systems stifle the African

American community and political expression. In her autobiography, she touches on what it means to be an African American woman in a racially and sexually divided society. She explores this issue in greater detail in her works on the problems of racial division within the women's movement, *Women, Race, and Class* and *Women, Culture, and Politics.* Many critics claim that in presenting her ideas from a decidedly Marxist perspective, Davis deprives her writing of personal insight. Most contend, however, that in spite of her ideological viewpoint, she gives a unique and passionate voice to the experience of African American women.

Angela Y. Davis (Library of Congress)

Angela Davis

TYPE OF WORK: Autobiography
FIRST PUBLISHED: 1974

Angela Davis: An Autobiography, Davis's most notable literary work, is the personal narrative of her development as an African American and feminist political activist. The autobiography explores how the forces of institutionalized racism shaped her consciousness as an African American and compelled her to seek political solutions. Her personal account also explores how her experiences as a woman in a movement dominated by males affected her awareness of the special challenges African American women face in overcoming sexism and racism.

The autobiography opens not with Davis's birth but with her flight from California legal authorities. She was charged with murder and kidnapping in relation to a failed escape attempt at a California courthouse. Her constant self-awareness as an African American woman attempting to evade discovery within an overwhelmingly white society underscores the problems African Americans have in establishing their identity. From the writer's perspective, the charges against her stemmed not from a legal system that seeks justice but from a legal system that works to destroy those who fight to change the system.

As a child in racially segregated Birmingham, Alabama, Davis's fight to establish such an identity began at an early age. Growing up on "Dynamite Hill," a racially mixed neighborhood that acquired its name from the frequent bombings of African American residences, she was, as a child, aware of the danger of simply being black and of fighting for the right to have an equal voice in society. In detailing her experiences within the Black Liberation movement, Davis expresses her growing awareness of attempts to stifle the voices of African American women in particular within the movement. Communism, she contends, would eradicate all such oppression.

Davis is further convinced of the oppressive nature of the American legal system after she is captured and incarcerated to await trial. She describes continual attempts by the prison authorities to control the minds of her fellow prisoners through humiliating and nonsensical rules. She also gives an account of attempts to deprive her of her basic rights as a prisoner. When she is finally acquitted, Davis sees the verdict not as a vindication of the legal system but as a vindication of the political efforts to fight racial oppression. Many critics contend that Davis's constant focus on political ideology prevents her from giving an honest and insightful account of her experiences in her autobiography. Most agree, however, that, in spite of such perceived flaws, the autobiography presents a powerful portrait of an African American woman passionately devoted to her battle against oppression.

SUGGESTED READINGS

Ashman, Charles R. *The People vs. Angela Davis.* New York: Pinnacle, 1972.
Jackson, George. *Soledad Brother.* New York: Coward, McCann, 1970.
Perkins, Margo V. *Autobiography as Activism: Three Black Women of the Sixties.* Jackson: University Press of Mississippi, 2000.
Smith, Nelda J. *From Where I Sat.* New York: Vantage, 1973.

—Lisa R. Aunkst

Samuel R. Delany

BORN: New York, New York; April 1, 1942

Delany is an intensely self-analytical explorer of the linguistic and imaginative possibilities of science fiction.

TRADITIONS: African American
PRINCIPAL WORKS: *The Jewels of Aptor*, 1962; *Babel-17*, 1966; *The Einstein Intersection*, 1967; *Nova*, 1968; *Dhalgren*, 1975; *Triton*, 1976; *The Jewel-Hinged Jaw*, 1977; *The American Shore*, 1978; *Heavenly Breakfast*, 1979; *Tales of Nevèrÿon*, 1979; *Nevèrÿona*, 1983; *Flight from Nevèrÿon*, 1985; *The Bridge of Lost Desire*, 1987; *The Motion of Light in Water*, 1988; *Silent Interviews*, 1994; *Atlantis: Three Tales*, 1995; *Times Square Red, Times Square Blue*, 1999

Samuel Delaney's early science fiction is remarkable for its vivid imagination, its pyrotechnic style, and its interest in linguistic science. Several essays collected in *The Jewel-Hinged Jaw* began an analysis of the distinctive ways in which meaning is generated in texts that refer to imaginary worlds. This analysis is a central preoccupation of his academic writing and played a vital part in shaping his later fiction. *The Einstein Intersection* is the first of his novels that makes the creator visible within the text and that links the process of fictional creation to his parallel life experiences.

The increasing openness of the science-fiction field allowed Delany to move on to an explicit and very elaborate examination of homosexual identity in *Dhalgren*. The intense introspective analysis of *Dhalgren* is inverted in *Triton*, which extrapolates the personal into the political with flamboyance in its analysis of a future "heterotopia" in which all kinds of sexual identities are readily accommodated and available for sampling.

Delany began to subject his life to an unusually candid and thoughtful analysis. The primary product of this analysis is *The Motion of Light in Water*, a detailed autobiographical account of his life between 1957 and 1965. The semiautobiographical novella *Heavenly Breakfast* deals with an experiment in communal living in the late 1960's. "Citre et Trans" (in *Atlantis*) describes a black American writer's erotic experiences in Greece in the mid-1960's. *Silent Interviews* is a collection of dialogues in which Delany responds in detail to various inquisitors. The remarkable fiction "The Tale of Plagues and Carnivals" (in *Flight from Nevèrÿon*), which offers a searching part-allegorical and part-autobiographical analysis of the advent of acquired immunodeficiency syndrome (AIDS), is the most complex and powerful of his works in this introspective vein.

The hallmark of all Delany's self-analytical work is a remarkable frankness, especially in matters of sexuality, although there is nothing self-aggrandizing in his examinations of his own sex life or the imaginary sex lives of characters like him. His curiosity about his experience as a gay black man is utterly scrupulous in its quest for honest expression and true explanation, and his attempts to understand and explain the different experiences of others are marked by great generosity of spirit and critical insight. His occasional adventures in pornography, recounted without embarrassment, demonstrate that his attempts to understand the erotic workings of the human mind are uninhibited by fear of stigmatization.

The Motion of Light in Water
TYPE OF WORK: Memoir
FIRST PUBLISHED: 1988

The Motion of Light in Water: Sex and Science Fiction Writing in the East Village, 1957-1965 is an account of the late adolescence and early adulthood of one of the finest science-fiction writers to emerge in the 1960's. Delany was the first black writer to rise to eminence in the genre and was one of the first writers to take advantage of the decline of censorship in the investigation of sexual identities. This memoir stops short of the period when he became a literary pioneer, but it examines in great detail the personal experiences that were later to feed that work. Its primary concern is the awakening of the author's homosexual identity, augmented—and slightly confused—by his early marriage to Marilyn Hacker, a white poet, and their setting up home on the Lower East Side of Manhattan.

The memoir describes—but not in strictly chronological order—Delany's unsteady emergence from the educational hothouse of the Bronx High School of Science into the "real world" of work and marriage. It contemplates, with slightly self-demeaning but sympathetic fascination, his early and precocious adventures in science-fiction writing and the gradual forging of his highly distinctive literary voice. It ends, after an astonishing profusion of erotic encounters, with his setting forth from the city of his birth to cross the Atlantic and explore the Old World, modestly recapitulating the kind of experiential quest pursued by all the heroes of his early novels.

The text of *The Motion of Light in Water* is broken up into brief numbered subchapters, some of which have further subchapters presumably introduced as elaborations and afterthoughts, emphasizing that it grew in a mosaic fashion rather than being written in a straightforward, linear manner. The second edition of the book is further augmented, offering additional testimony to the relentless curiosity with which the author has repeatedly worked through the catalog of his experiences.

The Motion of Light in Water is remarkable for its frankness and for its scrupulousness. It attains a paradoxical combination of warm intimacy and clinical objectivity that is unique. The analysis of actual experiences is combined with and subtly tempered by an extended reflection on the vagaries of memory. The metaphorical title refers to the essential elusiveness of the process by which the filtration of memory converts the raw material of incident and confrontation into the wealth of self-knowledge. There are very few works that capture the elusiveness of memory and celebrate its mercurial quality as well as Delany's.

Triton
TYPE OF WORK: Novel
FIRST PUBLISHED: 1976

Triton has two sections: The first is "Some Informal Remarks Toward the Modular Calculus, Part One," and the second is "An Ambiguous Heterotopia." The first section's title links *Triton* to a series of Delany's quasi-allegorical fictions, including the appendix to *Tales of Nevèrÿon* (1979), "Some Informal Remarks Toward the Modular Calculus, Part Three," and his remarkable memoir and analysis of the advent of acquired immunodeficiency syndrome (AIDS) in New York, "The Tale of Plagues and Carnivals: Or, Some Informal Remarks Toward the Modular Calculus, Part Five" (in *Flight from Nevèrÿon*, 1985). A calculatedly convoluted essay on the language of science fiction appears at the end of *Triton* as "Appendix B."

Triton's second section's title refers to the subtitle of Ursula K. Le Guin's *The Dispossessed: An Ambiguous Utopia* (1974) and stresses the fact that unlike most Utopian novels, *Triton* describes a society in which the differences among individuals—especially differences in sexuality—are not merely tolerated but encouraged to flourish, thus lending the anarchy of difference a constructive and creative thrust. The addition of this element of calculated flamboyance to the traditional story of the ideal society does not rob Delany's Utopia of its ambiguity. An ambiguity arising from Utopian fiction is the truth that one person's Utopia is another person's hell. The hero of *Triton*, Bron Helstrom, retains the only sexual trait that can still be called a perversity in the book's utopia: an inability to exploit in a fully satisfying manner the Utopia's rich potential for pleasure. This personal perversity is reflected in the plot on a larger scale when the scrupulously nonaggressive society of Triton is horribly maimed by the war fought between the Outer Satellites and the conservative Worlds of the inner solar system.

Unlike many of Delany's protagonists, Helstrom is not a version of the author. Delany's memoir *The Motion of Light in Water* (1988) includes an account of the young author's meeting with a prawn fisherman named Ron Helstrom, who seems to have provided a model for the character's stubborn masculinity. The fictional Helstrom is a kind of negative image of Delany's own sexuality and values. The author's identity is not only mirrored in The Spike—the novel's writer character—but also is transfigured and magnified into the Tritonian society to which Helstrom cannot adapt.

Although it did not have the commercial success of *Dhalgren* (1975), from the year before, *Triton* is tremendously impressive as an exploration of the personal and social possibilities inherent in freedom from traditional gender roles. The book is even more spectacular in its deployment of the narrative strategies of science fiction; it is a landmark work within the genre.

SUGGESTED READINGS

Barbour, Douglas. *Worlds out of Words: The SF Novels of Samuel R. Delany.* Frome, England: Ban's Head, 1979.

Broderick, Damien. "The Multiplicity of Worlds, of Others." *Foundation 55* (Summer, 1992): 66-81.

_____. *Reading by Starlight: Postmodern Science Fiction.* London: Routledge & Kegan Paul, 1995.

Fox, Robert Eliot. *Conscientious Sorcerers: The Black Postmodernist Fiction of LeRoi Jones/Amiri Baraka, Ishmael Reed, and Samuel R. Delany.* Westport, Conn.: Greenwood Press, 1987.

McEvoy, Seth. *Samuel R. Delany.* New York: Frederick Ungar, 1983.

Sallis, James, ed. *Ash of Stars: On the Writing of Samuel R. Delany.* Jackson: University Press of Mississippi, 1996.

—*Brian Stableford*

Michael Dorris

BORN: Louisville, Kentucky; January 30, 1945
DIED: Concord, New Hampshire; April 11, 1997

Dorris's works are among the best examples of fiction and nonfiction featuring Native Americans.

TRADITIONS: African American, American Indian
PRINCIPAL WORKS: *Native Americans: Five Hundred Years After*, 1977; *A Guide to Research on North American Indians*, 1983 (with Arlene B. Hirschfelder and Mary Gloyne Byler); *A Yellow Raft in Blue Water*, 1987; *The Broken Cord: A Family's Ongoing Struggle with Fetal Alcohol Syndrome* (1989; *The Broken Cord: A Father's Story*, 1990); *The Crown of Columbus*, 1991 (with Louise Erdrich); *Cloud Chamber*, 1997

Michael Dorris's involvement with Native American affairs came quite naturally. The only child of a non-Native American mother and a Modoc father, Dorris spent childhood vacations with relatives who lived on reservations in Montana and Washington. His disdain for being called a Native American writer stemmed from these early experiences; he learned to think of people as human beings rather than as members of particular ethnic groups.

After his father's death, Dorris was raised by his mother, aunts, and grandmothers. The result of this feminine influence is apparent in his novel *A Yellow Raft in Blue Water*, a story about three generations of women, narrated in their own voices.

In 1981, Dorris married Louise Erdrich, another author of mixed ancestry. Dorris attributed his literary success to Erdrich, making her another of his women-as-mentors. Dorris and Erdrich collaborated as they wrote, producing works that authentically showcase Native Americans.

After his adopted son, Abel, was diagnosed with fetal alcohol syndrome, a preventable but debilitating condition caused by alcohol consumption during pregnancy, Dorris began writing *The Broken Cord: A Family's Ongoing Struggle with Fetal Alcohol Syndrome*. The book includes a touching autobiographical account provided by Abel.

The Broken Cord's focus on alcohol abuse reflects Dorris's concern that government policies are plunging Native Americans into a health and education crisis, and continues his work as a Native American activist. While a professor at Dartmouth, Dorris founded the Native American Studies Program and received the Indian Achievement Award. His empathy for Native Americans is apparent in his literary characters, who dramatize the often difficult living conditions of contemporary tribal members.

Despite the focus on Native Americans in his works, the common experiences of humanity fueled Dorris's passion for writing. As an anthropologist who valued differences, Dorris used his literary voice to promote acceptance of diversity, touching on the basic elements of life that connect all people.

A Yellow Raft in Blue Water
TYPE OF WORK: Novel
FIRST PUBLISHED: 1987

A Yellow Raft in Blue Water, Dorris's first novel, chronicles incidents in the lives of his three women narrators. Readers have embraced the book, finding the story to be a compelling look at mothers and daughters. The novel opens with Rayona, a fifteen-year-old girl who is part Native American and part black. When her mother moves her to Montana to stay with her grandmother on a reservation, Rayona's mixed heritage makes her the target of prejudiced teens, damaging her already fragile self-esteem.

Eventually Rayona leaves the reservation and meets an understanding couple, who invite her to live with them. In Sky and Evelyn's modest home, Rayona feels accepted and begins to value commitment, self-sacrifice, and honesty as prime ways to define oneself. By the novel's end, Rayona develops the confidence and self-respect she needs to function in the tribal community and to be accepting of its diverse members.

Rayona learns to accept Christine and Ida, the other two main characters. Early in Christine's story, her sense of identity is complicated by an emotionally distant mother, who insists on being called "Aunt Ida." Christine's belief that she started life "in the hole" sends her on a quest for acceptance that leads to promiscuity, alcohol abuse, the fathers of her two children, and, finally, a fatal illness. As her life is ending, she moves toward harmony with herself, finally content simply to be Christine, a woman defined

Michael Dorris, with Louise Erdrich. (Jerry Bauer)

by the love of a good friend and forgiving family members.

Ida's story weaves together the autobiographies of all three women. During her teen years, her identity is negated by a family secret: She is not Christine's mother but her half sister. Ida's father and aunt, Christine's biological parents, persuade Ida to pretend the baby is hers, saving the family from embarrassment. Ida's true sense of self is obscured by the roles she plays and the tales she has been spinning for forty years. As her story closes, she is tentatively considering an honest relationship with Rayona.

That Rayona, Christine, and Ida are Native American women struggling with poverty and abandoned by most of the men in their lives motivates their strength and independence. Diverse readers have identified with the three's emotions and experiences.

SUGGESTED READINGS

Broyard, Anatole. "Eccentricity Was All They Could Afford." Review of *A Yellow Raft in Blue Water*, by Michael Dorris. *The New York Times Book Review*, June 7, 1987, 92-97.

Chavkin, Allan, and Nancy Feyl Chavkin, eds. *Conversations with Louise Erdrich and Michael Dorris.* Jackson: University Press of Mississippi, 1994.

Owens, Louis. "Erdrich and Dorris's Mixedbloods and Multiple Narratives." In *Other Destinies: Understanding the American Indian Novel.* Norman: University of Oklahoma Press, 1992.

Rayson, Ann. "Shifting Identity in the Work of Louise Erdrich and Michael Dorris." *Studies in American Indian Literatures* 3 (Winter, 1991): 27-36.

Weil, Ann. *Michael Dorris.* Austin, Tex.: Raintree Steck-Vaughn, 1997.

—Lynne Klyse

Frederick Douglass
(Frederick Augustus Washington Bailey)

BORN: Tuckahoe, Talbot County, Maryland; February, 1817?
DIED: Washington, D.C.; February 20, 1895

Douglass wrote one of the most artistic, articulate, and insightful slave narratives and lived a life dedicated to championing black civil rights.

TRADITIONS: African American

PRINCIPAL WORKS: *Narrative of the Life of Frederick Douglass: An American Slave*, 1845; *My Bondage and My Freedom*, 1955; *The Life and Times of Frederick Douglass*, 1881

Frederick Augustus Bailey, who changed his name to Frederick Douglass after escaping slavery, was the son of a slave mother and a white man, probably his mother's master, Captain Aaron Anthony. He grew up in a variety of slavery conditions, some very harsh. He nevertheless taught himself to read and write and became a skilled caulker at the Baltimore shipyards.

In 1838, he escaped to New York disguised as a free sailor. After marrying Anna Murray, a freewoman who had helped him escape, he moved with her to Massachusetts. He took the name Douglass and began working for the abolitionist cause. For four years he was a popular and eloquent speaker for antislavery societies and in 1845 published his *Narrative of the Life of Frederick Douglass: An American Slave*, one of the finest slave narratives.

As a precaution against recapture following the publication of his autobiography, Douglass went to England to lecture on racial conditions in the United States. In late 1846, British friends purchased and manumitted Douglass, and the following year he returned to New York a free man.

Moving to Rochester, Douglass began an abolitionist newspaper, *The North Star* (later renamed *Frederick Douglass' Paper*), became an Underground Railroad agent, wrote in support of women's rights and temperance, and revised and expanded his autobiography. In 1859, he narrowly escaped arrest following John Brown's raid at Harpers Ferry. Although Douglass had not supported the raid, he was a friend of Brown. He fled to Canada, then England, returning months later when he learned of his daughter Annie's death.

During the Civil War, Douglass urged the recruitment and equal treatment of blacks in the military (his two sons were early volunteers) and became an unofficial adviser to Abraham Lincoln on matters of race. After Lincoln's death, he opposed Andrew Johnson's procolonization stance and worked for black civil rights, especially suffrage.

A loyal supporter of the Republican Party, he was appointed to various posts by five presidents. In 1881, Douglass again updated his autobiography. The following year Anna Murray Douglass died. Two years later, Douglass married Helen Pitts, his white secretary, a marriage that shocked many. In 1889, President Benjamin Harrison appointed Douglass minister to Haiti. Douglass retired in 1891 but remained a powerful voice speaking out for racial equality until his death in 1895. He is remembered as not only the most prominent black American of his era but also a man whose life of commitment to the concept of equality made him an outstanding American for all times.

Frederick Douglass (Library of Congress)

Narrative of the Life of Frederick Douglass

TYPE OF WORK: Autobiography
FIRST PUBLISHED: 1845

Frederick Douglass's *Narrative of the Life of Frederick Douglass: An American Slave*, one of the finest nineteenth century slave narratives, is the autobiography of the most well-known African American of his time. The narrative chronicles Douglass's early life, ending soon after his escape from slavery when he was approximately twenty. It focuses on formative experiences that stand out in his life for their demonstration of the cruelty of slavery and of his ability to endure and transcend such conditions with his humanity intact.

Douglass's work follows the formula of many slave narratives of his day. He structures his story in a linear fashion, beginning with what little information he knew about his origins and progressing episodically through to his escape North. His recurring theme is the brutal nature of slavery, with an emphasis on the persevering humanity of the slaves despite unspeakable trials and the inhumanity of slave owners. Other themes common to Douglass's and other slave narratives are the hypocrisy of white Christianity, the linkage of literacy to the desire for and attainment of freedom, and the assurance that with liberty the former slave achieved not only a new sense of self-worth but also an economic self-sufficiency. Douglass's work is characteristic of the nineteenth century in that it is melodramatic and at times didactic.

Despite its conventional traits, however, Douglass's work transcends formulaic writing. The author's astute analyses of the psychology of slavery, his eloquent assertions of self, and his striking command of rhetoric lift this work above others in its genre. Particularly memorable scenes include young Frederick's teaching himself to read, the fight with the slave breaker Covey, the author's apostrophe to freedom as he watches sailboats on Chesapeake Bay, and his interpretation of slave songs as songs of sorrow.

When Douglass wrote this work in 1845, he had already earned a reputation as one of the most eloquent speakers for the Massachusetts Anti-Slavery Society. The *Narrative of the Life of Frederick Douglass* was published with a preface written by William Lloyd Garrison, which was followed by a letter by Wendell Phillips. An immediate success, the *Narrative of the Life of Frederick Douglass* soon went through five American and three European editions.

Douglass revised and enlarged the autobiography with later expansions, *My Bondage and My Freedom* (1855) and *The Life and Times of Frederick Douglass* (1881, 1892). Although these later versions are of historical value for their extension of Douglass's life story and for their expansion on matters—such as his method of escape—that Douglass purposefully avoided in his first publication, critics generally agree that the spareness and immediacy of the original *Narrative of the Life of Frederick Douglass* renders it the most artistically appealing of the autobiographies.

Today Douglass's book has become canonical as one of the best of the slave narratives, as an eloquent rendering of the American self-made success story, as a finely crafted example of protest literature, and for its influence on two important genres of African American literature—the autobiography and the literary treatment of slavery.

SUGGESTED READINGS

Bontemps, Arna. *Free at Last: The Life of Frederick Douglass.* New York: Dodd, Mead, 1971.

Chesebrough, David B. *Frederick Douglass: Oratory from Slavery.* Westport, Conn.: Greenwood Press, 1998.

Dexter, Fisher, and Robert B. Stepto, eds. *Afro-American Literature.* New York: Modern Language Association of America, 1979.

Ernest, John. *Resistance and Reformation in Nineteenth-Century African-American Literature: Brown, Wilson, Jacobs, Delany, Douglass, and Harper.* Jackson: University Press of Mississippi, 1995.

Jackson, Blyden. *A History of Afro-American Literature.* Baton Rouge: Louisiana State University Press, 1989.

Lawson, Bill E., and Frank M. Kirkland, eds. *Frederick Douglass: A Critical Reader.* Malden, Mass.: Blackwell, 1999.

McFeely, William S. *Frederick Douglass.* New York: W. W. Norton, 1991.

Preston, Diopkon J. *Young Frederick Douglass: The Maryland Years.* Baltimore: The Johns Hopkins University Press, 1980.

Quarles, Benjamin. *Frederick Douglass.* Washington, D.C.: Associated Publishers, 1948.

Smith, Valorie. "Form and Ideology in Three Slave Narratives." In *Self-Discovery and Authority in Afro-American Narrative.* Cambridge, Mass.: Harvard University Press, 1987.

Stephens, Gregory. *On Racial Frontiers: The New Culture of Frederick Douglass, Ralph Ellison, and Bob Marley.* New York: Cambridge University Press, 1999.

—Grace McEntee

Rita Dove

BORN: Akron, Ohio; August 28, 1952

Dove's poems give voice to the African American woman whose concerns are wider than region or race.

TRADITIONS: African American

PRINCIPAL WORKS: *The Yellow House on the Corner*, 1980; *Museum*, 1983; *Fifth Sunday*, 1985; *Thomas and Beulah*, 1986; *The Other Side of the House*, 1988; *Grace Notes*, 1989; *On the Bus with Rosa Parks: Poems*, 1999

Rita Dove acknowledges that her writing is influenced by a range of experiences. Consequently, Dove consistently avoids being pigeonholed. As an undergraduate at Miami University in Oxford, Ohio, she spent a year on a Fulbright Scholarship at the University of Tübingen, in West Germany, where she realized that a writer cannot have a limited view of the world. Although her earlier work was influenced by African American writers of the 1960's, she stands apart from African American writers who write primarily of the politics of ethnicity. Well-educated, Dove allows her poetry to reflect her wide interests. Many poems allude to the visual arts and music. Poems in *Museum* discuss Catherine of Alexandria, Catherine of Siena, William Shakespeare, Friedrich Hölderlin, and Giovanni Boccaccio. The cross-cultural thrust of her writing is indicative of the influence that Dove's European experience had on her.

Dove's poetry uses family history as raw material. In *Thomas and Beulah*, Dove mixes fact and imagination to describe the lives of her maternal grandparents. A book-length narrative, the story of her family employs two separate points of view, that of her grandfather and that of her grandmother. Race is central to the story, but Dove focuses on the relationship that they had, in spite of the difference between their families. Winner of the 1987 Pulitzer Prize in poetry, the volume shows her concern with the voices of ordinary people. Through these lives she addresses more communal concerns. Dove's work acknowledges the existence of race problems but allows the human spirit to triumph.

Marriage to Fred Viebahn in 1979 produced one daughter, Aviva Chantal Tamu Dove-Viebahn. Dove's poetry of the time explores mother-daughter relationships, especially when the child is biracial. Such poems are evident in *Grace Notes*. Dove experiments with other literary forms. She has produced a verse play, short stories, and a novel. *Through the Ivory Gate*, her first novel, explores the interplay between autobiography and artifice. Virginia King, a

Rita Dove (Fred Viebahn)

character reflecting Dove's experiences, returns to Akron to work with young students. Learning the stories of her family confirms Virginia in her desire for a career in the theater.

In 1993, Dove became poet laureate of the United States. In that role, she worked with emerging writers, encouraging them to gain the breadth and depth of experience that would fuel their writing.

Grace Notes
TYPE OF WORK: Poetry
FIRST PUBLISHED: 1989

In *Grace Notes*, Dove explores the implications of being an African American who is prepared to step forward into a world broader than any limiting labels would suggest. Many poems focus on the relationship between her biracial child and herself, revealing how the child discovers and accepts these differences. Others show the daughter learning what it means to become a woman. Still other poems question the effect that the development of identity can have on the artist.

Dove sets the stage with the first poem, "Summit Beach, 1921," which examines the risk of being at the edge of development. A girl watches her friends dance as she rests her broken leg. She had climbed to the top of her father's shed, then stepped off. Dove shows that the girl wants to date but that her father had discouraged her. This poem suggests that the search for identity does not occur without risks because the search involves making choices.

Married to a German, Dove's daughter learns to belong in both worlds. "Genetic Expedition" contains images which delve into the physical differences between the black mother and her biracial child. Beginning with images of her own body, Dove mentions that she resembles pictures of natives in the *National Geographic* more than she does her own daughter. Because of the *National Geographic*'s sensual, naked women, her father had not allowed the children to read the magazine. While Dove identifies physically with the bodies of these women, she acknowledges that her daughter's features and hair reflect her biracial heritage. Thus the poem exemplifies Dove's rootedness in her own culture while being open to other cultures.

Other poems that feature Dove's daughter show the child as she discovers her mother's body, the source of her life and future. "After Reading *Mickey in the Night Kitchen* for the Third Time Before Bed" describes a tender moment between mother and daughter as the daughter compares her budding body with her mother's mature body. Dove emphasizes the daughter's innocent curiosity and her delight at realizing what her future holds.

Several poems discuss artists searching for ways to express who they have come to be through their art. "Canary" looks at the difficulty of such inquiry. Focusing on Billie Holiday, the poem describes the downward spiral of her life. Whether it was more difficult for her to be black or to be female is the question of identity that Dove explores, suggesting that circumstances conspired to take away Holiday's power to carve out her own identity. Dove's poems allow the questions and implications of a search for identity to take shape as an ongoing process.

SUGGESTED READINGS

Costello, Bonnie. "Scars and Wings: Rita Dove's *Grace Notes*." *Callaloo* 14, no. 2 (1991): 434-438.

McDowell, Robert. "The Assembling Vision of Rita Dove." *Callaloo* 25 (Winter, 1985): 61-70.

Shaughnessy, Brenda. "Rita Dove: Taking the Heat." *Publishers Weekly* 246 (April 12, 1999): 48.

Steinman, Lisa M. "Dialogues Between History and Dream." *Michigan Quarterly Review* 26 (Spring, 1987): 428-438.

Vendler, Helen. *The Given and the Made: Recent American Poets.* London: Faber & Faber, 1995.

Wallace, Patricia. "Divided Loyalties: Literal and Literary in the Poetry of Lorna Dee Cervantes, Cathy Song, and Rita Dove." *MELUS* 18, no. 3 (Fall, 1993): 3-19.

—Martha Modena Vertreace

W. E. B. Du Bois

BORN: Great Barrington, Massachusetts; February 23, 1868
DIED: Accra, Ghana; August 27, 1963

Du Bois was the foremost African American intellectual of the twentieth century and a leader in civil rights and pan-Africanism.

TRADITIONS: African American
PRINCIPAL WORKS: *The Philadelphia Negro: A Social Study,* 1899; *The Souls of Black Folk: Essays and Sketches,* 1903; *Darkwater: Voices from Within the Veil,* 1920; *Vospominaniia,* 1962 (*The Autobiography of W. E. B. Du Bois: A Soliloquy on Viewing My Life from the Last Decade of Its First Century,* 1968)

W. E. B. Du Bois was a towering intellectual who created a new language of protest and ideas to understand and guide the African American experience. He wrote fiction and nonfiction, infusing his writings with eloquence and anger. He envisioned a world with equality for all people, emphasizing social justice for Africans and their descendants throughout the New World.

Du Bois's chronicle of his childhood begins with a tale of small-town conventionality in rural Massachusetts, where he experienced a loving home. In 1888, he entered Fisk University and saw firsthand the "color line" dividing the South. After graduating from Fisk, he returned to Massachusetts, where he earned a doctorate in history at Harvard.

His first important academic position was a marginal one at the University of Pennsylvania, but it resulted in his brilliant exposition, *The Philadelphia Negro.* In that work he outlines the historical background of the black community in Philadelphia and documents its patterns of daily life.

In 1897, he accepted a position at the University of Atlanta, where he worked until 1910. He held a yearly conference, resulting in a series of edited books on such topics as African Americans and business, religion, and social life. In 1903, Du Bois published the literary masterpiece *The Souls of Black Folk,* the first of four autobiographies that connect his personal experience with that of his community.

In 1909, Du Bois helped organize the National Association for the Advancement of Colored People (NAACP). He became the first editor of their journal *Crisis* in 1910. For the next quarter century, Du Bois was a center of debate on pressing social issues, and he was personally responsible for many columns, opinions, and reviews in the journal.

By 1935, Du Bois was increasingly at odds with the leadership at the NAACP. He resigned his position there and returned to the University of Atlanta. He helped found the journal *Phylon,* which continues to provide an

W. E. B. Du Bois (Library of Congress)

important voice for African American scholarship. Beginning in the 1920's, Du Bois turned his attention to international affairs, organizing pan-African conferences and observing the racist and classist practices of the Western nations. He became a Marxist and was attacked by other intellectuals. Du Bois was indicted by the United States for being an agent of a foreign power; the indictment was the result of his peace activism and leftist politics during the Cold War. Although he was acquitted, the accusation that his government made against him remained a source of bitterness.

Du Bois traveled widely around the world–after at first being denied a passport–and eventually settled in Ghana, whose leader, Kwame Nkrumah, was his friend. In Ghana, in his nineties, he began work on an encyclopedia of African culture. Much of Du Bois's vision of racial equality and African American achievement remained unfulfilled at his death in 1963.

The Autobiography of W. E. B. Du Bois
TYPE OF WORK: Autobiography
FIRST PUBLISHED: *Vospominaniia*, 1962 (English edition, 1968)

The Autobiography of W. E. B. Du Bois: A Soliloquy on Viewing My Life from the Last Decade of Its First Century is the inspiring story of a foremost African American intellectual and civil rights leader of the twentieth century. Du Bois discusses his individual struggles and accomplishments, as well as his major ideas dedicated to promoting racial equality for Africans and African Americans. Moving from the reconstruction era after the U.S. Civil War, through World Wars I and II, to the height of the Cold War and the atomic age, Du Bois's personal reflections provide a critical, panoramic sweep of American social history. Du Bois did not simply observe the American scene; he altered it as a leader of African Americans in the American Civil Rights movement.

The chronological structure of *The Autobiography of W. E. B. Du Bois* begins with five chapters on his travels to Europe, the Soviet Union, and China. After these travels, Du Bois announces the crowning ideological decision of his life: his conversion to communism. The remainder of *The Autobiography of W. E. B. Du Bois* answers the question: How did Du Bois arrive at this crucial decision in the last years of his life? Du Bois chronicles his life patterns of childhood, education, work for civil rights, travel, friendships, and writings. This information is written in such a way that it explains his decision to adopt communism as his political worldview.

Perhaps the most fascinating section of the book is Du Bois's account of his trial and subsequent acquittal in 1950 and 1951 for alleged failure to register as an agent of a foreign government, a sobering story of public corruption. His fundamental faith in American institutions, already strained by racism, was destroyed. He moved to Ghana and threw his tremendous energies into that nation as it shed its colonial experience.

The autobiography is subtitled as a soliloquy, but this categorization reflects the political realities of 1960 more than the specific literary form of speaking to oneself. At the time, the Cold War between the United States and the Soviet Union made communism an abhorrent choice to many Americans. The autobiography finally appeared in English in 1968, at a publishing house known for its communist writings. The autobiography is the least read of

Du Bois's autobiographies, although it is an engaging exposition in which Du Bois shows his continuing growth and faith in human nature during his tenth decade.

The Souls of Black Folk

TYPE OF WORK: Essays
FIRST PUBLISHED: 1903

The Souls of Black Folk is the passionate and eloquent story of an individual, W. E. B. Du Bois, and a group, African Americans. Du Bois could not forget that his world was divided by a color line. Du Bois calls the experience generated by the color line the veil and allows his readers to walk with him within the veil. He does this with songs of sorrow that introduce each chapter.

The second chapter begins with the famous lines: "The problem of the twentieth century is the problem of the color line." These prophetic words tell the story of American slaves and their descendants. One way to address these issues is to work for gradual change, as advocated by Booker T. Washington. Du Bois's criticism of Washington created a public debate about how to fight discrimination.

Du Bois then tells of entering Fisk University in Nashville, Tennessee. He experiences the Jim Crow world of the South and teaches children who must endure its cruelty. Du Bois soon moves from the elementary school to higher education, but before leaving the South, he travels through it. Jim Crow railway cars physically and socially segregate black and white passengers. Plantations dot the landscape, recalling the slavery that maintained them and continuing their legacy through tenant farming.

Du Bois reveals how the "faith of our fathers" is a communal heritage. Music and lyrics create a heritage from the past that lives in the present. Du Bois's faith is tested by the death of his first and only son, Burghardt, who was refused medical care because of the color line. Du Bois's keening cry against the evil that murdered his baby is heart-wrenching.

People are able to survive and triumph behind the veil, nevertheless, and the African American leader is the key to ending the color line. Alexander Crummell, a friend of Du Bois, was such a hero. Ordinary people can be revealed to be extraordinary too. Their paths may be hard, but their triumphs cause joy and celebration.

This book is a literary masterpiece that articulates the cost of hatred and the power to resist it. Although it has never been out of print, it was especially important in the 1960's, when it helped inspire the American civil rights struggle. Du Bois continued to tell his life story and the story of a people during the rest of his long, productive life. *The Souls of Black Folk*, however, is unique in its passion and eloquence. His inspirational language reaches all people who resist hatred.

SUGGESTED READINGS

Andress, Lillian, ed. *Critical Essays on W. E. B. Du Bois.* Boston: G. K. Hall, 1985.

Baber, Willie L. "Capitalism and Racism." *Critique of Anthropology* 12, no. 3 (1992): 339-363.

Du Bois, W. E. B. *W. E. B. Du Bois: A Reader*, edited by David Levering Lewis. New York: Henry Holt, 1995.

Horne, Gerald, and Mary Young, eds. *W. E. B. Du Bois: An Encyclopedia.* Westport, Conn.: Greenwood Press, 2000.

Lewis, David Levering. *W. E. B. Du Bois: Biography of a Race, 1868-1919.* New York: Henry Holt, 1993.

Stull, Bradford T. *Amid the Fall, Dreaming of Eden: Du Bois, King, Malcolm X, and Emancipation.* Carbondale: Southern Illinois University Press, 1999.

—Mary Jo Deegan

Paul Laurence Dunbar

BORN: Dayton, Ohio; June 27, 1872
DIED: Dayton, Ohio; February 9, 1906

Dunbar was one of the most popular American poets of his time and America's first professional black writer.

TRADITIONS: African American

PRINCIPAL WORKS: *Oak and Ivy*, 1893; *Majors and Minors*, 1895; *Lyrics of Lowly Life*, 1896; *Folks from Dixie*, 1898; *Lyrics of the Hearthside*, 1899; *The Strength of Gideon and Other Stories*, 1900; *The Sport of the Gods*, 1902; *Lyrics of Love and Laughter*, 1903; *The Heart of Happy Hollow*, 1904

Paul Laurence Dunbar's creative genius and personal and professional tragedies have often been misunderstood by readers who neglect to consider the poet in the context of his time, which was not just marked, but defined, by all-encompassing racial politics. At the end of the nineteenth and beginning of the twentieth centuries, commonly referred to by scholars of African American history as the nadir, Dunbar was a singular phenomenon, trapped between his audience's demands that he be the voice of his race and his own creative mandate that he not be restricted to any given subject matter. Dunbar wrote not merely evocative but enduring work, particularly as a poet. In addition to six volumes of verse, he also wrote four collections of short stories and four novels in the twelve prolific years before his untimely death at the age of thirty-three. Best known for his poems and stories about the Southern rural black world from which he came, Dunbar also wrote verse in standard English, often on black themes. His "We Wear the Mask" is a classic revelation of what it means to be black and American, and his "Sympathy" ("I know why the caged bird sings!") is an ode to freedom with universal appeal.

Dunbar was the only surviving child of Joshua and Matilda Glass Burton Murphy Dunbar, former slaves who had taught themselves to read and write. They nurtured their son with stories of their Kentucky plantation years, the Underground Railroad, the Civil War, and emancipation. These accounts became an important part of Dunbar's consciousness of himself as an inheritor of a particular history and a voice for that identity. Ironically, however, white audiences exploited this work, even as they championed it, seeing it as a black confirmation of their stereotypical plantation tradition. Despite Dunbar's apparent compromise in this regard, black audiences reveled in and memorized his verses, representing as they did the first national exposure of the black experience rendered in high art.

In 1898, Dunbar married Alice Ruth Moore, a Creole from New Orleans

143

and a writer. The couple separated, however, in 1902, the result of tensions from within the marriage, including her family's disdain for the dark-skinned Dunbar and the demands of his professional life. These pressures contributed to Dunbar's failing health from tuberculosis and his general melancholy, from which his late work suffered. He died childless and broken in spirit in the house he shared with his mother in Dayton.

Poetry

PRINCIPAL WORKS: *Oak and Ivy*, 1893; *Majors and Minors*, 1895; *Lyrics of Lowly Life*, 1896; *Lyrics of the Hearthside*, 1899; *Lyrics of Love and Laughter*, 1903; *Lyrics of Sunshine and Shadow*, 1905; *Complete Poems*, 1913

The poetry of Paul Laurence Dunbar provided America with its first widely read view of black America in verse. Dunbar's poems may be considered America's first experience with an African American poet's perspective on himself and his people and his conflicts with his world. Most of Dunbar's poetry is written in standard English and recalls in form, subject matter, and language the influences of the classic English and American poets. The work most quoted and criticized, however, is that which reflects the identity and experience of African Americans. Dunbar's race-conscious work is influenced by his appreciation for the oral tradition, by black folklore and mores, by the beliefs and expressive language of the black church, and by the historical works of black scholars such as George Washington Williams. Against the prevailing social and literary stereotype of black people as ignorant, contented, and comic, as seen in the work of Southern white writers, Dunbar tried to present his people realistically, in the fullness of their humanity and culture, with their particularities, and in their own voices. Sometimes, however, Dunbar's character depictions were too gently deepened, and the poet was criticized for

Paul Laurence Dunbar (Library of Congress)

his alleged conciliatory tone, as in "Home Longings," in which the speaker claims to want to "Drop the pen an' take the plow," a symbolically antiprogressive wish that a white racist could, clearly, misread.

Common themes in Dunbar's dialect poetry include a longing for and celebration of the South as home for the black community ("Goin' Back," "Possum Trot," and "A Letter"), the affirmation of family and love relationships to be found there ("A Negro Love Song" and "Little Brown Baby"), and the celebration of black humanism and cultural gifts ("When Malindy Sings"). In "When Malindy Sings," rhythmic language, rhyme, and exaggeration combine to praise Malindy's innate ability and compare it favorably to Miss Lucy's questionable learned skills. Often Dunbar's more lighthearted poetry seems simply designed to amuse, but closer examination reveals his satiric awareness of social injustice ("Accountability" and "An Ante-Bellum Sermon").

Dunbar's race-conscious poems in standard English reflect the perils, heroism, and survival techniques that come from living in a potentially violent, rigidly segregated, and racist society. Some poems eulogize black heroes and white allies of the freedom struggle ("Frederick Douglass" and "Robert Gould Shaw"). Others expose and condemn those who perpetuate injustices toward black people ("The Haunted Oak" and "To the South"). Still others praise the glory of the African race ("Ode to Ethiopia"). Dunbar's most popular and enduring poems express his awareness of his dilemma as a black man and poet in a restrictive society ("We Wear the Mask" and "Sympathy").

SUGGESTED READINGS

Braxton, Joanne M., ed. *The Collected Poetry of Paul Laurence Dunbar.* Charlottesville: University Press of Virginia, 1993.

Hudson, Gossie Harold. *A Biography of Paul Laurence Dunbar.* Baltimore: Gateway Press, 1999.

Martin, Jay, ed. *A Singer in the Dawn: Reinterpretations of Paul Laurence Dunbar.* New York: Dodd, Mead, 1975.

Martin, Jay, and Gossie H. Hudson, eds. *Paul Laurence Dunbar Reader.* New York: Dodd, Mead, 1975.

Revell, Peter. *Paul Laurence Dunbar.* Boston: Twayne, 1979.

—Cynthia Packard

Andrea Dworkin

BORN: Camden, New Jersey; September 26, 1946

Dworkin, a radical feminist, presents alternative views of sexuality and gender roles in society.

TRADITIONS: Jewish

PRINCIPAL WORKS: *Woman Hating: A Radical Look at Sexuality*, 1974; *Our Blood: Prophecies and Discourses on Sexual Politics*, 1976; *Pornography: Men Possessing Women*, 1981; *Right-Wing Women*, 1983; *Ice and Fire*, 1986; *Intercourse*, 1987; *Letters from a War Zone*, 1989; *Mercy*, 1990; *Scapegoat: The Jews, Israel, and Women's Liberation*, 2000

Andrea Dworkin was born to left-wing Jewish parents. Inspired by the peace movement of the 1960's, Dworkin participated in a number of antiwar demonstrations. It was at one of these demonstrations that she had the experience that changed her life. At eighteen she was arrested and taken to the Women's House of Detention. Her treatment there was brutal: bullying, harsh internal examinations, and authoritarian contempt left her emotionally and physically scarred. Released after four days, Dworkin hemorrhaged vaginally for two weeks. She spoke out publicly about her trauma in an attempt to find out why any woman should be humiliated in so sexual a way. Her marriage to a Dutch anarchist awakened her to the reality of sexual violence in relationships; he beat her severely until she escaped from him with the help of feminist friends. She was an intelligent, educated woman who had been graduated from Bennington College, but she could not prevent herself from being hurt.

Dworkin describes her childhood as one that taught her to defy convention. As a Jewish child, she refused to sing Christmas carols such as "Silent Night" at school. When her brush with the law and her nightmarish marriage left her horrified by the status of women, she took action.

Woman Hating: A Radical Look at Sexuality, Dworkin's first major work, echoes the pain of her personal experiences of misogyny. Later books, such as *Our Blood: Prophecies and Discourses on Sexual Politics* and *Intercourse*, go further into the implications of the sexual act itself. Dworkin analyzes the historical perceptions of rape and possession and of the biology of sexual contact. She also studies pornographic magazines in an attempt to understand how women are demeaned by pornography. Since many critics, such as one reviewer from the *London Review of Books*, find Dworkin's lack of makeup, her unflattering clothes, and her heaviness to be unattractive, Dworkin has had to relate to a double standard of beauty that does not apply to male writers, no matter how polemic they may be. As do other feminist writers, Dworkin enlightens women about gender roles in society.

Intercourse
TYPE OF WORK: Essay
FIRST PUBLISHED: 1987

Intercourse, one of Andrea Dworkin's most powerful books on sexuality in a repressive culture, is about self-disgust and self-hatred. Dworkin's "Amerika" is the modern world, or rather, the world that lives within the modern American. In "Amerika," sex is good and liking it is morally right. In "Amerika," sex is defined solely as vaginal penetration. In "Amerika," women are happy to be passive and accepting while their men are aggressive and demanding. *Intercourse* attempts to question the rigid sexual roles that define the male as literally and figuratively on top of the woman and the symbolic implications of sexual contact—entry, penetration, and occupation.

Intercourse, documenting a series of literary excerpts and comments by and for women, develops Dworkin's theory that sexual congress is an act in which, typically, men rape women. The book's theory is that because the penis of a man goes inside a woman during the sexual act, intercourse is a hostile act of occupation, ready to degenerate into gynocide and cannibalism. Dworkin describes a woman's individuality as being surrounded by her body and bordered by her skin. The privacy of the inner self is essential to understanding exactly who one is. Thus, having no boundaries between one's own body and the body of another makes one feel invaded and skinless. The experience of being skinless is the primary force behind "Amerika's" sexuality, since "Amerikan" sexuality relies so heavily on the man being superior or on top of the woman.

Strictly speaking, however, it is not only the act of heterosexual penetration that causes one to lose one's sense of individuality. In *Intercourse,* even lesbianism seems to be no answer to the repressive society that Dworkin describes. The "real privacy" of the body can be as violated by another woman's objectification of her lover as it can be by a heterosexual rape. So long as women can stay outside each other's skins, metaphorically speaking, then and only then will they escape sexual domination of one another. One of Dworkin's earlier books, *Woman Hating: A Radical Look at Sexuality* (1974), describes heterosexual contact as being acceptable so long as men do not insist on the superiority of an erect penis. In *Intercourse,* even a flaccid member does not negate female suppression in the sexual act. Dworkin's preoccupation is the obscenity of the ordinary; she encourages women to closely examine what they may have originally thought to be harmless, even trivial.

SUGGESTED READINGS

Blakely, Mary Kay. "Is One Woman's Sexuality Another Woman's Pornography?" *Ms.* 13 (April, 1985): 37-38.

Dworkin, Andrea. Letter to *The New York Times Book Review,* May 3, 1992, 15-16.

Glastonbury, Marion. "Unsisterly." *New Statesmen* 106, no. 2732 (July 29, 1983): 57-64.

Heller, Zoe. "Mercy." *The Times Literary Supplement,* October 5, 1990, 1072.

Jenefsky, Cindy, with Anne Russo. *Without Apology: Andrea Dworkin's Art and Politics.* Boulder, Colo.: Westview Press, 1998.

O'Driscoll, Sally. "Andrea Dworkin: Guilt Without Sex." *The Village Voice* 26, no. 29 (July 15-21, 1981): 26-29.

Rosenthal, Carole. "Rejecting Equality." *Ms.* 5, no. 8 (February, 1977): 86-90, 114.

Sage, Lorna. "Staying Outside the Skin." *The Times Literary Supplement,* October 16, 1987, 49-54.

–Julia M. Meyers

Stanley Elkin

BORN: Brooklyn, New York; May 11, 1930
DIED: St. Louis, Missouri; May 31, 1995

Through dark humor and inventive use of language, Elkin captures a unique Jewish American identity.

TRADITIONS: Jewish

PRINCIPAL WORKS: *Boswell: A Modern Comedy*, 1964; *Criers and Kibitzers, Kibitzers and Criers*, 1965; *A Bad Man*, 1967; *The Six-Year-Old Man*, 1968; *The Dick Gibson Show*, 1971; *Searches and Seizures*, 1973; *The Franchiser*, 1976; *The Living End*, 1979; *Stanley Elkin's Greatest Hits*, 1980; *George Mills*, 1982; *Early Elkin*, 1985; *Stanley Elkin's the Magic Kingdom*, 1985; *The Rabbi of Lud*, 1987; *The MacGuffin*, 1991; *Pieces of Soap: Essays*, 1992; *Van Gogh's Room at Arles: Three Novellas*, 1993; *Mrs. Ted Bliss*, 1995

Stanley Elkin wrote darkly humorous works. About half of his characters are Jewish, mostly secular Jews. Many of them, however, resist assimilation into mainstream American life. In his short stories and novels, Elkin establishes Jewish identity in two major ways. He captures Jewish humor through the unique intonations of Jewish American speech, and he casts his characters in professions often entered by Jewish men.

A consummate stylist, Elkin often presents his characters as caught between their religious heritage, which they consider anachronistic and from which they have distanced themselves, and late twentieth century American society, into which they refuse to integrate. To repair a tattered self-image, the gentile protagonist in *Boswell: A Modern Comedy* forms a club for famous and successful people; he then cannot sacrifice his individuality by joining.

Although Elkin considered himself a novelist, *Criers and Kibitzers, Kibitzers and Criers*, which clearly established his identity as a Jewish writer, caused many readers and some critics to consider Elkin essentially as a short-story writer. Elkin clearly established his identity as a novelist, however, by producing more than ten novels.

Aside from *Criers and Kibitzers, Kibitzers and Criers*, about half of whose stories treat Jewish subjects, Elkin deals with Jews and Jewish themes in a number of his other books. *A Bad Man* focuses on Leo Feldman, a department store owner hemmed in by a crazy father and a tedious son. In "The Condominium," a novella in *Searches and Seizures*, Elkin focuses on shiva, the Jewish funeral rite.

In *The Franchiser*, Elkin puts Ben Flesh, adopted by Julius Finsberg during the Depression, into an unbelievable family of eighteen twins and triplets, all afflicted with degenerative diseases. In *George Mills*, however, in which the protagonists are gentile, Elkin sacrifices ethnic identity for universality.

The Franchiser

TYPE OF WORK: Novel
FIRST PUBLISHED: 1976

The protagonist of *The Franchiser* suffers from multiple sclerosis, a disease that deteriorates the nervous system. Between attacks of the disease, Ben Flesh roams the American landscape, "the packed masonry of states," looking after the massive network of franchises he has built upon an inheritance from his godfather, Julius Finsberg, an industrial kingpin. What Ben inherits from Finsberg, who has cheated Ben's father out of his share of a successful business, is not a substantial sum of money but the prime interest rate—"Not money but the use of money." With the low interest rates of the preinflationary 1960's, Ben is able to build up a financial empire consisting entirely of franchises—Fred Astaire Dance Studios, Kentucky Fried Chicken restaurants, Baskin-Robbins Ice Cream parlors. In fact, Ben has his hand in literally every

Stanley Elkin (Miriam Berkley)

franchise in the United States. Along with the interest rate, Ben has inherited a responsibility for Finsberg's children, eighteen in all. Like Ben, each of the Finsbergs suffers from an incurable disease, which is their physical inheritance from old Julius, bearer of bad genes. As he invests their money in his franchises, Ben becomes a lover to each of the Finsberg daughters and a confidant to each son, so that, between Ben and the children, business and familial relationships are interchangeable.

In his ramblings, Flesh might be seen as a reader and interpreter of cultural signs. He observes the minute phenomena of the human world and attempts to make connections between the scattered manifestations of life and death. Ben spends a lot of time with Patty Finsberg, who refers to herself as "The Insight Lady" because she is obsessed with the parallels to be drawn among disparate cultural events. While some of her insights are breathtaking, it is clear that Patty is paranoically concerned with "connections." From her, Ben learns that there is order in disorder, contradiction in synthesis. Flesh as a character is, then, like a reader of his own novel, who interprets his life and observations as a commentator might discuss the patterns and repetitions of a fiction. Then, too, Flesh is like a writer: As a franchiser, he both organizes and disseminates the separated units of his financial network. Almost continually in physical discomfort and confronting the visible evidence of his own death, Flesh looks outward, on life, for the external order that will confer meaning upon his existence.

Elkin has always been interested in the exaggerated peculiarities of the individual vision and voice; he is a master of intonation and nuance. Perhaps no other contemporary writer has so successfully captured the varied life-styles and patois of contemporary Americans as they have been affected by the avid consumerism of their culture.

The MacGuffin
TYPE OF WORK: Novel
FIRST PUBLISHED: 1991

Set in a large unnamed American city in the Midwest that seems much like St. Louis, *The MacGuffin* is the story of some two days in the life of Bobbo Druff, commissioner of streets. The novel successfully functions on many levels; it exhibits a multifaceted complexity in that it is the story of a family, a love intrigue of the husband with mistress, a murder mystery, a tale of smuggling, and a political statement. While being all of these, it is mostly about Bobbo Druff and "The MacGuffin," his psychological other and controlling self.

Bobbo Druff, the narrator and main character of the story, is truly the only subject of this complex novel that has so many other threads and aspects. He represents the modern American, and his life embodies, for Elkin at least, life in America in the 1990's. He is materialistic and corrupt; he is neurotic, psychotic, and schizophrenic (and, importantly, justly so); he is intellectual, witty, and smart; he is hopelessly middle-class; he finds relief in life by incessantly getting high on coca leaves and taking at least four different prescription medicines; he is both humor and pathos—a strangely correct mixture.

Elkin's main purpose is to reveal the hopeless and meaningless entanglements of life in the United States in the 1990's—for the thinking and thoughtless alike. There is no escape from problems, no solution to them, only an awareness of facts that add up to craziness (a matter blended with humor and bitterness) in a world in which borderline insanity is necessary for survival. Bobbo Druff is not, however, insane; he is victimized by society and politics and legalities—but yet entirely by self. Survival requires some control of the system in which one lives. For Druff and other characters, that system is corrupt, somehow defunct yet going on anyway.

The MacGuffin succeeds in making significant and correct statements about modern politics. The global situation is so involved that even such traditional enemies as the Arabs and Jews cannot disentangle themselves from the complexity of the various problems. They depend upon one another to have someone to hate, to have an enemy; just as certainly and more important, however, they depend upon one another to fund and sustain their own problems and hatreds.

Local politics, as exemplified by Druff, the mayor, other commissioners, and even the two chauffeurs, parallels the mess and havoc of larger problems. No one can be trusted in a world where friends serve the causes of enemies and, conversely, enemies serve the causes of friends—all knowingly, but never openly.

It is internal politics with which Elkin is doubtless most concerned. This is represented in Druff's family life with both his wife and son, and with his relationship with himself and The MacGuffin. The context of family politics finally makes it impossible for Druff to make sense out of the entanglements around him, even when he has full knowledge of all the facts. In *The MacGuffin*, Elkin's goal is to make a statement not merely about problems in the Middle East (he is actually little concerned about relations between Jews and Arabs) but rather about problems in self-definition facing all readers.

SUGGESTED READINGS

Bailey, Peter J. *Reading Stanley Elkin.* Champaign: University of Illinois Press, 1985.

Bargen, Doris G. *The Fiction of Stanley Elkin.* Bern, Switzerland: Lang, 1980.

Charney, Maurice. "Stanley Elkin and Jewish Black Humor." In *Jewish Wry: Essays on Jewish Humor,* edited by Sarah Blacher Cohen. Bloomington: Indiana University Press, 1987.

Delta, no. 20 (February, 1985). Special issue.

Edwards, Thomas R. Review of *The MacGuffin,* by Stanley Elkin. *The New Republic* 204 (May 20, 1991): 44-47.

Elkin, Stanley. "A Conversation with Stanley Elkin." Interview by David C. Dougherty. *Literary Review* 34 (Winter, 1991): 175-195.

Emerson, Ken. "The Indecorous, Rabelaisian, Convoluted Righteousness of Stanley Elkin." *The New York Times Magazine,* March 3, 1991, 40-43.

Guttmann, Allen. *The Jewish Writer in America.* New York: Oxford University Press, 1971.

Saltzman, Arthur M., and Mark Axelrod, eds. *The Review of Contemporary Fiction: Stanley Elkin, Alasdair Gray.* Normal, Ill.: Review of Contemporary Fiction, 1995.

—R. Baird Shuman/Patrick O'Donnell/Carl Singleton

Ralph Ellison

BORN: Oklahoma City, Oklahoma; March 1, 1914
DIED: New York, New York; April 16, 1994

*In his writings, Ellison emphasizes his belief in integration and
pluralism in American society.*

TRADITIONS: African American

PRINCIPAL WORKS: *Invisible Man*, 1952; *Shadow and Act*, 1964; *Going to the
Territory*, 1986; *The Collected Essays of Ralph Ellison*, 1995; *Flying Home and
Other Stories*, 1996; *Juneteenth*, 1999

A native of rural Oklahoma, Ralph Ellison moved to New York City in 1936,
where he met fellow black writer Richard Wright. Wright helped Ellison
begin his writing career. In 1938, Ellison joined the Federal Writers' Project,
which launched his educational and literary life, which was dedicated to
exploring social and personal identities as defined by racial lines.

In 1945, Ellison, who was then exploring and espousing leftist views,
began work on *Invisible Man*, a novel based on his post-World War II interest
in racial identity, ethnic unity, and social justice. *Invisible Man* won the
National Book Award and the Russwarm Award in 1953, catapulting Ellison
into national prominence as an important black author. *Invisible Man* traces
the life of a young African American male who is attempting to define his
identity in the context of his race and of society as a whole. Ellison received
numerous honors, including the 1969 Medal of Freedom Award for his
leadership in the black literary community.

Shadow and Act and *Going to the Territory* are considered his spiritual and
literary autobiographies. They are collections of essays, criticism, and reviews
advocating integration and plurality. Describing "geography as fate," Ellison
wrote much about growing up in Oklahoma and about his deep interest in
the creative process, in black folklore and myth, in vernacular and popular
styles versus traditional and elite cultures, in jazz, in the blues, in literary
modernism, and particularly in the dynamics of race.

Ellison frequently focuses on the complexity of these dynamics, which, for
him, impose the obligation to question and challenge codified portrayals of
African American life and to embrace the promise of American democracy
despite its historic betrayals of the black community. Ellison's individualism
often moved against the grain of public opinion; for example, his essay "The
Myth of the Flawed White Southerner" defends Lyndon Johnson, then president of the United States, against the attacks of anti-Vietnam War protesters.
He claimed he was an integrationist of the imagination, where ideas are

difficult to control by social, economic, and political processes. Such ideas made him a target of black nationalists during the 1960's and early 1970's. Ellison is often compared to Mark Twain, William Faulkner, and Ernest Hemingway, all of whom Ellison spoke of as literary mentors.

Invisible Man
TYPE OF WORK: Novel
FIRST PUBLISHED: 1952

Frequently discussed as a novel addressing racial identity in modern, urban America, *Invisible Man* is also discussed regarding the larger issue of personal identity, especially self-assertion and personal expression in a metaphorically blind world. In the novel, the unnamed young black narrator is invisible within the larger culture because of his race. Race itself, in turn, is a metaphor for the individual's anonymity in modern life. The novel is scathing, angry, and humorous, incorporating a wide range of African American experiences and using a variety of styles, settings, characters, and images. Ellison uses jazz as a metaphor, especially that of the role of a soloist who is bound within the traditions and forms of a group performance.

The novel describes a series of incidents that show how racism has warped the American psyche. As a boy, the nameless narrator hears his grandfather say: "Undermine 'em with grins, agree 'em to death and destruction." Later, the youth sees a social function degenerate into a surrealistic and barbarous paroxysm of racism. Next, the narrator is expelled from a black college and heads north. After a job in a paint factory ends in shock treatment, the narrator heads to the big city and falls in with the Brotherhood, a group of political radicals. After realizing that the Brotherhood is just as power-hungry and manipulative as the

Ralph Ellison (National Archives)

other organizations and institutions that have victimized him, the narrator leaves the Brotherhood. He comes to understand that racism denies personal identity: As long as he is seen by others as a sample of a group rather than as an individual, he is invisible. The narrator finally becomes an urban hermit, living anonymously in a cellar and using pirated electricity.

The novel's narrator is typically viewed as representing a generation of intelligent African Americans born and raised in the rural South before World War II who moved to large cities such as New York to widen their opportunities. Such historical context aside, readers also see him as a black Everyman, whose story symbolically recapitulates black history. Attending a Southern black college, the narrator's idealism is built on black educator Booker T. Washington's teaching that racial uplift will occur by way of humility, accommodation, and hard work. The narrator's ideals erode, however, in a series of encounters with white and black leaders. The narrator learns of hypocrisy, blindness, and the need to play roles even when each pose leads to violence. The larger, white culture does not accept the narrator's independent nature. Accidents, and betrayals by educators, Communists, and fellow African Americans, among others, show him that life is largely chaotic, with no clear pattern of order to follow. The narrator's complexity shatters white culture's predetermined, stereotyped notions of what role he should play. He finds himself obliged as a result to move from role to role, providing the reader a wide spectrum of personalities that reflect the range of the black community.

In the end the narrator rejects cynicism and hatred and advocates a philosophy of hope, a rejection mirroring Ellison's desire to write a novel that transcended protest novels, emphasizing rage and hopelessness, of the period. The narrator decides to look within himself for self-definition, and the act of telling his story provides meaning to his existence, an affirmation and celebration preceding his return to the world. He has learned first of his invisibility, second of his manhood.

In his later years, Ellison realized that his novel expands the meaning of the word "invisible." He observed that invisibility "touches anyone who lives in a big metropolis." A winner of numerous awards, including the National Book Award in 1953, *Invisible Man* has continually been regarded as one of the most important novels in twentieth century American literature.

SUGGESTED READINGS

Bloom, Harold, ed. *Ralph Ellison.* New York: Chelsea House, 1986.

Busby, Mark. *Ralph Ellison.* Boston: Twayne, 1991.

Hersey, John, ed. *Ralph Ellison: A Collection of Critical Essays.* Englewood Cliffs, N.J.: Prentice-Hall, 1974.

Margolis, Edward. "History as Blues: Ralph Ellison's *Invisible Man.*" In *Native Sons: A Critical Study of Twentieth Century Black American Writers.* Philadelphia: J. B. Lippincott, 1966.

Reilly, John M., ed. *Twentieth Century Interpretations of "Invisible Man": A Collection of Critical Essays.* Englewood Cliffs, N.J.: Prentice-Hall, 1970.
Stephens, Gregory. *On Racial Frontiers: The New Culture of Frederick Douglass, Ralph Ellison, and Bob Marley.* New York: Cambridge University Press, 1999.

—Wesley Britton

Louise Erdrich

BORN: Little Falls, Minnesota; June 7, 1954

Erdrich's poetry and novels represent some of the most creative and accessible writing by a Native American.

TRADITIONS: American Indian

PRINCIPAL WORKS: *Jacklight*, 1984; *Love Medicine*, 1984 (expanded version, 1993); *The Beet Queen*, 1986; *Tracks*, 1988; *Baptism of Desire*, 1989; *The Crown of Columbus* (with Michael Dorris), 1991; *The Bingo Palace*, 1994; *Tales of Burning Love*, 1996; *The Antelope Wife*, 1998

Louise Erdrich's identity as a mixed blood, the daughter of a Chippewa mother and a German American father, is at the heart of her writing. The oldest of seven children and the granddaughter of the tribal chair of the Turtle Mountain Reservation, she has stated that her family was typical of Native American families in its telling of stories, and that those stories became a part of her and are reflected in her own work. In her poetry and novels, she explores Native American ideas, ordeals, and delights, with characters representing the European American and Native American sides of her heritage. Erdrich entered Dartmouth College in 1972, the year the Native American Studies Department was formed. The chair of that department was Michael Dorris, who later became her trusted literary collaborator and eventually her husband. Her work at Dartmouth was the beginning of a continuing exploration of her ancestry, the animating influence in her novels.

Erdrich frequently weaves stories in nonchronological patterns with multiple narrators. Her characters are multidimensional and entertaining while communicating the positives and negatives of Native American life in the twentieth century. Family relationships, community relationships, issues of assimilation, and the roles of tradition and religion are primary motifs in her novels. *Tracks*, *The Beet Queen*, *Love Medicine*, and *The Bingo Palace* form a quartet that follows four families living in North Dakota between the early 1930's and the late 1980's, exploring the relationships among themselves and within the larger cultures. The novel *The Crown of Columbus*, written with coauthor Michael Dorris, explores many of the same ideas and is a literary adventure story. In these novels about the search for identity, some of her characters are hopelessly caught between worlds, but most of her characters battle the hurt caused by mixed identities with humor, tenacity, and a will to construct their own sense of identity.

The result is some of the most accomplished and popular ethnic fiction available. The excellence of her work has earned for her numerous awards, including the National Book Critics Circle Award in 1984, and each of her five novels has achieved *The New York Times* best-seller list.

Louise Erdrich (Michael Dorris)

The Beet Queen
TYPE OF WORK: Novel
FIRST PUBLISHED: 1986

Erdrich's second novel, *The Beet Queen*, is centered in the fictional little town of Argus, somewhere in North Dakota. Unlike her other novels of people living on reservations, the characters in this story are mostly European Americans, and those Native Americans who exist have very tenuous ties to their roots and to the reservation that lies just outside the town. Racism, poverty, and cultural conflict are not in the foreground in this novel, which makes it different from most novels by Native American authors. Instead, European Americans, Native Americans, and mixed bloods are all in the same economic and cultural situation, and each of them is involved in a search for identity.

The prose in *The Beet Queen* is lyrical and finely crafted, as is evident in the description of Mary Adare, the novel's central character. Abandoned by a mother who literally vanishes in the air, she builds her identity by developing a solid grounding. She is described as heavy and immovable, and she makes a home for herself in a butcher shop that is described as having thick walls and green, watery light coming through glass block windows. She has found an earthy den, which attaches her to the one thing that will never abandon her—the earth. Her brother, Karl, is her opposite. Thin, flighty, always moving, he is a European American who fits perfectly the archetype of the Native American trickster figure. He is the destroyer, lover of men and women, game-player, and cocreator of the character who ties the main characters of the novel together, his daughter, Dot.

Dot is a strong, willful girl who is adored by her mother, a strong, mixed blood Chippewa woman named Celestine, her Aunt Mary, and Walter Pfef, a town leader and her father's former lover. It is Dot, the Beet Queen in a contest fixed by Pfef, who brings together the web of characters who are otherwise loosely joined in fragile relationships. During the Beet Celebration in which she is to be crowned, her father returns. Pfef, Celestine, and Mary are also there, and Russell, Celestine's paralyzed war-hero brother, is the centerpiece of a float honoring veterans. Mary's vain cousin, Sita, is also there, although she is dead. When the day is over, the circle of family is complete. Poetic and graceful, *The Beet Queen* is widely recognized as one of Erdrich's finest accomplishments.

Love Medicine
TYPE OF WORK: Novel
FIRST PUBLISHED: 1984

A dazzling meld of Native American storytelling and postmodern literary craft, Erdrich's first novel, *Love Medicine*, was an immediate success. It quickly made the best-seller lists and gathered an impressive group of awards, including the National Book Critics Circle Award for fiction, the American Academy and Institute of Arts and Letters Award for best first novel, the Virginia McCormack Scully Prize for best book of 1984 dealing with Indians or Chicanos, the American Book Award, and the *Los Angeles Times* award for best novel of the year.

Sad and funny, realistic and lyrical, mystical and down-to-earth, the novel tells the story of three generations of four Chippewa and mixed-blood families–the Kashpaws, Morriseys, Lamartines, and Lazarres–from the 1930's to the 1980's. Seven separate narrators tell their own stories in a discontinuous time line, each a puzzle piece of its own, but by the novel's end there is one story, one jigsaw puzzle picture of lost identities and the often humorous but always meaningful efforts of a fragmented people to hold on to what is left to them.

The characters in *Love Medicine* experience individual forms of alienation caused by physical and emotional separation from the communal root of their existence. They contend with the United States government and its policies of allotment and commodities; the Catholic Church, which makes no allowances for the Chippewas' traditional religion; and with the seductive pull of life off the reservation, a life that cuts them off from the community whose traditions keep them centered and give them a sense of their identities. These three factors place the characters under the constant threat of loss of their culture. Erdrich makes this clear, but she presents the lives of her Native American characters as human experiences that readers who have no background in Native American cultures can readily understand. The three generations of characters in *Love Medicine* surface as human beings who deal with an unfair world with strength, frailty, love, anger, and most of all, a sense of humor.

Where I Ought to Be

Type of work: Essay
First published: 1988

In the essay *Where I Ought to Be: A Writer's Sense of Place*, Erdrich explores the ways in which a sense of place changes the ways in which people think of themselves. Using examples from American authors of the last hundred and fifty years, she carefully compares and contrasts the approaches of European Americans and of Native Americans to a sense of place.

She begins the essay with a description of the Tewa Pueblo people's creation story. In that narrative, Grandmother Spider shows the people the Sandia Mountains and tells them the mountains are their home. Erdrich explains that the Tewa listening to that story would be living in the place where their ancestors lived, and the story would be a personal story and a collective story, told among lifelong friends and relatives.

In contrast with this view of a timeless, stable world, that of pre-invasion Native American cultures, Erdrich suggests that European American writers are invested in establishing a historical narrative for their landscapes. European American writers are interested in recording place, even predicting destruction, before their world changes again.

Erdrich proposes that the threat of destruction of place, such as in the extreme case of nuclear obliteration, may be one reason that writers catalog and describe landscapes so thoroughly. She takes the reader into a world of complete destruction, where nothing is left, and then she asks the reader to consider that this unthinkable thing has actually happened to the Native American population. "Many Native American cultures were annihilated more thoroughly than even a nuclear disaster might destroy ours, and others live on with the fallout of that destruction, effects as persistent as radiation—poverty, fetal alcohol syndrome, chronic despair." She points out that because of this, Native American writers have a different task. They "must tell the stories of contemporary survivors while protecting and celebrating the cores of cultures left in the wake of catastrophe."

She ends her essay with a description of her own sense of place, the area of North Dakota where she lived as a child. She points out that it is truly knowing a place that provides the link between details and meaning. A sense of place is, then, at the foundation of a sense of identity.

SUGGESTED READINGS

Allen, Paula Gunn. *The Sacred Hoop: Recovering the Feminine in American Indian Traditions.* Boston: Beacon Press, 1986.

Bartlett, Mary, ed. *The New Native American Novel: Works in Progress.* Albuquerque: University of New Mexico Press, 1986.

Beck, Peggy V., and Anna Lee Walters. *The Sacred: Ways of Knowledge, Sources of Life.* Tsaile, Ariz.: Navajo Community College Press, 1977.

Beidler, Peter G., and Gay Barton. *A Reader's Guide to the Novels of Louise Erdrich.* Columbia: University of Missouri Press, 1999.

Chamberlin, J. E. *The Harrowing of Eden: White Attitudes Toward Native Americans.* New York: Seabury Press, 1975.

Coltelli, Laura. *Winged Words: American Indian Writers Speak.* Omaha: University of Nebraska Press, 1990.

Erdrich, Louise, and Michael Dorris. "On Native Ground: An Interview with Louise Erdrich and Michael Dorris." Interview by Sharon White and Glenda Burnside. *Bloomsbury Review* 8, no. 4 (1988): 16-18.

Hobson, Geary, ed. *The Remembered Earth.* Albuquerque: University of New Mexico Press, 1981.

Ortiz, Alfonso. *The Tewa World: Space, Time, Being, and Becoming in a Pueblo Society.* Chicago: University of Chicago Press, 1969.

Owens, Louis. *Other Destinies: Understanding the American Indian Novel.* Norman: University of Oklahoma Press, 1992.

Rainwater, Catherine. "Reading Between Worlds: Narrativity in the Fiction of Louise Erdrich." *American Literature* 62 (1990): 405-422.

—*Jacquelyn Kilpatrick*

Jessie Redmon Fauset

BORN: Snow Hill, New Jersey; April 27, 1882
DIED: Philadelphia, Pennsylvania; April 30, 1961

Fauset's fiction depicts an unusual perspective of middle-class African American life.

TRADITIONS: African American
PRINCIPAL WORKS: *There Is Confusion,* 1924; *Plum Bun: A Novel Without a Moral,* 1929; *The Chinaberry Tree: A Novel of American Life,* 1931; *Comedy, American Style,* 1933

Jessie Fauset, believing that black writers could more accurately depict their race, wrote to "put the best foot of the race forward." Writing about the people she knew–the middle class–Fauset presents images different from those of other New Negro novelists of the Harlem Renaissance.

In Fauset's first novel, *There Is Confusion,* the main character, Joanna Marshall, daughter of middle-class parents, believes that African Americans "can do everything anybody else can." Only after experiencing discrimination in her attempt to become a dancer does she realize the problems posed by race. Joanna, her boyfriend Peter Bye, and a neighbor, Maggie Ellersley, overcome the difficulties of race, family, and class distinctions; Joanna's initial belief is affirmed by the novel's end. The characters, and by extension all African Americans, can triumph in spite of the hardships they have endured.

In her second novel, *Plum Bun: A Novel Without a Moral,* Fauset complicates the race issue by creating characters light enough to pass for white. The protagonist, Angela Murray, also from a middle-class family, grows up observing her mother occasionally pass. In order to realize her dreams of becoming an artist, Angela passes, which has its consequences. By denying her only sister, Virginia, Angela is isolated from family. Rejected by her boyfriend, Roger, because they are not of the same economic class, Angela learns that being white does not ensure happiness. When Rachel, a black art student, is denied a scholarship to study abroad, Angela turns down her own prize and acknowledges her race. The novel ends with a happier, wiser Angela continuing her art training in Paris. Revealing the problems facing African Americans who pass, Fauset suggests that values are more important than race.

In her final novel, *Comedy: American Style,* Fauset examines the consequences of color consciousness within the family. The color-obsessed Olivia Blanchard marries Dr. Christopher Cary because he is also light enough to pass. They have three children, Teresa, Christopher, Jr., and Oliver, whose lives are affected by their mother's obsession. Teresa marries a Frenchman she does not love. Oliver, who is too dark to pass and is therefore mistreated by his mother, commits suicide. Christopher, Jr., survives and marries a blond, blue-eyed black woman. When the novel ends, Olivia is in Europe while her family seeks to recover from her mania.

In her novels, Fauset explores the problems of identity through characters who triumph by accepting their race, class, and gender.

The Chinaberry Tree
TYPE OF WORK: Novel
FIRST PUBLISHED: 1931

The Chinaberry Tree: A Novel of American Life, Fauset's third novel, is her attempt to illustrate that "to be a Negro in America posits a dramatic situation." Believing that fate plays an important role in the lives of blacks and whites, Fauset depicts the domestic lives of African Americans who are not struggling with the harsh realities of day-to-day existence.

The Chinaberry Tree relates the story of two cousins, Laurentine Strange and Melissa Paul. Because Laurentine is the product of an illicit romantic relationship between a former slave and her master, Laurentine accepts the community's opinion that she has "bad blood." Rejection from a male suitor reinforces her feelings of inadequacy and propels her to further isolation from the community. The young Melissa, although the daughter of an adulterous relationship between Judy Strange and Sylvester Forten, believes herself superior. Sent to Red Brook to live with her relatives, Melissa meets and falls in love with Malory Forten, who, unknown to her, is her half brother. The "drama" of the novel is the exploration of both women's responses to being innocent victims of fate. Laurentine overcomes her feelings of inadequacy, and Melissa learns that she too is a product of "bad blood."

The Chinaberry Tree is also Fauset's attempt to prove that African Americans are not so vastly different from any other American. To illustrate this, Fauset creates characters such as Dr. Stephen Denleigh (whom Laurentine eventually marries) and Mrs. Ismay and Mrs. Brown, wives of prominent physicians, who enjoy the leisurely pursuits of bridge and whist and travel to Newark or Atlantic City to view moving pictures or to shop. There are also their offspring, children who attend private schools, enjoy winter sports, and have servants. Fauset's characters are not very different in their daily lives from financially comfortable whites.

Fauset's characters experience the joys and sorrows of love. Sarah's and Colonel Halloway's was a forbidden love; they were denied marriage because of the times in which they lived. He could not marry Sarah, but Colonel Halloway provided a comfortable home for Sarah and Laurentine. Although

Laurentine experiences rejection by her first suitor, she attains love and happiness after she learns to accept herself. Melissa, who cannot marry Malory, is loved by Asshur Lane, someone she initially rejects because he aspires to be a farmer. Fauset argues that the African American is "endowed with the stuff of which chronicles may be made." In this novel Fauset addresses issues of identity in terms of race and social standing amid the disorder of her characters' daily lives.

SUGGESTED READINGS

Feeney, Joseph. "Greek Tragic Patterns in a Black Novel: Jessie Fauset's *The Chinaberry Tree.*" *CLA Journal* 18 (December, 1974): 211-215.

Lupton, Mary. "Bad Blood in Jersey: Jessie Fauset's *The Chinaberry Tree.*" *CLA Journal* 27 (June, 1984): 383-392.

Sylvander, Carolyn. *Jessie Redmon Fauset: Black American Writer.* Troy, N.Y.: Whitston, 1981.

Wall, Cheryl. *Women of the Harlem Renaissance.* Bloomington: Indiana University Press, 1995.

—Paula C. Barnes

Harvey Fierstein

BORN: Brooklyn, New York; June 6, 1954

Fierstein's work challenges assumptions regarding the lives of gay and bisexual Americans.

TRADITIONS: Jewish
PRINCIPAL WORKS: *Torch Song Trilogy,* pr. 1979, pb. 1981; *La Cage aux Folles,* pr. 1983

Harvey Fierstein's 1981 trio of one-act plays titled *Torch Song Trilogy* successfully introduced gay characters to the American stage without apology. The central character, Arnold Becker, is a drag queen with a desire to live a life consistent with the American Dream. He wants to secure a loving family life and sees no reason why he should be denied the opportunity of creating one simply because of his sexual orientation. The uniqueness of the play's statement lies in the fact that the work was premiered at the end of the sexual revolution of the 1970's, when gay life was viewed by many as simply a series of casual encounters. Americans seemed content with a view of gays as emotional children who lived strange, uncommitted lives. Fierstein's characters challenge this view.

The son of a handkerchief manufacturer and a librarian, Fierstein grew up in a tight family unit that accepted his gayness. His first encounters with the lifestyle were through family friends who shared long-term, committed relationships. These were his role models, who helped him develop his somewhat conservative view of gay life.

Fierstein's reworking of the popular French film *La Cage aux Folles* (1978) is another example of the playwright's ability to present fully developed gay characters for mixed audiences. Fierstein received a Tony Award for the best book for a musical in 1984. The musical enjoyed a long run in the United States and abroad. Like *Torch Song Trilogy,* the play is an old-fashioned love story espousing the virtues of family and commitment.

Fierstein's writing style is a fusion of his several identities. His work is distinguished by a mixture of Jewish and gay humor interspersed with poignant self-revelation. It is this combination that has endeared him to straight and gay audiences. Through laughter and dramatic truth, his characters are able to tap the human thread that brings all people together.

Although best known as a playwright, Fierstein is also an actor who has played various roles on stage, on national television, and in film, most notably as Frank, the gay brother in the film *Mrs. Doubtfire* (1993). In addition to his work as an artist, Fierstein is active in various gay rights organizations and devotes considerable time and energy as an activist for causes relating to the acquired immunodeficiency syndrome (AIDS).

Torch Song Trilogy
TYPE OF WORK: Drama
FIRST PRODUCED: 1979; first published, 1981

Torch Song Trilogy is Fierstein's groundbreaking portrait of a gay man's struggle for respect and love in a homophobic world. The play, comprising three one acts titled "International Stud," "Fugue in a Nursery," and "Widows and Children First," chronicles the journey of the central character, Arnold Becker, from a life of transitory sexual encounters with strangers in the back rooms of New York's gay bars to his insistence on relationships based on commitment, respect, and love.

In the first play, "International Stud," Arnold meets Ed Reiss in a gay bar. For Arnold, the encounter offers the possibility of an honest relationship that will put an end to his loneliness. Ed, however, sees his meeting with Arnold as simply a one-night stand and returns to his developing relationship with Laurel. He describes himself as bisexual but chooses to hide his homosexuality for fear of public opinion. Ed attempts to terminate the relationship but finds himself returning to Arnold and is even able to acknowledge his love for Arnold. Arnold, however, cannot accept an undercover and uncommitted relationship and finally walks away.

"International Stud" presents the reader with two characters who are at different places regarding their understanding of themselves. Arnold is comfortable with himself as a gay man and is in search of a lover who is also a friend. Ed, however, is in denial as to his sexuality and, therefore, incapable of giving himself to anyone as either friend or lover.

"Fugue in a Nursery" takes place one year after "International Stud." By this time Ed and Arnold have what each wanted; Arnold has Alan, an eighteen-year-old model, and Ed is involved in a relationship with Laurel. The action of the play takes place on an oversized bed. Arnold and Alan have been invited to spend a weekend with Ed and Laurel. In a brilliantly written series of overlapping lines and interwoven actions, the playwright demonstrates the confusion of each character as he or she attempts to resolve the conflict between what one has and what one wants. It becomes clear that none of the characters has found all that he or she was seeking. In Alan, however, Arnold has found someone who loves and respects him.

"Fugue in a Nursery" continues the argument of "International Stud." It clearly demonstrates that one cannot give love until one has learned to love oneself. Alan and Arnold have a better chance of building a solid relationship because each is aware of who he is and can, therefore, be honest with the other. Ed, however, can talk to Laurel about his confusions but cannot confront the truth of his attraction to and preference for Arnold.

The final play in the trilogy, "Widows and Children First," takes place five years after the preceding play. Arnold has lost Alan to a mob of gay-bashers and is currently in the process of adopting David, a gay teenager. Ed's marriage to Laurel has failed, and he is temporarily staying with Arnold. The action of the play centers around a visit from Arnold's recently widowed mother and her inability to accept her son's need for love and the security of a family. Although she is aware of Arnold's lifestyle, she does not accept it. She is insulted when he compares his suffering at the death of Alan to her loss of her husband, and she questions the morality of a gay man rearing a child. A series of arguments ensues, and Arnold states that his mother is unwelcome in his life unless she can respect him and the validity of his feelings and desires. She leaves. David affirms his love for his soon-to-be father, and Ed finally confronts the truth of his desire to be with Arnold.

Torch Song Trilogy addresses the issue of gay identity and asks its audience to deal with the broader questions of honesty and respect regardless of sexual preference or lifestyle.

SUGGESTED READINGS

Kroll, Jack. "His Heart Is Young and Gay." *Newsweek,* June 13, 1983, 36.
Winn, Steven. "Anything but a Drag: Gay Theater Takes New Directions and More Risks." *San Francisco Chronicle,* January 9, 2000, DAT 33.

—Don Evans

Rudolph Fisher

BORN: Washington, D.C.; May 9, 1897
DIED: New York, New York; December 26, 1934

Fisher depicts the layers of Harlem life during the 1920's with humor, wit, and satirical grace.

TRADITIONS: African American
PRINCIPAL WORKS: "The City of Refuge," 1925; *The Walls of Jericho*, 1928; *The Conjure-Man Dies: A Mystery Tale of Dark Harlem*, 1932

Rudolph Fisher was educated in the arts and sciences. His first short story, "The City of Refuge," was published while Fisher was in medical school, and throughout his life he maintained careers as a doctor and as a writer of fiction and medical research.

For all his medical degrees, Fisher wanted to be known as a writer who could interpret Harlem life. Little seemed to have escaped his vision and analysis. He saw Harlem as a vast canvas upon which he painted characters from several different levels of life. There were the "rats," a Harlem term for the working class; the "dickties," which was Harlemese for upper-class aspirants to white values; Pullman porters; gangsters; barbers; pool hall owners; doctors; lawyers; misguided white liberals; and white celebrants and aspirants to Harlem culture. In the novel *The Walls of Jericho*, Fisher brings all of the economic, racial, and political strata of Harlem together at the annual costume ball. The dickties and the rats mingle with whites who are in search of what they think is black bohemia. The dance hall setting that Fisher enlivens in *The Walls of Jericho* was modeled after the Harlem cabarets and nightclubs he frequented.

Fisher achieved remarkable balance between the medical and artistic worlds. His short stories were published in national magazines in which other Harlem Renaissance writers could not publish. *The Walls of Jericho* was well received. The detective novel *The Conjure-Man Dies* was hailed as a first. From 1929 to 1934, Fisher was a hospital superintendent, a roentgenologist, a first lieutenant in the medical division of the 369th Infantry, and a lecturer at the 135th Street Branch of the New York Public Library.

Fisher seemed to know that working-class blacks in Harlem led lives that were far removed from the artistic renaissance popularized by intellectuals. In such short stories as "The City of Refuge" and "Vestiges, Harlem Sketches," he sympathetically depicts the struggles of many who have come from the South and who are disappointed or tricked by the fast, indifferent ways of the city. Characters such as Jinx Jenkins, Bubber Brown, and Joshua "Shine"

Jones in *The Walls of Jericho* are subject to the competition and physical dangers of furniture moving. A maid in *The Walls of Jericho* is viewed by her white employer as slightly better than most blacks because of her light skin.

In 1934, Fisher died of cancer caused by X-ray exposure. A retinue of Harlem artists, including Countée Cullen and Noble Sissle, joined Fisher's wife and son to mourn the loss of one of Harlem's visionaries.

The Conjure-Man Dies
TYPE OF WORK: Novel
FIRST PUBLISHED: 1932

In *The Conjure-Man Dies: A Mystery Tale of Dark Harlem*, Fisher combines his talent and comedic wit with his knowledge of medicine to produce the first-known detective novel by an African American. Fisher introduces a variety of Harlem characters, including Jinx Jenkins and Bubber Brown, unemployed furniture movers who also appear in *The Walls of Jericho* (1928). Other characters include John Archer, the doctor who helps Harlem police solve the murder.

The complex plot highlights characters and settings popularized in Fisher's works. When Jinx and Bubber discover the murdered conjure man, they become suspects with several others: a numbers-runner, Spider Webb, who works in Harlem's illegal lottery system; a drug addict named Doty Hicks; a railroad worker; and a church worker. Mr. Crouch, mortician and owner of the building in which the conjure man is a tenant, and Crouch's wife Martha are quickly dismissed as suspects. When the corpse disappears and reappears as the live conjure man, Archer and Detective Dart know that there has been a murder but are unable to find the corpse. The conjure man is seen burning a body in the furnace. The body is of his servant, who was mistakenly killed instead of the conjure man. The conjure man adamantly insists he is innocent and helps to set a trap for the real murderer, but the conjure man is fatally shot by the railroad worker. Distraught that he has killed her lover, Martha assaults the railroad man, and all discover he is none other than the avenging Mr. Crouch, in disguise.

The detective story framework of *The Conjure-Man Dies* does not overshadow Fisher's depiction of several issues of Harlem life. Residents of Harlem resort to creative means to survive as the Depression makes their difficult economic situations worse. Bubber becomes a self-appointed detective for spouses who suspect their partners are being unfaithful. The numbers racket provides a living for many, including the conjure man. African Americans who are "firsts" to achieve a specific rank are under pressure to prove themselves worthy. Such is the case for detective Dart, who privately thanks Dr. Archer for promising that the city administration will be informed that Dart solved the murder.

Although Fisher's development of the hard-boiled character may have been influenced by the detective fiction of Dashiell Hammett, his most remarkable character is the conjure man, N'Gana Frimbo, a Harvard-educated West African king who imparts the traditions of his culture to Dr. Archer. Frimbo reflects Fisher's interest in the connections among blacks in Harlem, the Caribbean, and Africa. In the spirit of the Harlem Renaissance, Fisher creates a new path with *The Conjure-Man Dies*, one that would influence later writers such as Chester Himes and Walter Mosley.

SUGGESTED READINGS

De Jongh, James. *Vicious Modernism: Black Harlem and the Literary Imagination.* New York: Cambridge University Press, 1990.

Gloster, Hugh M. *Negro Voices in American Fiction.* Chapel Hill: University of North Carolina Press, 1948.

Gosselin, Adrienne Johnson. "The World Would Do Better to Ask 'Why Is Frimbo Sherlock Holmes?'" *African American Review* 32 (Winter, 1998): 607.

Kramer, Victor, ed. *The Harlem Renaissance Re-examined.* New York: AMS Press, 1987.

Lewis, David Levering. *When Harlem Was in Vogue.* New York: Oxford University Press, 1989.

—Australia Tarver

Charles Fuller

BORN: Philadelphia, Pennsylvania; March 5, 1939

*Fuller has helped break a long tradition of stereotyping blacks,
especially black men, in literature.*

TRADITIONS: African American
PRINCIPAL WORKS: *The Village: A Party*, pr. 1968; *An Untitled Play*, pr. 1970; *In
My Many Names and Days*, pr. 1972; *The Candidate*, pr. 1974; *First Love*, pr.
1974; *In the Deepest Part of Sleep*, pr. 1974; *The Lay Out Letter*, pr. 1975; *The
Brownsville Raid*, pr. 1976; *Sparrow in Flight*, pr. 1978; *Zooman and the Sign*,
pr. 1980, pb. 1982; *A Soldier's Play*, pr. 1981, pb. 1982; *Sally*, pr. 1988; *Prince*,
pr. 1988 (*Sally* and *Prince* performed together as *We*, 1989); *Jonquil*, pr. 1990

Charles Fuller wrote and produced his first play, *The Village: A Party*, in 1968.
His place as a significant and talented playwright in contemporary African
American theater is marked by an impressive number of dramas, among
them *Zooman and the Sign*, for which he received two Obie Awards for best
play and best playwright in 1980, and *A Soldier's Play*, which received the New
York Drama Critics Circle Award for best American play, the 1982 Pulitzer
Prize for Drama, and a film contract in 1984.

Fuller was reared in comfortable circumstances in an extended family of
many foster children in North Philadelphia. He attended a Roman Catholic
high school with his lifelong friend, Larry Neal, and attended Villanova
University from 1956 to 1958. After a four-year hiatus in the U.S. Army in
Japan and Korea, he returned to complete his undergraduate studies at
LaSalle College from 1965 to 1968. Fuller began writing short stories, poetry,
and essays in the 1960's in Philadelphia mostly at night after working various
daytime jobs. His interest in literature, largely a result of assuming the
responsibility of proofreading his father's print jobs, began early and served
as the fertile source for a formal writing career, which developed from his
short stories long after he began writing.

In addition to his Pulitzer Prize-winning *A Soldier's Play*, a number of his
best-known plays have been produced by the Negro Ensemble Company,
notably *The Brownsville Raid*, *Zooman and the Sign*, and the *We* plays.

As a social reformer, Fuller is concerned with brushing away deeply rooted
stereotypes and uprooting preconceptions in order to explore the complexities of human relationships—particularly black-white relationships in America—and rectify the portrayals that distort African Americans, especially the
black male. Critical of black hatred for and treatment of other blacks, Fuller

is just as critical of the negative portrayal of the black male by the white media. Convinced that the stage is a powerful medium that can effectively rectify the stereotyped image of blacks shaped by white media, Fuller combined the mystery genre with his knowledge of the military structure of the U.S. Army to expose some of the real conflicts of white and black, and of black and black in America.

A Soldier's Play
TYPE OF WORK: Drama
FIRST PRODUCED: 1981; first published, 1982

A Soldier's Play, which won the Pulitzer Prize in drama in 1982, is a murder mystery in which Fuller examines many social issues and poses provocative questions. The play won the New York Drama Critics Circle Award, with a citation for best American play. The screenplay adaptation, *A Soldier's Story* (1984), which Fuller wrote, garnered an Academy Award nomination for adapted screenplay.

A play in two acts, *A Soldier's Play* examines and evaluates the causes of oppression of African Americans and the obstacles to their advancement. Unlike Fuller's two other award-winning plays, *The Brownsville Raid* (1976) and *Zooman and the Sign* (1979), *A Soldier's Play* has no particular, actual historical source. The play very realistically describes, however, the complex social issues that pervade his work: institutional, systemic racism in the U.S. Army during World War II; race relations; black genocide and the search for the meaning and definition of blackness in America; the meaning of democracy and the place of African Americans in it; and what it means to be black in a racially biased society.

Outside a segregated U.S. Army camp in Tynin, Louisiana, during World War II, a tyrannical technical sergeant, Vernon Waters, is murdered. The local brass has succeeded in playing down the murder until a Howard-trained attorney, Captain Davenport, is sent by Washington, D.C., to investigate the case. Initially assumed to be racially motivated, the murder's prime suspects are the white townspeople. The Ku Klux Klan is the first suspect, then two white officers. Davenport's thorough investigation, conducted in an atmosphere of racial hostility, mistrust on all sides, and condescension, leads to a surprising discovery of the murderer and the motives for the murder. The murderer is Private Peterson, the least-likely suspect.

Strong, outspoken, and opinionated, Peterson faces off with Waters, whose militant agenda for black destiny causes the innocent, naïve C. J. to commit suicide. Waters's heinous, sinister, and obsessive master plan to cleanse the black race of "geeches" such as C. J. meets its match in Peterson's own calculated perspective of how to refashion the black image. Mutual hatred eventually leads to murder, not before, however, Waters realizes the flaw in his inhumane master plan, grieves his obsession with blackness, and challenges the source of his misdirected self-justifying posture.

In focusing on the character of Waters rather than on the murder or the murderer, Fuller is able to engage and address the major causes and effects of the race problem, particularly the psychological. The play indicts all of the characters—white and black, except C. J.—for racially motivated violence informed by pervasive prejudice and dangerous stereotypical assumptions.

SUGGESTED READINGS

Anadolu-Okur, Nigun. *Contemporary African American Theater: Afrocentricity in the Works of Larry Neal, Amiri Baraka, and Charles Fuller.* New York: Garland, 1997.

Carter, Steven R. "The Detective as Solution: Charles Fuller's *A Soldier's Play.*" *Clues* 12, no. 1 (Spring-Summer, 1991): 33-42.

Demastes, William W. *Beyond Naturalism: A New Realism in American Theater.* Westport, Conn.: Greenwood Press, 1988.

Harriot, Esther. *American Voices: Contemporary Playwrights in Essays and Interviews.* Jefferson, N.C.: McFarland, 1988.

Hughes, Linda, and Howard Faulkner. "The Roles of Detection in *A Soldier's Play.*" *Clues* 7, no. 2 (Fall/Winter, 1986): 83-97.

—Pamela J. Olubunmi Smith

Ernest J. Gaines

BORN: Oscar, Louisiana; January 15, 1933

Gaines's regionalist short stories and novels are distinguished contributions to modern African American fiction.

TRADITIONS: African American
PRINCIPAL WORKS: *Catherine Carmier*, 1964; *Of Love and Dust*, 1967; *Bloodline*, 1968; *The Autobiography of Miss Jane Pittman*, 1971; *In My Father's House*, 1978; *A Gathering of Old Men*, 1983; *A Lesson Before Dying*, 1993

Born on a southern Louisiana plantation, Ernest J. Gaines was raised by a disabled aunt who became the model for the strong women in his works, including Miss Jane Pittman. There was no high school for Gaines to attend, so he left Louisiana in 1948 to live with relatives in California, where he suffered from the effects of his displacement. Displacement—caused by racism, by Cajuns' acquisition of land, or by loss of community ties—is a major theme for Gaines.

Young Gaines discovered works by John Steinbeck, William Faulkner, and Anton Chekhov, who wrote about the land. Not finding acceptable literary depictions of African Americans, Gaines resolved to write stories illuminating the lives and identities of his people. After completing military service, he earned a degree in English, published his first short stories, and received a creative writing fellowship at Stanford University.

Gaines rejected California as a subject for fiction, chose southern Louisiana as his major setting, and, like the Southern literary giant Faulkner, invented his own county. *Catherine Carmier*, an uneven apprentice novel, is the first of Gaines's works revealing Louisiana's physical beauty and folk speech.

Receiving a grant from the National Endowment for the Arts, Gaines published *Of Love and Dust*, inspired by a blues song about an African American who escapes prison by doing hard labor on a Louisiana plantation. This and other works by Gaines are not protest fiction, but they are concerned with human rights, justice, and equality.

Years of listening to the conversations of plantation folk led Gaines to employ multiple narrators in "Just Like a Tree" in *Bloodline*, a short-story collection. He also employs the technique in *A Gathering of Old Men*, which gives new form to another favorite theme, the achievement of manhood. Twelve elderly African American men, after a lifetime of passivity, stand up against ruthless Cajuns and rednecks who have mistreated them, taken over

Ernest J. Gaines (Jerry Bauer)

their farmland, and threatened to destroy their past, represented by family homes and graveyards. In Gaines's somber moral drama, *A Lesson Before Dying*, an African American teacher who has difficulty being a man in his segregated society learns to love. He helps to humanize an illiterate teenager wrongly condemned for murder and to convince the boy to die courageously. With a firmer personal and racial identity, the teacher becomes dedicated to educating young African Americans.

Gaines has served as a teacher in his position as writer-in-residence at a Louisiana university. His honors include a Guggenheim Fellowship and awards from the American Academy and Institute of Arts and Letters and the MacArthur Foundation.

The Autobiography of Miss Jane Pittman
TYPE OF WORK: Novel
FIRST PUBLISHED: 1971

In *The Autobiography of Miss Jane Pittman* the heroine and many African Americans in south Louisiana move from passivity to heroic assertion and achieve a new identity. Gaines's best-known novel is not an autobiography but a first-person reminiscence of a fictional 110-year-old former slave whose memories extend from the Emancipation Proclamation to Martin Luther King, Jr. *The Autobiography of Miss Jane Pittman* tells her unschooled but adept version of state and national occurrences and personalities (Huey Long, the flood of 1927, the rise of black athletes such as Jackie Robinson and Joe Louis). Her version of history is given to a tape-recording young school-teacher who wants historical facts; Jane helps him to understand the dynamics of living history, the way she remembers it. Her accounts are loving, sane, and responsible. Her language–speech patterns and pronunciations–is authentic, since Gaines read interviews with former slaves.

Renamed Jane Brown by a Union soldier because Ticey (her original name) is "a slave name," Jane wears her new designation proudly, as a badge of her identity as a free woman, when she and other former slaves attempt to escape from Louisiana. Many of them are brutally murdered by Klansmen. Jane, who is about ten at the time, escapes along with a small orphan, Ned. Jane becomes Ned's mother and during Reconstruction she raises him when they settle on another plantation as field hands. Ned receives some schooling and as a teenager is involved in civil rights struggles. His life in danger, Ned escapes to Kansas. Jane chooses to remain in Louisiana.

Ned represents the first of three African American males in Jane's life who struggle to define their racial and personal identities. The second is Joe Pittman, with whom Jane lives after Ned leaves. Joe loves Jane and wants her with him even though she is barren as a result of childhood beatings. He finds personal fulfillment in breaking wild horses on a Texas ranch; he accepts danger and the risk of death unflinchingly. Like Ned, who is murdered after he returns to Louisiana and sets up a school for black children, Joe is also killed fulfilling his destiny. Ned describes his identity as that of a black American who cares, and will always struggle. With these men, Jane finds a personal identity as a woman and demonstrates her desire to work with her black men but not to control them.

When Jimmy, a young civil rights worker much loved by Jane and others, is murdered, Jane—age 110—goes into the nearby town to drink from the segregated water fountain at the courthouse. She moves from the safety of silence and obscurity to join the ranks of African Americans who assert themselves and who risk losing their homes and lives but gain courage, dignity, and a heroic identity.

SUGGESTED READINGS

Babb, Valerie. *Ernest Gaines.* Boston: Twayne, 1991.

Bryant, Jerry H. "Ernest J. Gaines: Change, Growth, and History." *Southern Review* 10 (October, 1984): 851-864.

Lowe, John, ed. *Conversations with Ernest Gaines.* Jackson: University Press of Mississippi, 1995.

Rowell, Charles H. "The Quarters: Ernest Gaines and the Sense of Place." *Southern Review* 21 (1985): 733-750.

Simpson, Anne K. *A Gathering of Gaines.* Lafayette: University of Southwestern Louisiana, 1991.

—Philip A. Tapley

Allen Ginsberg

BORN: Newark, New Jersey; June 3, 1926
DIED: New York, New York; April 5, 1997

Ginsberg helped inaugurate major literary, social, and cultural changes in the post-World War II United States through his role as one of the members of the Beat generation.

TRADITIONS: Jewish
PRINCIPAL WORKS: *Howl*, 1956; *Kaddish and Other Poems*, 1961; *The Fall of America: Poems of These States, 1965-1971*, 1972; *Death and Fame: Poems, 1993-1997*, 1999; *Deliberate Prose: Selected Essays, 1952-1995*, 2000

Allen Ginsberg's earliest literary influences were his childhood experiences among the politically disenfranchised: socialists, communists, the working class, Russians, and Jews. His mother, Naomi, a teacher, was a Russian Jewish immigrant whose family was active in the Communist Party. Louis, his father, a teacher and poet, was a child of Russian Jewish immigrants and was active in the Socialist Party.

Ginsberg's earliest ambition was to become a labor lawyer. As Ginsberg grew older, his concerns for class inequities continued, even when he decided to give up law school for literary ambitions. In college he became less inclined to hide his homosexuality, and in his writing he increasingly sought to legitimize gay and bisexual experience. These identities—socialist, communist, gay, bisexual—are most fully realized in *Howl*, a major poem that broke the hegemony of the impersonal, academic poetry that had dominated much of the century. The poem eulogizes "the best minds" of the era, those imprisoned or driven mad by

Allen Ginsberg (George Holmes)

179

their resistance to the sexual and political uniformity of postwar American capitalist culture. In 1957, *Howl* was seized by San Francisco authorities and declared obscene.

Ginsberg won the subsequent trial, the first of his many encounters with political and legal establishments. In 1965 he was expelled from Cuba and Czechoslovakia because of his adamant support for gay civil rights in those countries. His later poetry, including *The Fall of America* and *Plutonian Ode* (1982), is influenced by his work in the United States in support of gay rights, the peace movement, freedom of speech, and drug decriminalization.

Ginsberg's career was marked by the convergence of Western and Eastern religious practices. He took vows as a Tibetan Buddhist in 1972. In 1974, he cofounded the Jack Kerouac School of Disembodied Poetics at the Naropa Institute, in Boulder, Colorado, the first accredited Buddhist college in the Western world.

Howl

TYPE OF WORK: Poetry
FIRST PUBLISHED: 1956

The protagonists of *Howl*, Ginsberg's best-known book, are marginalized because of their rejection of, or failure to measure up to, the social, religious, and sexual values of American capitalism. The poem "Howl," central to the book, is divided into three sections. Part 1 eulogizes "the best minds of my generation," whose individual battles with social, religious, and sexual uniformity leave them "destroyed by madness, starving hysterical naked." Ginsberg said that his use of the long line in *Howl*, inspired by Walt Whitman, is an attempt to "free speech for emotional expression." The poem is structured to give voice to those otherwise silenced by the dominant culture, to produce from their silence a "cry that shivers the cities down to the last radio."

Part 2 focuses on Moloch, the god for whom parents burned their children in sacrifice. Moloch symbolizes the physical and psychological effects of American capitalism. From America's "mind" of "pure machinery" emerges Moloch's military-industrial complex, whose bomb threatens to destroy the world.

Part 3 is structured as a call-and-response litany, specifically directed to Carl Solomon, whom Ginsberg met in 1949 when both were committed to the Columbia Presbyterian Psychiatric Institute. Solomon, to whom the poem is dedicated, represents the postwar counterculture, all of those whose "madness basically is rebellion against Moloch." The addendum to the poem, "Footnote to Howl," celebrates the holy cleansing that follows the apocalyptic confrontation dramatized in the poem.

Ginsberg termed crucial those elements of the poem that specifically describe the gay and bisexual practices of his protagonists as "saintly" and "ecstatic." Drawing from Ginsberg's experiences as a gay man in the sexually conformist 1940's and 1950's, the poem affirms gay eroticism as a natural form of sexual expression, replacing, as he said, "vulgar stereotype with a statement of act." The sexual explicitness of the poem prompted the San Francisco police to seize *Howl* and to charge Ginsberg's publisher, Lawrence Ferlinghetti, with obscenity. The judge in the case found the book to be "not obscene" because of its "redeeming social importance." The *Howl* case remains a landmark victory for freedom of expression in the twentieth century.

Kaddish

TYPE OF WORK: Poetry
FIRST PUBLISHED: 1961

Kaddish is Ginsberg's elegy for his mother, Naomi. In *Kaddish* Ginsberg portrays the course of Naomi's mental illness and its effect on the extended Ginsberg family. The perceptions of Ginsberg, the narrator, are crucial to understanding how sexual and religious themes of identity work in the poem. Naomi's worsening condition coincides with Ginsberg's realization as a young boy that he is gay, and with his emerging discomfort with traditional American religious institutions.

Invoking both "prophesy as in the Hebrew Anthem" and "the Buddhist Book of Answers," section 1 remembers Naomi's childhood. Naomi passes through major American cultural institutions—school, work, marriage—all of which contribute to her illness. Section 2 details her descent into madness and its harrowing effects on the family. Throughout the poem, Ginsberg seeks rescue from Naomi's madness, yet recognizes that her condition also inspires his own critique of the United States. "Naomi's mad idealism" frightens him; it also helps him understand the sinister qualities of middle-class American institutions. As he admits Naomi's condition caused him sexual confusion, he also confers imaginative inspiration to her. She is the "glorious muse that bore me from the womb, gave suck/ first mystic life"; and it was from her "pained/ head I first took vision." Unlike Naomi, the truly mad in *Kaddish* are those incapable of compassion, such as the psychiatric authorities who brutalize Naomi with electroshock treatments, leaving her "tortured and beaten in the skull."

By the end of *Kaddish*, Ginsberg seeks to redeem Naomi's life according to the Eastern and Western religious traditions which inform the poem. The final sections of *Kaddish* seek to transform the trauma of Naomi's illness into sacred poetry. The key to this transformation is Ginsberg's revision of the Kaddish, the Jewish prayer for the dead. The Kaddish was not said at Naomi's grave because the required minimum of ten Jewish adults—a *minyan*, in traditional Judaism—was not present, as required by Jewish law. Therefore, the poem accomplishes what Naomi's original mourners could not: Ginsberg eulogizes

Naomi with his Kaddish, and by doing so he offers his own revision of traditional Judaic law.

SUGGESTED READINGS

Caveney, Graham. *Screaming with Joy: The Life of Allen Ginsberg.* New York: Broadway Books, 1999.

Hyde, Lewis, ed. *On the Poetry of Allen Ginsberg.* Ann Arbor: University of Michigan Press, 1984.

Miles, Barry. *Ginsberg: A Biography.* New York: Simon & Schuster, 1989.

Portugés, Paul. *The Visionary Poetics of Allen Ginsberg.* Santa Barbara, Calif.: Ross-Erikson, 1978.

Rosenthal, M. L. *The New Poets: American and British Poetry Since World War II.* New York: Oxford University Press, 1967.

Schumacher, Michael. *Dharma Lion: A Critical Biography of Allen Ginsberg.* New York: St. Martin's Press, 1992.

Tonkinson, Carol, ed. *Big Sky Mind: Buddhism and the Beat Generation.* New York: Riverhead Books, 1995.

Tytell, John. *Naked Angels: The Lives and Literature of the Beat Generation.* New York: McGraw-Hill, 1976.

—*Tony Trigilio*

Nikki Giovanni
(Yolande Cornelia Giovanni, Jr.)

BORN: Knoxville, Tennessee; June 7, 1943

Giovanni's works have earned critical acclaim and have remained in print in an era when poetry typically does not sell.

TRADITIONS: African American

PRINCIPAL WORKS: *Black Feeling, Black Talk*, 1968; *Black Judgement*, 1970; *Re:Creation*, 1970; *Gemini*, 1971; *Spin a Soft Black Song: Poems for Children*, 1971; *My House*, 1972; *Ego-Tripping and Other Poems for Young People*, 1973; *The Women and the Men*, 1975; *Cotton Candy on a Rainy Day*, 1978; *Vacation Time: Poems for Children*, 1980; *Those Who Ride the Night Winds*, 1983; *Sacred Cows and Other Edibles*, 1988; *Racism 101: A Collection of Essays*, 1994; *Selected Poems of Nikki Giovanni*, 1996; *Love Poems*, 1997; *Blues: For All the Changes*, 1999

When Nikki Giovanni began, in journal publications and readings, to appear on the literary scene in the late 1960's, she was hailed as one of its most noted black poets. Critics praised her work for its themes of militancy, black pride, and revolution. The majority of poems in her volumes, however, address themes such as love, family, and friendship. Her militant poems received more attention, however, and they reflected Giovanni's own activism. It is then, arguably, not accurate when critics argue that Giovanni abandoned the cause of black militancy when, in the 1970's, her poems became more personal. The change was not as marked as some believed.

Giovanni's work took on a different perspective in 1970, when she became a mother. That year she published *Re:Creation*, whose themes are black female identity and motherhood. In *My House*, Giovanni more clearly addresses issues of family, love, and a twofold perspective on life, which is revealed in the two divisions of the book. With poems about the "inside" and "outside," Giovanni acknowledges the importance of not only the personal but also the world at large. Another dimension of this two-part unity is seen in *The Women and the Men*. Giovanni's poetry, over time, also seems to have undergone another change—an increased awareness of the outside world. Giovanni's poetry since 1978 reflects her interest in the human condition. The poems become more meditative, more introspective, and eventually more hopeful as they focus upon life's realities. Examined as a whole, Giovanni's work reveals concerns for identity, self-exploration, and self-realization. These concerns also appear in her works of other genres: recorded poetry, read to music; children's poetry, which she wrote to present positive images to black children; and essays. Giovanni's most consistent theme is the continual, evolving exploration of personal identity and individualism amid familial, social, and political realities.

Black Feeling, Black Talk
TYPE OF WORK: Poetry
FIRST PUBLISHED: 1968

Although Giovanni's reputation as a revolutionary poet is based upon this work, fewer than half of its poems address the theme of revolution. Critics point to often quoted incendiary poems in this collection to indicate Giovanni's revolutionary stance. They also note the poems about political figures and poems addressing black identity to illustrate Giovanni's militancy. These poems are important in this volume, but they are not Giovanni's sole concern.

What has been overlooked are the highly personal poems. In tallying the themes that appear in this work, it becomes apparent that love, loss, and loneliness are important to Giovanni. She also writes personal tributes and reminiscences to those who helped shape her life and ideology. Then there are Giovanni's personal responses to political events. She mourns the deaths of John F. Kennedy, Martin Luther King, Jr., and Robert Kennedy. She states that the 1960's were one long funeral day. She also notes atrocities in Germany, Vietnam, and Israel and compares them to 1960's America.

Black Feeling, Black Talk, then, is a compilation of political and personal poetry. Amid calls for revolution and affirmations of blackness are an

Nikki Giovanni (Jill Krementz)

insistence on maintaining one's individuality in the face of the political. There is also the importance of acknowledging the contributions of others in one's development. Thus, what is central to Giovanni's revolution is helping people to think about new ways of viewing and understanding their lives, personally and politically. *Black Feeling, Black Talk* is not a call for revolution that will destroy the world. The book is about how people, in the words of its final poem, may "build what we can become when we dream."

Gemini
TYPE OF WORK: Essays
FIRST PUBLISHED: 1971

Giovanni identifies her first work of prose, *Gemini*, in its subtitle as "an extended autobiographical statement on my first twenty-five years of being a black poet." *Gemini* is in a sense neither an autobiography nor an extended statement; rather, it is a collection of thirteen essays, about half of which discuss aspects of Giovanni's life. Readers learn something of Giovanni's life, but *Gemini* reveals more of her ideas. All of the essays involve personal observations mingled with political concerns, as the final lines of the essay "400 Mulvaney Street" illustrate: "They had come to say Welcome Home. And I thought Tommy, my son, must know about this. He must know we come from somewhere. That we belong." These lines are a capsule of Giovanni's major themes: family and belonging, identity, and one's relationship to the world. As the people of Knoxville come to hear her, Giovanni realizes her connection to a place and people. Sharing this with her son underscores the importance of family and passing on legacies, a lesson for not only him but also all blacks. To know that they come from somewhere and therefore belong is part of the message in this work.

The central message in *Gemini* is love. Giovanni claims, "If you don't love your mama and papa then you don't love yourself." This includes racial love; Giovanni provides tributes to black writer Charles Waddell Chesnutt and to black musicians Lena Horne and Aretha Franklin. Giovanni states that black people "must become the critics and protectors" of black music and literature. Love of oneself leads to a sense of identity: This is Giovanni's second message.

Giovanni cautions blacks against carelessly adopting "white philosophies." Her advice is to "know who's playing the music before you dance." Giovanni discusses respect as an outgrowth of love and identity, particularly for blacks of other nationalities and for the elderly. In Giovanni's discussion of the black revolution, she emphasizes the need to change the world. She addresses what one should be willing to live for: hope to change the world or some aspect of it. The essays of *Gemini* combine to give readers a sense of Giovanni, her world, and their world.

SUGGESTED READINGS

Fabio, Sarah Webster. "Black Feeling, Black Talk, Black Judgment." *Black World*, December, 1970, 102-104.

Fowler, Virginia. *Nikki Giovanni.* New York: Twayne, 1992.

Gaffke, Carol T., ed. *Poetry Criticism: Excerpts from Criticism of the Works of the Most Significant and Widely Studied Poets of World Literature.* Vol. 19. Detroit: Gale Research, 1997.

Jago, Carol. *Nikki Giovanni in the Classroom.* Urbana, Ill.: National Council of Teachers of English, 1999.

Jordan, June. Review of *Gemini*, by Nikki Giovanni. *The New York Times Book Review*, February 13, 1972, 6, 26.

Lee, Don L. *Dynamite Voices I: Black Poets of the 1960's.* Detroit: Broadside Press, 1971.

Mitchell, Carolyn. "Nikki Giovanni." In *Black Women in America: An Historical Encyclopedia*, edited by Darlene Clark Hine. New York: Carlson, 1993.

—Paula C. Barnes

Jessica Tarahata Hagedorn

BORN: Manila, Philippines; 1949

Hagedorn expresses the "tough and noble" lives of Asian immigrants who feel only partially assimilated.

TRADITIONS: Filipino American

PRINCIPAL WORKS: *Dangerous Music,* 1975; *Pet Food and Tropical Apparitions,* 1981; *Dogeaters,* 1990; *Danger and Beauty,* 1993; *Charlie Chan Is Dead: An Anthology of Contemporary Asian American Fiction,* 1993 (editor); *The Gangster of Love,* 1996

Born and raised in the Philippines, Jessica Hagedorn experienced the United States through the eyes of her mother and through images provided by American textbooks and movies. "The colonization of our imagination was relentless," she has said. Only when she started living in California in 1963 did she begin to appreciate what was precious in the Filipino extended family, a cultural feature partially left behind. In California, she began to feel allied with persons of various national origins who challenged American myths. Kenneth Rexroth, who had been patron of the Beat generation in San Francisco during the 1950's, introduced her to the poets who gathered at the City Lights bookstore. In 1973, Rexroth helped her publish her first poems, later collectively titled "The Death of Anna May Wong." Her principal concern was the exploitation of Filipino workers.

Her poetry became more and more influenced by the rhythms of popular street music. In 1975, she gathered together a volume of prose and poetry called *Dangerous Music.* That same year Hagedorn formed her band, The West Coast Gangster Choir, and sang lyrics of her own invention with them. In 1978, she left San Francisco without her band and established herself in New York City. There, along with Ntozake

Jessica Tarahata Hagedorn (Nancy Wong)

187

Shange and Thulani Davis, she performed her poetry at Joseph Papp's Public Theater. In 1981, Hagedorn published her second collection of mixed prose and poetry. During the 1980's she worked on her first novel, *Dogeaters*, which exposes corruption in her homeland as a result of Ferdinand Marcos's years of "constitutional authoritarianism." *Dogeaters* is also a novel that she has described as a love letter to her motherland. The characters in her novel for the most part are trapped by consumerism; this plight is caused by the Filipinos' long history as a colony and by their dreams of success, which too often come from American soap operas. Hagedorn's work is devoted to substituting for such stereotypes the complexities visible among people in Metro Manila and the urban reaches of the American coasts. Her anthology, *Charlie Chan Is Dead*, signifies a new image for Asians.

Dangerous Music
TYPE OF WORK: Poetry
FIRST PUBLISHED: 1975

The poems in *Dangerous Music* were composed after Hagedorn began "discovering myself as a Filipino-American writer" in California. Orientalist Kenneth Rexroth had placed five of her early poems in his 1973 anthology, *Four Young Women Poets*. "The Death of Anna May Wong," included in that edition, signified the poet's rejection of Hollywood stereotypes of Asian women as demure or exotically sinister. *Dangerous Music* continues the author's search for authentic images of non-Europeans that describe her own situation as well as those of other minorities. The intensity of many of these lyrics, written while she was performing with her West Coast Gangster Choir, became a way of expressing whole dimensions of society largely ignored or misunderstood by generations of European Americans. Although on the page such poems resemble songs without music, their occasional arrangement in ballad quatrains sometimes imitates blues music. The influence of Latino or African music is visible in the more jagged, syncopated lines of such poems as "Latin Music in New York" or "Canto Negro."

The cultural environment that is so much a part of the voices she assumes in *Dangerous Music* can readily be imagined. "Something About You," for example, affectionately connects Hagedorn with fellow artists Ntozake Shange and Thulani Davis, with whom she performed poems set to music for New York's Public Theater. Other poems identify her with Puerto Rican or Cuban musicians. More typical poems, however, describe a love-hate relationship with the American Dream. In "Natural Death," a Cuban refugee seems satisfied with fantasies of cosmetic splendor, though warned about bodies buried in saran wrap on a California beach. Loneliness and anger are conveyed by the mocking refrain: "o the grandeur of it." Yet the Philippines, which is remembered in "Sometimes" ("life is very cheap"), is equally far from being ideal. "Justifiable Homicide" warns of urban dangers anywhere in the world, when differences among people become cause for mutual indifference.

The only defense against the insanity that comes from cultural and economic stress is found in singing, according to "Sorcery" and "Easter Sunday," even if the songs themselves are passionate outcries of pain, not lullabies. The unacceptable alternative to release through song is to surrender one's memories of better dreams or, as in the case of "The Blossoming of Bongbong," the one prose fantasy included with these poems, total forgetfulness of one's personal identity.

SUGGESTED READINGS

Casper, Leonard. *Sunsurfers Seen from Afar: Critical Essays, 1991-1996.* Metro Manila, Philippines: Anvil, 1996.

Kim, Elaine H. *Asian American Literature.* Philadelphia: Temple University Press, 1982.

Lee, Rachel C. *The Americas of Asian American Literature: Gendered Fictions of Nation and Transnation.* Princeton, N.J.: Princeton University Press, 1999.

Zapanta Manlapaz, Edna. *Songs of Ourselves.* Metro Manila, Philippines: Anvil, 1994.

—Leonard Casper

Lorraine Hansberry

BORN: Chicago, Illinois; May 19, 1930
DIED: New York, New York; January 12, 1965

*Hansberry is credited with being the first African American woman
playwright to have a play produced on Broadway.*

TRADITIONS: African American
PRINCIPAL WORKS: *A Raisin in the Sun*, pr., pb. 1959; *The Sign in Sidney
Brustein's Window*, pr. 1964, pb. 1965; *To Be Young, Gifted, and Black*, pr.
1969, pb. 1971

With the successful Broadway opening in 1959 of *A Raisin in the Sun*, Lorraine
Hansberry became a major voice in behalf of racial, sexual, economic, and
class justice. During Hansberry's childhood, her father, a successful real estate
broker, and her mother, a schoolteacher, were involved in politics and were
active supporters of the National Association for the Advancement of Colored People and its causes. Hansberry grew up in a Chicago household where racial issues, oppression, African American identity, and the struggle against discrimination were major concerns. Her early intellectual development was influenced by her uncle, William Leo Hansberry, a professor and scholar at Howard University and writer of African history. He put Hansberry in contact with her African roots and introduced her to a world of articulate black artists and thinkers who personified the struggle to overcome discrimination in American society.

Lorraine Hansberry (Library of Congress)

Hansberry was a student in the segregated Chicago public school system. She proceeded to the University of Wisconsin, where she became the first African American woman to live in her dormitory. At the university she was active in politics and developed an interest in the theater and its power.

Dropping out of school, Hansberry moved to New York and became a writer and associate editor for the progressive newspaper *Freedom.* She championed civil rights causes, writing not only on behalf of blacks but also on behalf of other socially repressed groups, including women and gays. With encouragement and inspiration from such luminaries as W. E. B. Du Bois, Langston Hughes, and Paul Robeson, her active professional and intellectual life in Harlem soon blossomed into stories, poems, and plays.

After marrying Robert Nemiroff in 1953, Hansberry left *Freedom* to devote all her attention to writing. Drawing upon her Chicago experiences, she completed *A Raisin in the Sun,* a play that explores the tensions that arise as a black family in Chicago tries to escape the ghetto. The family faces white hostility as it plans to move into a white neighborhood. The play was a phenomenal success.

Hansberry's second Broadway production, *The Sign in Sidney Brustein's Window,* explores such topics as prostitution, marriage, homosexuality, and anti-Semitism. The play's depictions of the plight of those oppressed and discriminated against and of the nature of society's reaction to injustice and prejudice are vivid and thoughtful. Hansberry died from cancer at the age of only thirty-four. Her call for justice and human sympathy continues to reverberate in the work she left behind.

A Raisin in the Sun

TYPE OF WORK: Drama
FIRST PRODUCED: 1959; first published, 1959

A Raisin in the Sun, Hansberry's most celebrated play, is a realistic portrait of a working-class black family struggling to achieve the American Dream of careers and home ownership while gripped by the reality of their lives as African Americans who must survive in a racist society.

Hansberry based her play on her knowledge of life in Chicago's black ghetto and the families to whom her father, a successful real estate broker, rented low-income housing. The action takes place in the cramped, roach-infested apartment of the Youngers, where three generations of the family have resided for years. With the death of her husband, Lena (Mama) becomes the head of the family. She has the right to decide how to use the $10,000 in life insurance money that has come with her husband's death.

Tensions develop quickly. Mama dreams of using the money to move out of the apartment into a new, large home where her family can breathe the free, clean air outside the ghetto. Her son Walter, seeing himself as the new head of the family, envisions the money as a way to free himself and his family from poverty by investing in a liquor store. Walter's intellectual sister hopes the windfall may be a way for her to break racist and sexist barriers by getting a college education and becoming a doctor.

As the play unfolds, Hansberry explores issues of African American identity, pride, male-female relationships within the black family, and the problems of segregation. Mama makes a down payment on a house in a white neighborhood. Fearing that her exercise of authority will diminish her son's sense of masculine self-worth, and in spite of her opposition to buying a liquor store, she reminds Walter of his sister's right to some of the money for a college education and entrusts him with what is left of the money after the down payment. When he returns despairingly after losing all of it, he considers that the only way to recoup the loss is to humiliate himself and his family by making a deal with the Clybourne Park Association, a group of white homeowners who want to buy back the new home in order to keep their neighborhood white.

In a dramatic conclusion, the disillusioned Walter enacts the dilemma of the modern African American male. Trapped at the bottom of the economic ladder, he must again submit to matriarchal authority. Mama despairs at having to take control and wield the authority she knows is destroying her son's masculine identity. Walter finally realizes that he cannot accept the degradation he would bring upon himself, his family, and his father's memory by accepting the association's offer. Discovering his manhood and his responsibility to his family and his race, he refuses to sell back the house. When the association's representative appeals to Mama to reverse her son's decision, she poignantly and pridefully says, "I am afraid you don't understand. My son said we was going to move and there ain't nothing left for me to say." The play closes with the family leaving their cramped apartment for their new home and the challenges that surely await them there.

To Be Young, Gifted, and Black
TYPE OF WORK: Drama
FIRST PRODUCED: 1969; first published, 1971

After Hansberry's untimely death, Robert Nemiroff, her former husband and literary executor, edited versions of her writings and adapted them for the stage under the title *To Be Young, Gifted, and Black*. He also expanded that work into an informal autobiography of the same title. In Nemiroff's words, the work is "biography and autobiography, part fact, part fiction, an act of re-creation utilizing first person materials as well as, inferentially, autobiographical projections of herself in her characters."

"Never before, in the entire history of the American theater, had so much truth of black people's lives been seen on the stage," James Baldwin said of

To Be Young, Gifted, and Black. Characters from Hansberry's plays, including the character of Lorraine Hansberry, portray and relate various strands of African American life in modern America. Walter Lee, for example, embodies the frustrations of black men trying to cope in an economic system that promises advancement but holds them back because of their race. His sister, Beneatha, is an example of the gifted, intelligent black woman (not unlike Hansberry herself) who aspires to participate fully in the American culture. She also, as does Asagai, the Africanist intellectual, strives to remember her African roots.

Then there is Sidney Brustein of *The Sign in Sidney Brustein's Window* (1964), the play most represented in *To Be Young, Gifted, and Black.* Sidney, after leading a life of sleepy noncommitment, grows to care about himself and his society; he takes action, political and otherwise, to improve things. This sort of character growth, in one way or another apparent in all of Hansberry's work, defines her own belief in the possibility for human goodness to prevail. It is this conviction that allows her to anticipate a healing of familial and social ills that comes when people are moved to dedicate themselves to change.

To Be Young, Gifted, and Black also addresses the deep connections between black Americans and emerging African nations, black empowerment, sexual relationships, the generation gap, and black art. Woven throughout *To Be Young, Gifted, and Black* is the character of Lorraine Hansberry herself, who, at the beginning of the work, states perhaps somewhat despairingly: "I was born on the South Side of Chicago. I was born black and female," but by the end is proclaiming proudly, "My name is Lorraine Hansberry. I am a writer." She has ceased allowing the ghetto, with its economic, social, and cultural deprivation, to define her. She has overthrown her enslavement by oppressive sexual stereotypes. In this, the character of Lorraine Hansberry and the playwright are one in the embodiment of a hope for the black race and the female sex. Just as they have, through commitment and perseverance, discovered and defined themselves in name and vocation, so, too, must their people insist on partaking of that vital experience and self-definition that leads to a discovery of self-worth, purpose, and genuine human sympathy.

SUGGESTED READINGS

Carter, Steven R. *Hansberry's Drama: Commitment and Complexity.* Champaign: University of Illinois Press, 1991.

Cheney, Anne. *Lorraine Hansberry.* Boston: G. K. Hall, 1984.

Scheader, Catherine. *Lorraine Hansberry: Playwright and Voice of Justice.* Springfield, N.J.: Enslow, 1998.

Sharadha, Y. S. *Black Women's Writing: Quest for Identity in the Plays of Lorraine Hansberry and Ntozake Shange.* New Delhi, India: Prestige Books, 1998.

Wilkerson, Margaret B. "The Dark Vision of Lorraine Hansberry: Excerpts from a Literary Biography." *Massachusetts Review* 28 (Winter, 1987): 642-650.

_____. "Lorraine Hansberry." In *African American Writers*, edited by Valerie Smith, Lea Baechler, and A. Walton Litz. New York: Charles Scribner's Sons, 1991.

—Richard M. Leeson

Joy Harjo

BORN: Tulsa, Oklahoma; May 9, 1951

Harjo's poetry has won acclaim for its substance, style, and themes, combining many elements of Native American and mainstream American experience.

TRADITIONS: American Indian
PRINCIPAL WORKS: *She Had Some Horses,* 1983; *In Mad Love and War,* 1990; *The Woman Who Fell from the Sky,* 1994; *A Map to the Next World: Poetry and Tales,* 2000

Joy Harjo's collections of poetry express a close relationship to the environment and the particularities of the Native American and white cultures from which she is descended. She is an enrolled member of the Creek tribe, the mother of two children (a son, Phil, and a daughter, Rainy Dawn), and a grandmother. Various forms of art were always a part of her life, even in childhood. Her grandmother and aunt were painters. In high school, she trained as a dancer and toured as a dancer and actress with one of the first Indian dance troupes in the country. When her tour ended, she returned to Oklahoma, where her son was born when she was seventeen years old. She left her son's father to move to New Mexico, enrolling at the university as a pre-med student. After one semester, she decided that her interest in art was compelling enough to engage in its formal study.

Educated at the Institute of American Indian Arts in Santa Fe, New Mexico, where she later worked as an instructor, she received a bachelor's degree from the University of New Mexico and a master's degree in

Joy Harjo

195

fine arts from the University of Iowa. She was a professor of English at both the University of Arizona and the University of New Mexico.

Harjo has received numerous awards for her writing, including the William Carlos Williams award from the Poetry Society of America, the Delmore Schwartz Award, the American Indian Distinguished Achievement in the Arts Award, and two creative writing fellowships from the National Endowment for the Arts. Harjo's poetry has been increasingly influenced by her interest in music, especially jazz. She plays the saxophone in a band, Poetic Justice, that combines the musical influences of jazz and reggae with her poetry. Many of her poems are tributes to the various musicians who have influenced her work, including saxophonists John Coltrane and Jim Pepper.

The history and mythology of her people and the current state of their oppression also are prominent themes in her work. As she states in the explanation of her poem "Witness," "The Indian wars never ended in this country . . . we were hated for our difference by our enemies."

In Mad Love and War
TYPE OF WORK: Poetry
FIRST PUBLISHED: 1990

In Mad Love and War is composed of two sections of poems expressing the conflicts and joys of Harjo's experiences as a Native American woman living in contemporary American culture. The poems draw on a wealth of experiences, including those relating to tribal tradition and sacredness of the land. Such positive experiences are compared with the sometimes grim realities inherent in the modern society in which Harjo lives.

The first section, titled "The Wars," offers poetry that imagistically develops themes relating to oppression and to survival in the face of daunting problems of poverty, alcoholism, and deferred dreams. In her notable poem "Deer Dancer," Harjo retells a traditional myth in the contemporary setting of "a bar of broken survivors, the club of shotgun, knife wound, of poison by culture." Through the dance, the deer dancer becomes "the myth slipped down through dreamtime. The promise of feast we all knew was coming." Like many of Harjo's poems, "The Deer Dancer" ends with beauty being experienced amid lost hope and despair.

Many of the other poems in "The Wars" are political in nature, containing stark images of violence and deprivation, most notably her poem dedicated to Anna Mae Pictou Aquash, a member of the American Indian Movement whose murdered body was found on the Pine Ridge Reservation, and the poems "We Must Call a Meeting," "Autobiography," "The Real Revolution Is Love," and "Resurrection."

The poems of the second section, "Mad Love," are more personal in their treatment of subject, more lyrical in their voice, and quieter in their tone. In a poem titled with the name of Harjo's daughter, "Rainy Dawn," Harjo concludes by expressing the joy of Rainy Dawn's birth.

> And when you were born I held you wet and unfolding, like a butterfly newly born from the chrysalis of my body. And breathed with you as you breathed your first breath. Then was your promise to take it on like the rest of us, the immense journey, for love, for rain.

In Mad Love and War encompasses a variety of styles, from narrative poems written in expansive lines to tightly chiseled lyrics. Many of the poems in the "Mad Love" section are prose poems, whose unlined stanzas create a notable incongruity with respect to the increasingly personal, softer mood of the pieces. The book offers a journey from the ruins of dislocation to the joys of membership and love. In the final masterful poem of the collection, "The Eagle," Harjo writes, "That we must take the utmost care/ And kindness in all things. . . . We pray that it will be done/ In beauty/ In beauty."

The Woman Who Fell from the Sky

TYPE OF WORK: Poetry
FIRST PUBLISHED: 1994

The Woman Who Fell from the Sky, Harjo's seventh collection of poetry, consists primarily of prose poems. The collection is divided into two sections, "Tribal Memory" and "The World Ends Here," which express the lore of Harjo's Native American ancestry and her observations of contemporary life. These poems show a concern for content over style. The poetry is presented without conventions of patterned rhyme or meter; the imagery is stark and unadorned.

Each poem is followed by an explanation that contextualizes the piece by offering a brief history of the genesis of the poem or commenting on themes elucidated by the writing. The majority of the book's poems are narrative, developing stories that explain the destinies of Native American characters who retain identity despite the onslaught of European culture, which strips away their language, lore, and religion. The poems create a universe of oppositions: darkness and light, violence and peace.

Other poems relate stories of ancestry on a more personal level, illuminating a view of many worlds existing at once, interconnected and affecting one another. In "The Naming," a grandmother "who never had any peace in this life" is "blessed with animals and songs"; after the birth of a "daughter-born-of-my-son . . . the earth is wet with happiness." As Harjo notes in the explanation of this piece, "When my granddaughter Haleigh was born I felt the spirit of this grandmother in the hospital room. Her presence was a blessing." In the world that Harjo creates, the living and the dead are united and the physical universe is animate, pulsing with feeling of its own.

"The World Ends Here" offers shorter and more concrete poems than those in "Tribal Memory." In addition, the poems are concerned with wounds suffered through a history of genocide inflicted upon Native Americans. "When a people institute a bureaucratic department to serve justice then be suspicious," Harjo warns in "Wolf Warrior." "The Indian wars never ended in this country," she writes in the postscript to "Witness." The poems do not, however, fall into despair. The beauty of nature, the rich rewards of friendship, the joys of music, and the hope of love are continually evident, emerging with their healing power. As Harjo writes in "Perhaps the World Ends Here," "The gifts of earth are brought and prepared, set on the table. So it has been since creation, and so it will go on."

SUGGESTED READINGS

Allen, Frank. Review of *The Woman Who Fell from the Sky*, by Joy Harjo. *Library Journal*, November 15, 1994, 70-71.

Leen, Mary. "An Art of Saying." *American Indian Quarterly* 19, no. 1 (Winter, 1995): 1-16.

McQuade, Molly. Review of *The Woman Who Fell from the Sky*, by Joy Harjo. *Publishers Weekly*, November 28, 1994, 54-55.

Pettit, Rhonda. *Joy Harjo*. Boise, Idaho: Boise State University Press, 1998.

Smith, Stephanie. "Joy Harjo." *Poets and Writers* 21, no. 4 (July/August, 1993): 23-27.

—Robert Haight

Michael S. Harper

BORN: Brooklyn, New York; March 18, 1938

Harper's poetry synthesizes diverse ethnic, racial, and historic components to create an inclusive perspective on American culture.

TRADITIONS: African American

PRINCIPAL WORKS: *Dear John, Dear Coltrane,* 1970; *History Is Your Own Heartbeat,* 1971; *Song: I Want a Witness,* 1972; *Debridement,* 1973; *Nightmare Begins Responsibility,* 1974; *Images of Kin: New and Selected Poems,* 1977; *Rhode Island: Eight Poems,* 1981; *Healing Song for the Inner Ear,* 1985; *Songlines in Michaeltree: New and Collected Poems,* 2000

The first son in his middle-class African American family, Michael S. Harper was encouraged to follow the career path of his grandfather and great-grandfather: medicine. An intense interest in the rhythms of language and in exploring the apparent schisms in American society, however, led Harper to his dual vocations of writer and scholar.

In the Harper home, music and poetry were important parts of family life. Poems by Langston Hughes were a familiar presence in Harper's childhood home. Harper's parents also owned an extensive collection of contemporary jazz recordings. The poet recalled spending many happy hours listening to, among others, Bessie Smith, Billie Holiday, Charlie Parker, and John Coltrane.

As an adolescent, Harper was forced into an awareness of racism in America. The family moved from New York to West Los Angeles, where African Americans were the targets of racial violence. During high school, Harper began experimenting with creative writing. In college, he continued writing in addition to working full time for the post office. He later attended the famous Iowa Writers Workshop at the University of Iowa in Iowa City.

As the only African American student in the poetry and fiction workshop classes, Harper endured misunderstanding and prejudice. These experiences motivated him to confront the dualism inherent in being an African American writer. Harper refused exclusive containment in either the African American or in the American category. Rather, he affirmed his identity in both groups.

Harper interrupted his studies at Iowa to enter the student teacher program at Pasadena City College in 1962. He became the first African American to complete the program, and after finishing his courses at Iowa, he accepted an instructorship at Contra Costa College in San Pablo, California. This was the beginning of an extensive and distinguished teaching career, including professorships at Colgate University, Brown University, and Harvard University. In addition to eight volumes of poetry, Harper has contributed to numerous journals and anthologies and has edited several anthologies of poetry.

Poetry

Michael S. Harper is a poet with a strong individual style. His poetry is notable for the variable rhythm of its lines. Harper's poems echo a variety of human speech patterns and rhythms. This characteristic distinguishes his rhythm from the more traditionally metric patterns of many poets. Harper's looser rhythms work along with such techniques as repetition, internal rhyme, and enjambment (lines flowing together without pause at the end) to modulate sound in the poem. Sound is important in Harper's poems; they are most effective when read aloud.

The content of Harper's poetry reflects a concern with unification. Harper's poetic speakers explore connections. For Harper, the poem evidences the connections between the poet's individual utterances and universal concerns that transcend time and place. A major theme through all of Harper's books is that of connections among racial and ethnic groups. Other major themes include the importance of an awareness of history, the relationship between the individual and the group, and the connections between one geographic location and another.

Harper's development of these major themes begins in *Dear John, Dear Coltrane.* The poems in this book pay homage to the greats of jazz and the blues. The musicians also represent individual and collective human achievement, achievement attained and achievement still possible.

The exploration of the individual's connection to history and possibility continues in *History Is Your Own Heartbeat.* This second book won the Poetry Award of the Black Academy of Arts and Letters. The idea that an awareness of individual and collective history is essential is further developed in *Song: I Want a Witness.* In the preface, Harper writes: "Where there is no history/ there is no metaphor." In other words, an individual ignorant of history has no basis for comparison (metaphors are comparisons), for testing feelings and attitudes.

In *Debridement* Harper narrows the theme of the importance of history to explore the historical relationships between black and white Americans. The poems collectively suggest that understanding of history is necessary for the individual's moving beyond misunderstanding and hatred. "Debridement" means surgically removing dead flesh from old wounds so that healing can begin.

In *Nightmare Begins Responsibility*, Harper metaphorically reviews his own personal history. In his two later books, *Images of Kin: New and Selected Poems* and *Healing Song for the Inner Ear,* Harper steps back somewhat from personal history to consider the universal traditions of black and white poets.

In addition to his books of thematically linked poetry, Harper has published in many journals and anthologies. His poems testify in the voice of the American trying to reconcile the past, present, and future of the individual's relationship with the nation.

SUGGESTED READINGS

Brown, Joseph A. "Their Long Scars Touch Ours: A Reflection on the Poetry of Michael Harper." *Callaloo* 9, no. 1 (Winter, 1986): 209-220.

Harper, Michael S. "It Is the Man/Woman Outside Who Judges: The Minority Writer's Perspective on Literature." *TriQuarterly* 65 (Winter, 1986): 57-65.

_____. "Interview with Michael S. Harper." Interview by David Lloyd. *TriQuarterly* 65 (Winter, 1986): 119-128.

_____. "My Poetic Technique and the Humanization of the American Audience." In *Black American Literature and Humanism*, edited by Miller R. Baxter. Lexington: University Press of Kentucky, 1981.

Nicholas, Xavier. "Robert Hayden and Michael S. Harper." *Callaloo* 17, no. 4 (Fall, 1994): 976-1016.

Stepto, Robert B. "Let's Call Your Mama and Other Lies About Michael S. Harper." *Callaloo* 13, no. 4 (Fall, 1990): 801-804.

Young, Al, Larry Kart, and Michael S. Harper. "Jazz and Letters: A Colloquy." *TriQuarterly* 68 (Winter, 1987): 118-158.

—Anne B. Mangum

Wilson Harris

BORN: New Amsterdam, British Guiana (now Guyana); March 24, 1921

As philosopher, novelist, and critic, Harris imagines recent world history and colonialism in order to present a vision of a possible human community that celebrates multiple, mixed, and interrelating identities.

TRADITIONS: African American, American Indian, Caribbean
PRINCIPAL WORKS: *Palace of the Peacock,* 1960; *The Secret Ladder,* 1963; *Tradition, the Writer, and Society: Critical Essays,* 1967; *Fossil and Psyche,* 1974; *The Tree of the Sun,* 1978; *The Womb of Space,* 1983; *Carnival,* 1985; *Jonestown,* 1996; *The Selected Essays of Wilson Harris,* 1999

Wilson Harris is an extremely eclectic and expansive writer. In *The Womb of Space,* he writes that "literature is still constrained by regional and other conventional suffocating categories." Harris has spent his career attempting to transcend notions of genre, tradition, and discipline, constructing texts founded on philosophical speculation. Harris attempts, in his writing, to promote new models for civilization and for creative art.

Influenced by Carl Gustav Jung, Martin Buber, Elizabethan poetry, William Blake, Native American folklore, and nineteenth century expedition literature, Harris investigates the ambiguities of life and death, of history and innovation, of self and other, and of reality and illusion. Harris questions received concepts of origin, history, and reality. It is Harris's hope that such inquisitions of the self may prove crucial in the development of a radical revision of history, origin, and identity.

Opening with a series of nightmare vignettes that awaken into each other, the narrator of Harris's *Palace of the Peacock* declares: "I dreamt I awoke with one dead eye seeing and one living eye closed." The novel hovers between reality and illusion, death and life, insight and blindness. It chronicles an expeditionary party's journey into the interior of Guyana. In this expedition into the territory of the self, each member of the party embodies a part of Guyanese identity. A European, an African, and a Native American set out together in a quest to retrieve renegade farmworkers but find along the way that they are, perhaps, the ghostly repetitions of a party that perished on the same river in the early days of European conquest. The allegorical and existential significances of the quest give Harris the opportunity to delve into the nature of narration, of time, of space, and of being. He asserts that humanity can alter fate through recognition of connections and by articulating and celebrating commonly held identities.

The themes *Palace of the Peacock* raises are also found in the novels that succeed it. In subsequent novels, Harris returns to elaborate and examine the psychological and existential structures by way of which identity ossifies and resists participation in change. By carefully constructing contradictory narrative puzzles, Harris leads his readers into ambiguous regions of understanding where opposites (life and death, reality and illusion, self and other) meet. It is his hope that such expeditions of the imagination will result in greater understanding of identity and community.

Fossil and Psyche
TYPE OF WORK: Essay
FIRST PUBLISHED: 1974

Fossil and Psyche articulates Wilson Harris's belief that "the potentiality for dialogue, for change, for the miracle of roots, for new community is real." Using the metaphor of archery (psychic arrows and fossil targets), he situates his novels and the work of other writers within a realm of attempts to reach architectonic (mythic) realities. He argues against the opposition of the material to the spiritual and critiques the borders by means of which the real is held separate from the imaginary. Harris asserts the potential of the imaginary to illuminate the transcendent possibilities of history and identity. Such possibilities, if realized, would result in a culturally heterogeneous world community and in an alteration of world power hierarchies.

The "idolatry of absolutes" holds readers and writers hostage to the temporal, spatial, and cultural limitations of literature when in fact those limitations are illusory. Arrows of language and imagination can reach the fossil targets of architectonic, mythic, eternal, atemporal, renewing experience. Novels by authors such as Patrick White and Malcolm Lowry, Harris claims, are dream-expeditions signaling humanity toward "a third perhaps nameless revolutionary dimension of sensibility" that evades commonly held notions of material and spiritual reality. Such an evasion is the key to enriching and understanding the value of the multiplicity of identities. Accessing these wells of timeless connection will "deepen and heighten the role of imaginative literature to wrestle with categories and to visualize the birth of community as other than the animism of fate."

Traditional oppositions lead to inadequate readings of imaginative literature and to misreadings of the processes that underlie imaginative composition. Literature, like every aspect of human experience, is lodged within a matrix of time and space. The literature Harris addresses in *Fossil and Psyche* attempts to transcend this matrix, to confound time and space, to mine the architectonic fossils of human community with present psychic projections of imagination.

Novels of expedition, then, revise history and reveal the hopeful, transformative energies of life locked away in even the most deadly and deadening acts of history. Writers who embrace such a process of revision renew the creative, psychic act of imagination. Such psychic projections of imagination join past to present and future and European to African and Native American.

The Womb of Space

TYPE OF WORK: Essays
FIRST PUBLISHED: 1983

Harris's *The Womb of Space: The Cross-Cultural Imagination* is a collection of critical essays that attempt to describe how multiculturalism can inform the reading of texts. "Imaginative sensibility," Harris asserts, "is uniquely equipped by forces of dream and paradox to mirror the inimitable activity of subordinated psyche." Harris's cross-cultural rereadings of specific texts in *The Womb of Space* reveal bridges of myth, imagination, and dream that link culture to culture, despite the appearance of disparity.

Harris interprets works by William Faulkner, Edgar Allan Poe, Ralph Ellison, Jean Toomer, Juan Rulfo, Raja Rao, Jean Rhys, Derek Walcott, Edward Brathwaite, and others in order to demonstrate the applicability of a cross-cultural analysis to world literature.

For example, Harris rereads Poe's *The Narrative of Arthur Gordon Pym* (1838) as a psychic text in which the unconscious subtext critiques the cultural hierarchy that the surface of the tale intends to uphold. Instead of emphasizing the tale's narrative focus on the consolidation of Western values, Harris underscores the unconscious "twinships" (pairings) of characters and events that point to an unconsciously scripted psychic, mythic dimension. Such a subversion of the text leads Harris to "perceive the decay of order conditioned by conquest; that order begins to review its daylight deeds . . . in the night-time rebellious dream life of the half-conscious and unconscious psyche." Despite the conscious intentions of Poe, the text is for Harris a revision of pre-Columbian mythic antecedents which illuminate the psychic, mythic, and communal dimensions of the literary imagination.

Harris generalizes that cross-cultural readings reveal, in literature, correlations and unity that spring from the dialectic of explicit statement and implicit subversion of that statement. Stressing the undermining of Western texts by consulting mythic, psychic (often non-Western) roots, Harris hopes to open a cultural dialogue among cultures and identities. Harris suggests that such a dialogue will encourage the growth of broader, multicultural, inclusive communities. The "womb of space" is the generative region where such a community may begin to develop.

"The paradox of cultural heterogeneity, or cross-cultural capacity, lies in the evolutionary thrust it restores to orders of the imagination, the ceaseless dialogue it inserts between hardened conventions and eclipsed or half-eclipsed otherness." By bringing the cross-cultural imagination to bear on a variety of texts in *The Womb of Space*, Wilson Harris affirms his particular vision of literature and of the role texts play in reconstructing identity, culture, and community.

SUGGESTED READINGS

Drake, Sandra E. *Wilson Harris and the Modern Tradition: A New Architecture of the World.* Westport, Conn.: Greenwood Press, 1986.
Gilkes, Michael. *Wilson Harris and the Caribbean Novel.* New York: Longman, 1975.
Harris, Wilson. *Tradition, the Writer, and Society: Critical Essays.* London: New Beacon, 1967.
Maes-Jelinek, Hena, ed. *Wilson Harris: The Uncompromising Imagination.* Aarhus, Denmark: Dangaroo, 1991.
Moore, Gerald. *The Chosen Tongue.* London: Longman, 1969.
The Review of Contemporary Fiction 17, no. 2 (Summer, 1997).

—Daniel M. Scott III

Robert Hayden

BORN: Detroit, Michigan; August 4, 1913
DIED: Ann Arbor, Michigan; February 25, 1980

*Hayden's poetry provides a learned, kind observer's view of major events
and figures in American and African American history.*

TRADITIONS: African American
PRINCIPAL WORKS: *Heart-Shape in the Dust*, 1940; *The Lion and the Archer*, 1948;
Figure of Time, 1955; *A Ballad of Remembrance*, 1962; *Selected Poems*, 1966;
Words in the Mourning Time, 1970; *The Night-Blooming Cereus*, 1972; *Angle of
Ascent: New and Selected Poems*, 1975; *American Journal*, 1978, 1982; *Collected
Prose*, 1984; *Collected Poems*, 1985

Robert Hayden's childhood independence was instrumental to his becoming
a scholar and poet. He was reared in a poor Detroit neighborhood, where
such distinctions were rare. Soon after he was born Asa Bundy Sheffey,
Hayden was adopted by the Haydens, neighbors of his birth parents. A
sufferer of extreme myopia as a child, Hayden was separated from his peers
into a "sight conservation" class; although his handicap kept him from
participating in most sports, the resulting time alone allowed him to read
(especially poetry, which demanded less of his vision), write, and play the
violin, thereby developing rhythmical and tonal sensitivities that would well
serve his eventual vocation.

Several fortuitous events and encounters in Robert Hayden's life supported his choosing texts in African American history, especially the narratives of rebellious slaves, as fruitful subjects for his verse. After attending
Detroit City College (which later became Wayne State University), Hayden,
in 1936, began working for the Federal Writers' Project of the Works Progress
Administration; he was assigned to research "Negro folklore." Two major
figures encouraged his ensuing interest in African American history. The first,
Erma Inez Morris, a pianist and a teacher in Detroit's public schools, became
Hayden's wife and, for a time, his financial support. She also introduced her
new husband to Countée Cullen, the Harlem Renaissance poet who admired
Hayden's first book, *Heart-Shape in the Dust*, and who motivated Hayden to
keep writing. Hayden also found inspiration from the British poet W. H.
Auden, also a folklorist, who instructed Hayden at the University of Michigan
when the younger poet began graduate work there.

In 1946, Hayden began a twenty-three-year tenure as a professor at Fisk
College in segregated Nashville. During this time Hayden wrote steadily,
despite being hampered by a heavy teaching load. The quality of Hayden's

work was recognized internationally—it was broadcast by the British Broadcasting Company, and his 1962 book *A Ballad of Remembrance* won the Grand Prize for Poetry at the First World Festival of Negro Arts in Dakar, Senegal—before he was discovered in the United States. Eventual recognition included invitations to teach at several universities and to edit anthologies of work by his poetic heroes and contemporaries. The year that *Angle of Ascent* was published, 1975, Hayden was elected fellow of the Academy of American Poets and Appointed Consultant in Poetry to the Library of Congress.

Hayden's greatest personal successes, however, occurred in the last few months of his life. The poet was publicly celebrated both by President Jimmy Carter, at "A White House Salute to American Poetry," and by his peers at the University of Michigan with "A Tribute to Robert Hayden," the latter occurring the day before Hayden died of a respiratory embolism at age sixty-six. Popular appreciation of Hayden's sensitive lyrics, dramatic monologues, and poignant remembrances has grown since his death.

Poetry

PRINCIPAL WORKS: *Heart-Shape in the Dust,* 1940; *The Lion and the Archer,* 1948; *Figure of Time,* 1955; *A Ballad of Remembrance,* 1962; *Selected Poems,* 1966; *Words in the Mourning Time,* 1970; *The Night-Blooming Cereus,* 1972; *Angle of Ascent: New and Selected Poems,* 1975; *American Journal,* 1978, 1982; *Collected Poems,* 1985

Much of Robert Hayden's poetry reflects one man's wrestling with the sway of poetic influence. His early verse echoes the themes and styles of many of his immediate forebears: Harlem Renaissance poets such as Langston Hughes and Countée Cullen, and American modernists such as Edna St. Vincent Millay and Hart Crane. The subjects of Hayden's later poetry reflect his belief that African American poets need not focus exclusively on sociological study or on protest. Early mentors such as Hughes and Cullen guided Hayden through his years of apprenticeship and obscurity, and defended Hayden during his later successful years, when he was often upbraided by some black poets for being insufficiently political. Hayden's persevering confidence in his poetic voice and learning inured him against such criticism.

Throughout most of his career as a poet, from the publication of *Heart-Shape in the Dust* to that of his breakthrough book, *Angle of Ascent,* Hayden was sustained by academic work—heavy teaching loads and an occasional funded research project—more than he was by popular acclaim. Working in the 1930's and 1940's as a researcher for the Federal Writers' Project, and in various university libraries, Hayden found the historical material for some of his most celebrated poems. Interested especially in the motivations of rebellious slaves, Hayden in "The Ballad of Nat Turner" imagines Turner's almost sympathetic understanding of his captors as the educated slave "Beheld the conqueror faces and, lo,/ they were like mine." In "Runagate Runagate" Hayden celebrates Harriet Tubman as "woman of earth, whipscarred," who has "a shining/ Mean to be free." The culmination of Hayden's study of his political heroes can be found in the perfectly crafted sonnet titled "Frederick Douglass," a poignant paean to "this man, this Douglass, this former slave, this Negro/ beaten to his knees, exiled, visioning a world/ where none is lonely, none hunted, alien."

Throughout his middle years Hayden himself might have felt like an alien, teaching at Fisk University in segregated Nashville. He was composing often formal, often disinterested poetry in a time when confessional poetry was fashionable. As was the case with Frederick Douglass a century earlier, Robert Hayden did not let his dissimilarity from those around him keep him from speaking his mind. An inherently peaceful person, Hayden was most upset by the violence of the 1960's; the title poem of his 1970 book *Words in the Mourning Time* mourns "for King for Kennedy . . . / And for America, self-destructive, self-betrayed." Himself feeling betrayed by America's policies in Vietnam, Hayden asks: "Killing people to save, to free them?/ With napalm lighting routes to the future?" Despite this expressed skepticism toward American nationalism, in the 1960's and 1970's Hayden was welcomed by the poetic and political establishment. Named poetry consultant at the Library of Congress and invited to read at the Carter White House, Hayden felt particularly gratified regarding his late ascendancy. His successes corroborated Hayden's belief that literature composed by African Americans should be judged objectively and should meet the same high standards as the best literature written in English.

SUGGESTED READINGS

Conniff, Brian. "Answering 'The Waste Land': Robert Hayden and the Rise of the African American Poetic Sequence." *African American Review* 33 (Fall, 1999): 487.

Fetrow, Fred M. *Robert Hayden*. Boston: Twayne, 1984.

Hatcher, John. *From the Auroral Darkness: The Life and Poetry of Robert Hayden*. Oxford, England: G. Ronald, 1984.

Nicholas, Xavier. "Robert Hayden and Michael S. Harper." *Callaloo* 17, no. 4 (Fall, 1994): 976-1016.

_____. "Robert Hayden: Some Introductory Notes." *Michigan Quarterly Review* 31, no. 3 (Summer, 1992): 8.

Williams, Pontheolla. *Robert Hayden: A Critical Analysis of His Poetry*. Champaign: University of Illinois Press, 1987.

—Andrew O. Jones

Le Ly Hayslip
(Phung Thi Le Ly)

BORN: Ly La, Vietnam; December 19, 1949

Hayslip's memoirs chronicle a largely successful merger of her Vietnamese ancestry with her acquired American identity.

TRADITIONS: Vietnamese American

PRINCIPAL WORKS: *When Heaven and Earth Changed Places: A Vietnamese Woman's Journey from War to Peace*, 1989 (with Jay Wurts); *Child of War, Woman of Peace*, 1993 (with James Hayslip)

Born Phung Thi Le Ly in 1949 to Buddhist peasants living under Vietnam's French colonial rule, Le Ly Hayslip ardently supported her nation's struggle for independence. Years later, when Viet Cong soldiers of the North wrongly accused her of treason, she fled her village in central Vietnam to live in Danang and, later, Saigon. After giving birth to her wealthy employer's son and witnessing the cruelty of Communist rebels against the peasants they purported to defend, she shifted her allegiance to the republican-backed American forces. She supported herself and her child through black market-eering and other illegal activity and entered into a series of unhappy love affairs with United States servicemen before marrying Ed Munro, an American contractor more than forty years her senior. In 1970, without notifying her family, she left Vietnam for the United States as Munro's bride and the mother of his infant son.

The pattern of being caught in the middle—between the North and the South or between allies and enemies—continued in her new home in suburban San Diego, where Hayslip experienced culture shock, homesickness, and racial antagonism. Soon after Munro's death in 1973, she married Dennis Hayslip, a mentally unstable man by whom she had her third son before he committed suicide. The resilient Hayslip supported herself in the United States as a maid, nurse's aide, and factory worker; with money from her late husband's insurance settlement and trust fund, she purchased stock options, real estate, and a share in a successful restaurant. Combining investment revenues with the proceeds from her memoir about her life in Vietnam (*When Heaven and Earth Changed Places*), Hayslip founded the nonprofit East Meets West Foundation, a humanitarian relief organization that delivers medical and relief supplies to the Vietnamese.

Child of War, Woman of Peace, the sequel to her first memoir and the account of her American acculturation and subsequent return trips to Vietnam, attests Hayslip's ability to endure and heal, which she attributes to her potential to forgive. That second memoir, cowritten with her eldest son, James Hayslip, reveals her ability to embrace America while reconnecting to her Vietnamese past. She explains that her philanthropy, financing her mission in Vietnam through resources acquired in the United States, is the means to bind her old country to her new one, "to sponsor a healing handshake across time and space." The two autobiographies form the basis for Oliver Stone's 1993 film, *Heaven and Earth*, about Hayslip's life in Vietnam and America.

When Heaven and Earth Changed Places
TYPE OF WORK: Memoir
FIRST PUBLISHED: 1989

When Heaven and Earth Changed Places: A Vietnamese Woman's Journey from War to Peace, cowritten with Jay Wurts, recounts Hayslip's life in war-ravaged Vietnam, her emigration to the United States in 1970, and her dangerous return visit to her homeland in 1986. As a young girl, Phung Thi Le Ly (her name before marriage) promises her father, a devote Buddhist farmer, that she will become a woman warrior. She interprets that charge to mean that she must stay alive in order to nurture other life and preserve her ancestral heritage. The memoir is her means of fulfilling that responsibility. She nevertheless offends her family by her presumed betrayal by marriage to an American civilian contractor and flight from Vietnam to join him in California. The autobiography is her tribute to her ancestral traditions and her testimony that she has not forsaken them.

Le Ly's loyalties shift throughout her autobiography. Like most peasants in her village on the border between North and South Vietnam, she supports the Viet Cong against the republican government and its American backers. She performs many daring acts to advance the Communist cause, but the Viet Cong wrongly suspect her of collaborating with the South. She evades their deadly reprisals by fleeing to Danang and, later, Saigon. There she pins her hope for a better life onto the American servicemen she comes to know as she struggles to support her illegitimate son and other family members by working as a nurse's assistant, black marketeer, and, briefly, a prostitute.

Although Le Ly leaves Vietnam during the war and enters the United States as the wife of one American and marries another when she is widowed, her expatriate status distresses her. She proudly regards her three sons—two born in Vietnam and one in the United States—as Americans but regrets that she is "something else: not quite Vietnamese anymore, but not so American as they." By returning to Vietnam with a fresh perspective to write the account of her family's suffering, she aids in their survival and recovery, thus reconciling with them and healing her divided sense of self. The memoir's dual time frames, which alternate chapters of Le Ly moving toward emigration with ones of her preparing to return, converge near the end of the book when her departure and homecoming are complete. The narrative strategy suggests that the difference between leaving home and remaining there is not significant. Rather than forsaking her homeland by emigrating, Le Ly has protected and prepared herself for the mission of telling its story and preserving its culture.

SUGGESTED READINGS

Hayslip, Le Ly, and James Hayslip. *Child of War, Woman of Peace.* New York: Doubleday, 1993.

Hoang, Trang. "*When Heaven and Earth Changed Places.*" *Amerasia Journal* 20, no. 2 (Spring, 1994): 119-121.

Rose, Phyllis, ed. *The Norton Book of Women's Lives.* New York: W. W. Norton, 1993.

Shipler, David. Review of *When Heaven and Earth Changed Places,* by Le Ly Hayslip. *The New York Times Book Review,* June 25, 1989, 1.

—Theresa M. Kanoza

Oscar Hijuelos

BORN: New York, New York; August 24, 1951

Hijuelos, a Latino writer, was awarded the 1990 Pulitzer Prize in fiction for The Mambo Kings Play Songs of Love.

TRADITIONS: Cuban American

PRINCIPAL WORKS: *Our House in the Last World*, 1983; *The Mambo Kings Play Songs of Love*, 1989; *The Fourteen Sisters of Emilio Montez O'Brien*, 1993; *Mr. Ives' Christmas*, 1995; *Empress of the Splendid Season*, 1999

Oscar Hijuelos's family came from Oriente province in Cuba. Hijuelos was reared amid two divergent worlds: that of Columbia University, teeming with scholars, and that of Morningside Park, overflowing with drug addicts and muggers. At age four, Hijuelos and his mother visited Cuba, and upon his return, he succumbed to nephritis. Bedridden, Hijuelos lingered in a hospital for two years. The theme of separation and isolation, especially from family, saturates Hijuelos's novels. After receiving his master's degree in 1976 from the City University of New York, Hijuelos moved to within a few blocks of his childhood home to begin his author's life, supported by a menial job in an advertising agency.

Oscar Hijuelos (Roberto Koch)

Our House in the Last World is a portrait of his family's exodus from Cuba. The work recalls Hijuelos's family relationships; he hated and loved his alcoholic father, and he misunderstood and miscommunicated with his mother. *The Mambo Kings Play Songs of Love* also recalls Hijuelos's family life. One of Hijuelos's uncles had been a musician with Xavier Cugat. The elevator operator in Hijuelos's building played music. Hijuelos jumbled these two characters into Cesar Castillo. Cesar and his brother Nestor reach the highest point in their lives when the Mambo Kings appear on the *I Love Lucy* television show. Later, the brothers are separated.

In *The Fourteen Sisters of Emilio Montez O'Brien*, Hijuelos addresses issues of cross-cultural identity with the connection of Cuban and Irish families in a marriage. In *Mr. Ives' Christmas*, Hijuelos examines father-son relationships from the father's perspective. Mr. Ives seeks penance and peace after the disaster of his son's murder.

The Mambo Kings Play Songs of Love
TYPE OF WORK: Novel
FIRST PUBLISHED: 1989

Hijuelos's life in an advertising agency had little to do with his passion for writing. When he first began thinking of the story that would become *The Mambo Kings Play Songs of Love*, he knew that an uncle and an elevator operator would be his models. The uncle, a musician with Xavier Cugat in the 1930's, and a building superintendent patterned after an elevator-operator-musician merged to become Cesar Castillo, the Mambo King. Cesar's brother, Nestor, laconic, retrospective, lamenting the loss of a lover he left behind in Cuba, writes the song in her memory that draws the attention of Ricky Ricardo. He hears "Beautiful María of My Soul" as he catches the Mambo Kings in a seedy nightclub where gigs are cheap but long. Ricky's interest changes their lives. The book altered Hijuelos's literary career by winning for him the Pulitzer Prize in fiction in 1990.

As the book opens, Cesar rots with his half-empty whiskey glass tipped at the television beaming reruns. He seeks the *I Love Lucy* spot featuring Nestor and him as the Mambo Kings. Nestor has died. Cesar pathetically broods on the aging process, cirrhosis, and the loss of flamboyant times. Cesar's old, scratchy records—brittle and warped—resurrect his music stardom. He laments his brother's death by leafing through fading pictures.

In *The Mambo Kings Play Songs of Love*, Hijuelos presents pre-Castro Cubans, who, after World War II, streamed to New York. All communities may strive for the American Dream, but in Latino quarters, music, the mainstream of a culture, sought to free the oppressed. Hijuelos pursues thematic progression: The Castillo brothers become, for a moment, cultural icons by their appearance on *I Love Lucy*. Their fame does not last, however; Cesar comforts his ego with debauchery, and Nestor dies suddenly. The ironically named Hotel Splendour is where Cesar commits suicide.

Mr. Ives' Christmas
TYPE OF WORK: Novel
FIRST PUBLISHED: 1995

Hijuelos, who was awarded the Pulitzer Prize in fiction in 1990 for his splendid rendition of a life going sour, *The Mambo Kings Play Songs of Love* (1989), presents, in *Mr. Ives' Christmas*, the somber Mr. Ives. Mr. Ives sanely goes through his life with no malice toward fellow man or woman. He seeks the rewards of work and patience that he has become accustomed to earning, but one date, Christmas Eve, consistently seems to interfere with his life.

Hijuelos, born in New York City, grew up in a humble, immigrant Cuban family. At age four, he was exiled from the family by nephritis, a kidney inflammation that crippled his youth with a two-year quarantine from home and loved ones. Perhaps that near-orphan status inspired Hijuelos to develop the Edward Ives of this novel. A widowed printmaker visits the orphan Edward Ives on Christmas Eve, and, a few Christmases later, adopts him. His adoptive father idyllically rears the dark-skinned child, inspires him to pursue his love for drawing, and eventually guides him to the Art Students League where he meets, on Christmas Eve, his future wife.

The picture postcard family image is shattered when, on Christmas Eve, the Ives's seventeen-year-old son is gunned down as he leaves church choir practice. A fourteen-year-old Puerto Rican kills the boy for ten dollars. Mr. Ives devotes his life to obsessive, unerring attempts to rehabilitate the murderer. Symbolically, Mr. Ives's favorite book is a signed copy of British novelist Charles Dickens's *A Christmas Carol* (1843). Hijuelos strongly relies on this book to link the two tales. The author emulates Dickens's populous canvases and uses his love of coincidence and contrivance as a metaphor for God's mysterious workings. The temperance of Mr. Ives allows him a longing for grace, a gift for contemplation, and a steady curiosity.

Hijuelos draws heavily on images from his New York neighborhood, his coterie of friends, and the milieu of gangs, muggers, and dope addicts at the end of his street. Differing from his other novels, *Mr. Ives' Christmas* leaves no doubt that Hijuelos speaks of faith; a faith that mysteriously probes emotions, tested by death and the opportunity of forgiveness.

SUGGESTED READINGS

Barbato, Joseph. "Latino Writers in the American Market." *Publishers Weekly* 238, no. 6 (February 1, 1991): 17-21.

Chávez, Lydia. "Cuban Riffs: Songs of Love." *Los Angeles Times Magazine*, April 18, 1993, 22-28.

Coffey, Michael. "Oscar Hijuelos." *Publishers Weekly* 236, no. 3 (July 21, 1989): 42-44.

Elias, Amy. "Oscar Hijuelos's *The Mambo Kings Play Songs of Love*, Ishmael Reed's *Mumbo Jumbo*, and Robert Coover's *The Public Burning.*" *Critique: Studies in Contemporary Fiction* 41, no. 2 (Winter, 2000).

Kamp, James, ed. *Reference Guide to American Literature*. 3d ed. Detroit: St. James Press, 1994.

—*Craig Gilbert*

Chester Himes

BORN: Jefferson City, Missouri; July 29, 1909
DIED: Moraira, Spain; November 12, 1984

Himes's work evokes the social and psychological burden of being a
black man in a white society.

TRADITIONS: African American
PRINCIPAL WORKS: *If He Hollers, Let Him Go,* 1945; *Lonely Crusade,* 1947; *The Third Generation,* 1954; *The Quality of Hurt,* 1972; *My Life of Absurdity,* 1976

Chester Himes wrote nearly twenty novels, two volumes of autobiography, and a series of popular crime thrillers. Whatever form his writing took, the dominant theme was usually racism: the pain it causes and the hateful legacy it creates. In *If He Hollers, Let Him Go,* Himes uses a wartime West Coast shipyard to set the central confrontation between an educated Northern black man and his poor Southern white coworkers. The results are violent. In spare, functional prose that highlights the psychological paths the novel charts, Himes describes what has been called the American dilemma, or the contrast

between a black man believing in democracy and the realities that bruise his dreams. Critics, while not always enamored with the novel, praised Himes for his relentless honesty.

Lonely Crusade, Himes's second novel, treats the betrayal, dislocation, and terror at the nexus of race and sex in United States society. The book makes a laudable effort to understand the relationship between the oppressed and the oppressor.

Third Generation, thought by many critics to be thinly veiled autobiography, dramatizes three generations in a family, from slavery to the middle of the twentieth

Chester Himes (Library of Congress)

century. It tellingly captures the fear and hatred that can fester in a troubled family, making it perhaps Himes's most ambitious and moving novel.

Himes left the United States in 1954 for Europe, where he received greater literary recognition than he had ever achieved at home. In France, Himes published ten sophisticated, fast-paced crime novels. The protagonists, a pair of cynical street-smart black detectives, were hailed by French critics. When, years later, the novels were finally printed in the United States, the series achieved wide success. Himes's two-volume autobiography, *The Quality of Hurt* and *My Life of Absurdity*, was written in Spain.

Autobiographies

FIRST PUBLISHED: *The Quality of Hurt*, 1972; *My Life of Absurdity*, 1976

"I grew to manhood in the Ohio State Penitentiary," writes Chester Himes in *The Quality of Hurt*, a book that is less an organized autobiography than a series of poignant sketches, in which he writes about the many hurts that poisoned his life in the United States. Himes is one of the least known, most prolific African American writers of the twentieth century. Over a fifty-year career, Himes wrote scores of novels, short stories, articles, and poems, all marked by a naked sincerity and raging anger at racism.

Himes began writing, drawing on his experiences as a young man in prison. He gained critical attention first with a short story, "To What Red Hell," a fictionalized account of the 1930 fire that killed more than three hundred inmates at the Ohio State Penitentiary.

Released during the Depression, Himes became involved with the Federal Writers' Project, the labor movement, and the Communist Party. He also worked as a journalist in Cleveland. In 1941, Himes moved to California, where he began writing novels of rage and frustration, including *If He Hollers, Let Him Go* (1945), *Lonely Crusade* (1947), and *Cast the First Stone* (1952). By 1953, disgusted with the racism he encountered and the lukewarm, when not hostile, reception his work received, Himes left for Europe.

My Life of Absurdity is not a deep examination of his life so much as a commentary on the meaning of being a black expatriate writer. "No American," he writes, "has lived a life more absurd than mine." In Europe, Himes published the series of detective stories that brought him fame in later years. Among them are *The Crazy Kill* (1959), *The Heat's On* (1966), and *Cotton Comes to Harlem* (1965). Himes also wrote stories that are sometimes painfully funny and often bitterly desolate. In them, cops, robbers, and all-around losers—the people Himes knew well in his youth—trade in the debased currency of lies and secrets.

Himes's work resounds with wit and indignation but is too often incorrectly identified simply as social protest. His novels made the best-seller lists in foreign countries as well as in the United States.

SUGGESTED READINGS

Fabre, Michel, Robert E. Skinner, and Lester Sullivan, comps. *Chester Himes: An Annotated Primary and Secondary Bibliography.* Westport, Conn.: Greenwood Press, 1992.

Margolies, Edward, and Michel Fabre. *The Several Lives of Chester Himes.* Jackson: University Press of Mississippi, 1997.

Milliken, Stephen. *Chester Himes: A Critical Appraisal.* Columbia: University of Missouri Press, 1976.

Skinner, Robert. *Two Guns from Harlem: The Detective Fiction of Chester Himes.* Bowling Green, Ohio: Bowling Green State University Popular Press, 1989.

—Barbara Day

Rolando Hinojosa

BORN: Mercedes, Texas; January 21, 1929

Hinojosa's fiction gives a view of Mexican American life in the Rio Grande Valley of Texas in the twentieth century.

TRADITIONS: Mexican American

PRINCIPAL WORKS: *Estampas del valle y otras obras/Sketches of the Valley and Other Works*, 1973 (English revision, *The Valley*, 1983); *Korean Love Songs from Klail City Death Trip*, 1978 (printed 1980); *Mi querido Rafa*, 1981 (*Dear Rafe*, 1985); *Rites and Witnesses: A Comedy*, 1982; *Partners in Crime*, 1985; *Klail City y sus alrededores*, 1976 (*Klail City: A Novel*, 1987); *Becky and Her Friends*, 1990; *The Useless Servants*, 1993; *Ask a Policeman*, 1998

Rolando Hinojosa began writing book-length works of fiction in the 1970's when he was in his forties and after he had established a successful academic career. He attended the University of Texas at Austin, but he left to serve in Korea before returning to complete his degree in Spanish in 1953.

In the 1950's, he taught at Brownsville High School. He next took a master's degree in Spanish from New Mexico Highlands University (1962) and a Ph.D. in Spanish from the University of Illinois (1969). From 1968 to the present, he has taught and held administrative posts at various universities in Texas.

Korean Love Songs from Klail City Death Trip, which is poetry, and his novels form the Klail City Death Trip series, which deals with ethnic identity, the perils and rewards of cultural assimilation, and the importance of education. Hinojosa's major characters undergo epic struggles with the issues of identity, moving from a discrete, self-contained Mexican American community of the 1930's into a world in which young Mexican American men fight and die for the institutions that have relegated them to second-class citizenry.

Hinojosa shows that life in the Rio Grande Valley must change. The Klail City Death Trip series in particular shows the subtle mid-century changes in the social and economic landscape of the small towns of the valley and the ways in which Mexican Americans began to demand equality.

Because many of Hinojosa's characters believe in the American Dream, they become more Americanized and less Chicano as the twentieth century moves forward. By the time of *Partners in Crime* and *Becky and Her Friends*, the main characters have achieved status within the Anglo community and appear to thrive within it.

Klail City

TYPE OF WORK: Novel
FIRST PUBLISHED: *Klail City y sus alrededores*, 1976 (English translation, 1987)

Klail City is part of the Klail City Death Trip, a chronicle of the Texas Rio Grande Valley. This novel moves between past and present so that the past and the present often appear to be the same. Like most of Hinojosa's novels, *Klail City* lacks linear plot development. A series of vignettes create a sense of place and ultimately present a picture of a changing world. Several narrators, including the main characters of the series, Rafe Buenrostro ("Buenostro" means "good face") and Jehú Malacara ("Malacara" means "bad face") tell the stories.

P. Galindo, Esteban Echevarría (a kind of wise man throughout the series), Rafe, and Jehú recount a variety of tales ranging from the story of a hastily arranged marriage between the pregnant Jovita de Anda and Joaquín Tamez to tales of the Texas Rangers' abuse of Mexican Americans to the story of how Alejandro Leguizamón planned the murder of Rafe's father, Jesús, and the revenge exacted by Jesús's brother, don Julián. There is also a kind of interior monologue by Jehú as he and Rafe attend their twenty-second high school class reunion.

The past is interwoven with the present, particularly in the scenes that occur in the bars, where the old men, the *viejitos*, sit drinking and talking until don Manuel Guzmán, Klail City's only Mexican American police officer, comes to take them home.

The section entitled "The Searchers" tells the stories of migrant workers as they leave their homes in the valley to travel north to pick produce. The narrator P. Galindo is introduced, and he reveals himself to be a kind of surrogate author for Hinojosa as he explains his interest in preserving a history of these people.

In addition, Rafe gives a personal account of what it was like in the 1940's for Mexican American students in the American high school, and Jehú recounts some of his experiences as an orphan, an acolyte, and a traveling evangelist with Brother Imás. Brother Imás's life story is told, as is Viola Barragán's (Hinojosa's prototype of the liberated woman), along with an account of how the whites used "bought" Mexicans to get their hand-picked candidates elected. This eclectic collection of vignettes makes up a book that, in 1976, won Latin America's most prestigious literary award, the Casa de las Américas prize.

SUGGESTED READINGS

Broyles, Yolanda Julia. "*Klail City y sus alrededores:* Oral Culture and Print Culture." In *The Rolando Hinojosa Reader*, edited by José David Saldívar. Houston, Tex.: Arte Público Press, 1985.

_____. "Texas Border Literature: Cultural Transformation and Historical Reflection in the Works of Américo Paredes, Rolando Hinojosa, and Gloria Anzaldúa." *Disposito* 16, no. 41 (1991): 13-27.

Hinojosa, Rolando. "The Texas-Mexico Border: This Writer's Sense of Place." In *Open Spaces, City Places: Contemporary American Writers on the Changing Southwest,* edited by Judy Nolte Temple. Tucson: University of Arizona Press, 1994.

Lee, Joyce Glover. *Rolando Hinojosa and the American Dream.* Denton: University of North Texas Press, 1997.

Penzenstadler, Joan. "La frontera, Aztlán, el barrio: Frontiers in Chicano Literature." In *The Frontier Experience and the American Dream,* edited by David Mogen, Mark Busby, and Paul Bryant. College Station: Texas A&M Press, 1989.

Saldívar, José David. "Chicano Border Narratives as Cultural Critique." In *Criticism in the Borderlands: Studies in Chicano Literature, Culture, and Ideology,* edited by Héctor Calderón and José David Saldívar. Durham, N.C.: Duke University Press, 1991.

–Joyce J. Glover

Garrett Kaoru Hongo

BORN: Volcano, Hawaii; May 30, 1951

Hongo writes lyrically and evocatively about personal history, place of origin, and ethnicity.

TRADITIONS: Japanese American
PRINCIPAL WORKS: *Yellow Light,* 1982; *The River of Heaven,* 1988; *Volcano: A Memoir of Hawai'i,* 1995

Garrett Hongo was born in the shadow of the Kilauea volcano but reared near Los Angeles. When he comes to terms with his origins during his first sojourn to Hawaii at middle age, he liberates his spirit with a moving insight that solidifies his sense of self. His poetry and prose are reverent, precise, and evocative, celebrating male ancestors, early Japanese poets, family, birthplace, and home.

Estranged from his past, Hongo was sheltered from the bitter truths of the World War II internment by his family. Gardena, California, the town where he grew up, boasted the largest community of Japanese Americans on the mainland United States at the time and was bordered on the north by the predominantly black towns of Watts and Compton and on the southwest by Torrance and Redondo Beach, white towns. Thus, Hongo was sensitized to issues of uneasy race relations and urban street life early in life.

Hongo studied in Japan for a year following graduation from Pomona College, then earned a master's degree in fine arts from the University of California at Irvine. As a poet in residence in Seattle, he founded and directed a local theater group called The Asian Exclusion Act. Hongo identifies largely with the West Coast, a mecca for many Asian American writers, and early became a friend and collaborator with Lawson Fusao Inada, a pioneer Japanese American poet. His marriage to white violinist Cynthia Thiessen and their rearing of two sons, Alexander and Hudson, have given Hongo particular sensitivity to the cultural terrain he calls "the borderlands."

The only Asian member of the faculty at the University of Oregon, Eugene, Hongo has directed the creative writing program there since 1989 and has received several extended leaves that allowed time in Hawaii to work on his prose memoirs, published in 1995 as *Volcano.* Among the most important influences he identifies is Wakako Yamauchi, a widely anthologized Japanese American short-story writer and playwrite, whose works Hongo collected and edited under the title *Songs My Mother Taught Me,* which was published in 1994.

Volcano

TYPE OF WORK: Memoir
FIRST PUBLISHED: 1995

Volcano: A Memoir of Hawai'i evocatively describes flora, fauna, and geographical features of an exuberantly lush and exotic landscape. The book contains biographical portraits of a handful of Hongo's flamboyant, melancholy, or mercenary ancestors, intriguing in themselves. In the artful way in which it combines place with personal history, and in which it seeks to reconcile Hongo's Japanese heritage with his American circumstances, the book explores a larger truth: To achieve true peace of mind, it is necessary to seek, acknowledge, and celebrate one's own ethnic, geographical, and biological origins.

Hongo's last name means "homeland," and he conducts a pilgrimage, crossing the Pacific Ocean to immerse himself in the birthplace he left when he was only a few weeks old, Volcano. Growing up near Los Angeles and living as an adult in Missouri and Oregon, Hongo first returns to Volcano when he is thirty years old, his Caucasian violinist wife and their infant son, Alexander, in tow. Having felt a profound sense of estrangement from his past, knowing little about his father or grandfather, Hongo soon makes acquaintances in Volcano with locals and distant relatives, who reveal painful truths about the ravages of the Japanese American internment on his family.

His cabin in the rainforest is in the shadow of the Kilauea volcano, which takes on symbolism as his narrative continues. He shops in the general store that his grandfather once owned. He witnesses a volcano erupting in the early morning and hikes around lava flows. He eats food such as poi and miso soup, which for him become a wayside of culture and memory.

The first visit makes Hongo eager to return, having given him particulars of ancestral memory and having shown him a way to belong in and to make sense of his world. In the poignancy and drama of coming face-to-face with ugly racial and personal secrets and also with the beauties of place that lift him above the pain, Hongo becomes inspired to compose the poetry that had been locked deep in-

Garrett Kaoru Hongo (Ellen Foscue Johnson)

side. The book ends with the wish that the reader achieve similar healing self-knowledge.

SUGGESTED READINGS

Chock, Eric, and Darrell H. Y. Lum, eds. *The Best of Bamboo Ridge: The Hawaii Writer's Quarterly*. Honolulu: Bamboo Ridge Press, 1986.

Filipelli, Laurie. *Garrett Hongo*. Boise, Idaho: Boise State University Press, 1997.

Hongo, Garrett. "A Vicious Kind of Tenderness: An Interview with Garrett Hongo." Interview by Alice Evans. *Poets and Writers* 20, no. 5 (September/October, 1992): 36-46.

Jarman, Mark. "The Volcano Inside." *The Southern Review* 32, no. 2 (Spring, 1996): 337-343.

Schama, Simon. *Landscape and Memory*. New York: Alfred A. Knopf, 1995.

—Jill B. Gidmark

Langston Hughes

BORN: Joplin, Missouri; February 1, 1902
DIED: New York, New York; May 22, 1967

Hughes's writings reflect on the struggles and triumphs of African American people, in the idiom of black America.

TRADITIONS: African American
PRINCIPAL WORKS: *The Ways of White Folks*, 1934; *The Big Sea*, 1940; *I Wonder as I Wander: An Autobiographical Journey*, 1956; *Selected Poems of Langston Hughes*, 1959; *The Best of Simple*, 1961; *The Panther and the Lash: Or, Poems of Our Times*, 1967

A prominent African American writer, Langston Hughes led an active literary life. His writings extend from the Harlem Renaissance of the 1920's to the Black Arts movement of the 1960's. Hughes's father abandoned his wife and infant son in 1903 to seek wealth in Mexico. His mother, unable to find even menial labor in Joplin, moved frequently to look for work. In his youth, Hughes lived predominantly with his maternal grandmother in Lawrence, Kansas. Hughes understood poverty, dejection, and loneliness, but from his grandmother he learned the valuable lessons of perseverance and laughter. Her resilience and ingenuity made a lasting impression upon Hughes's imagination, and she seems the prototype of his self-assured female characters.

After his grandmother's death, Hughes reunited with his mother in Lincoln, Illinois, but for a time was placed with his Auntie Reed and her husband, religious people who pressured Hughes into joining their church. Hughes marked this unsuccessful attempt at conversion as the beginning of his religious disbelief, as illustrated in the story "Salvation."

Hughes later moved to Cleveland, where his intellectual growth began in earnest. His earliest poems were influenced by Paul Laurence Dunbar and Carl Sandburg. He read the German philosophers Arthur Schopenhauer and Friedrich Nietzsche and was introduced to socialist ideas. When Hughes's father, having become prosperous, asked Hughes to join him in Mexico in 1920, Hughes rode a train across the Mississippi River at St. Louis and penned the famous "The Negro Speaks of Rivers" on the back of an envelope.

In Mexico, Hughes became dissatisfied with his father's materialism and his plans to send him to a European university. Hughes escaped and attended bullfights and studied Mexican culture. He wrote little of these experiences, although a few pieces were published in *The Brownies' Book*, founded by

225

W. E. B. Du Bois's staff at *Crisis*, the official journal of the National Association for the Advancement of Colored People (NAACP).

In 1921, Hughes enrolled at Columbia University. He was quickly disillusioned with Columbia's coldness and spent more time in Harlem and at Broadway productions. Consequently, Hughes failed most of his classes and dropped out. He worked odd jobs while devoting his free time to the shaping forces of the Harlem Renaissance. Hughes led a nomadic life for two years as a cabin boy on freighters that took him to Europe and Africa. On his initial voyage, he threw away his books because they reminded him of past hardships. He discovered how cities such as Venice had poor people too. These voyages and observations became the genesis of his first autobiography, *The*

Langston Hughes (Library of Congress)

Big Sea. Hughes made many influential friends, among them Countée Cullen, James Weldon Johnson, Carl Van Vechten, and Arna Bontemps. Van Vechten helped Hughes find a publisher for his work. Bontemps and Hughes later collaborated on numerous children's books and anthologies.

Hughes matriculated at Lincoln University in Pennsylvania in 1926, the year that his first book, *The Weary Blues*, was published. This book was soon followed by many others. During the 1930's, Hughes made trips to Haiti and to the Soviet Union. In 1937, he was a correspondent in Spain during that country's civil war. He wrote about these excursions in his second autobiography, *I Wonder as I Wander*. During the 1940's, he wrote columns for the *Chicago Defender*, formulating the humorous persona Jesse B. Semple, or "Simple," who would later become the basis of the "Simple" stories. In the 1950's, his politically edged writings made Hughes a brief target of Senator Joseph McCarthy's hunt for communists. In the last years of his life, Hughes continued to produce volumes of edited and creative work. Hughes died following prostate surgery at Polyclinic Hospital in New York City.

Autobiographies

FIRST PUBLISHED: *The Big Sea*, 1940; *I Wonder as I Wander*, 1956

In the opening of Hughes's first autobiography, *The Big Sea*, the author recalls how he heaved his books overboard at the start of his first journey to Africa in 1923. The gesture may be seen as adolescent and anti-intellectual, but it suggests the commencement of Hughes's role as a Renaissance man in Black American letters. The book chronicles the first twenty-seven years of Hughes's life, from the 1920's, when he explored the idiom and jazz rhythms of African Americans in his poetry, to the shift to his bitter prose of the 1930's.

The autobiography is written typically as a confession, but it remains comparatively impersonal. Only three guarded personal accounts appear in the text of *The Big Sea*. The first concerns a religious revival Hughes attended at age thirteen at which he waited in vain for Jesus. The second describes the morning in Mexico when he realized that he hated his father. The third, at the book's end, details the break with his patron and mentor, Charlotte Mason. He ties the latter experience to the other two: "The light went out with a sudden crash in the dark, and everything became like that night in Kansas when I had failed to see Jesus and had lied about it afterwards. Or that morning in Mexico when I suddenly hated my father."

Other than these specific episodes, controversy rarely enters the book. Instead, Hughes presents himself as a man who loves his race and is optimistic about his people. He nevertheless carries doubts and fears within himself. The book, furthermore, is peopled by Hughes's many friends, including Jean Toomer, Zora Neale Hurston, and others involved with the Harlem Renaissance. Hughes's publisher, Blanche Knopf, thought that the references were excessive, but Hughes convinced her to retain them. Consequently, *The Big Sea* is perhaps the best chronicle of the Harlem Renaissance.

The second autobiography, *I Wonder as I Wander*, received less favor than its predecessor, although Hughes thought that his second autobiography was more important to his future as a writer. Knopf rejected the book, claiming it was "pretty weighted . . . and not a book." Covering his life from 1929 to 1950, it includes his travels to Haiti, Spain, and Russia. More than half of the collection explores his 1932 trip to the Soviet Union, and a second long section covers his excursion to Spain during its civil war. The book seems less a literary life than a political commentary on his travels.

One of the criticisms directed at *I Wonder as I Wander* was its detachment from the personal and reflective. *The Big Sea* contains few enough personal reflections, but those that it contains are balanced between pain and joy. *I Wonder as I Wander* shows a Hughes who is more secure in his world and who is suffering less, despite his poverty (which fame did little to diminish). *I Wonder as I Wander* is a mature recollection, written without radicalism or prejudice.

Selected Poems of Langston Hughes
TYPE OF WORK: Poetry
FIRST PUBLISHED: 1959

The poems of *Selected Poems of Langston Hughes* were gathered by the poet from several of his earlier collections, including *The Weary Blues* (1926), *Fine Clothes to the Jew* (1927), *Dear Lovely Death* (1931), *Shakespeare in Harlem* (1942), *Fields of Wonder* (1947), *One Way Ticket* (1949), and *Montage of a Dream Deferred* (1951). Representative of the body of Hughes's poetry, the collection includes his best poems: "The Negro Speaks of Rivers," "The Weary Blues," "Song for a Dark Girl," "Sylvester's Dying Bed," "I, Too," "Montage of a Dream Deferred," and "Refugee in America."

Hughes's poetry is an exploration of black identity, not only the sorrows and tribulations faced by black Americans but also the warm joy and humor of Hughes's people. He writes in "Negro": "I am a Negro:/ Black as the night is black,/ Black like the depths of my Africa." This is a resolute proclamation confronting racial adversity: "The Belgians cut off my hands in the Congo./ They lynch me still in Mississippi." Hughes refuses, however, to allow his poetry to become a podium for anger; rather, he offers readers portraits of the black experience and, consequently, draws his readers into a nearer understanding of black identity.

One of the strongest of Hughes's poems is "The Negro Speaks of Rivers." The poem muses upon what rivers mean to black culture and how the rivers symbolize the strength and longevity of a proud race:

> I bathed in the Euphrates when dawns were young.
> I built my hut near the Congo and it lulled me to sleep.
> I looked upon the Nile and raised the pyramids above it.
> I heard the singing of the Mississippi when Abe Lincoln
>   went down to New Orleans, and I've seen its muddy
>   bosom turn all golden in the sunset.

The beauty of the poem, which reads like a hymn or spiritual, is unmistakable and permanent.

Elsewhere, Hughes experiments with blues rhythms and jazz improvisations, as in "The Weary Blues":

> In a deep song voice with a melancholy tone
> I heard that Negro sing, that old piano moan—
>   "Ain't got nobody in all this world,
>   Ain't got nobody but ma self.
>   I's gwine to quit ma frownin'
>   And put ma troubles on the shelf."
> Thump, thump, thump, went his foot on the floor.
> He played a few chords then he sang some more—
>   "I got the Weary Blues
>   And I can't be satisfied."

The blues touch upon black sorrow, but the music of the blues makes its listeners feel better. Some of Hughes's characters, as found in the "Madam to You" sequence, are not blue, or troubled, or even angry. Rather, they are secure and pleased with themselves. In "Madam's Calling Cards," Alberta K. Johnson tells the printer: "There's nothing foreign/ To my pedigree:/ Alberta K. Johnson—/ *American* that's me."

Ultimately, Hughes's objective seems to be to provide blacks with identities as Americans, living in a democracy that ensures life without prejudice. Thus, in "I, Too," a poem echoing Walt Whitman's *Leaves of Grass*, the poet looks to a future when a black man can "be at the table/ When company comes" and that "they'll see/ How beautiful I am/ And be ashamed."

The Ways of White Folks
Type of work: Short fiction
First published: 1934

During Hughes's travels to Russia in 1931, he became intensely interested in D. H. Lawrence's short fiction. As he later described in *I Wonder as I Wander*, he had never read Lawrence before and remarked that both "The Rocking Horse Winner" and "The Lovely Lady" had made his "hair stand on end." "I could not put the book down," he wrote. Furthermore, he wrote: "If D. H. Lawrence can write such psychologically powerful accounts of folks in England . . . maybe I could write stories like his about folks in America."

This fascination led to *The Ways of White Folks*, a collection of fourteen stories. The title is derived from the story "Berry," an account of a young black man who works as a handyman in a home for handicapped children. Berry is exploited and does more than his share of work for a pittance. He cannot understand why this happens and remarks, "The ways of white folks, I mean some white folks, is too much for me. I rekon they must be a few good ones, but most of 'em ain't good–least wise they don't treat me good. And Lawd knows, I ain't never done nothin' to them, nothin' a-tall."

Overall, the stories comment on the suffering the black community endures at the hands of white society. "Slave on the Block," for example, details how a white couple strives to make a young black artist fit into their aesthetic mold. Humorously, the young man, rebelling, runs off with the cook. In "Father and Son," Bert, a college student, returns home to the South but does not relinquish his independence. Despite warnings to respect white society, Bert ignores them and finds himself and his father hunted by a lynch mob. To save themselves from the disgrace of public hanging, Bert kills his father and himself before the mob overtakes them.

In "Home," Hughes writes of an elderly musician who has returned home; while his career had been successful elsewhere, he is murdered by locals offended by his talking to a white woman. "The Blues I'm Playing" describes how a white patron, a spinster who collects artists, tries to mold a talented black woman into a respectable classical pianist. While the young woman plays exceptional music, she often reverts to her first loves: gospel and blues. Oceola tells her patron, "This is mine. . . . Listen! . . . How sad and gay it is. Blue and happy–laughing and crying. . . . How white like you and black like me." Her music is rooted in "bass notes [that] throb like tomtoms deep in the earth." Her patron, who cannot understand this music's value, prefers looking at the stars, which are unattainable, futile, and distant.

Underlying most of this collection is the difficulty of black-white relationships. Hughes illustrates how blacks are never regarded as individuals but rather as members of a group, how they are always treated with mistrust and hate. Hughes makes it clear in *The Ways of White Folks* that white people do not comprehend their own actions.

SUGGESTED READINGS

Bloom, Harold, ed. *Langston Hughes*. New York: Chelsea House, 1989.

Emanuel, James A. *Langston Hughes*. New York: Twayne, 1967.

McLaren, Joseph. *Langston Hughes, Folk Dramatist in the Protest Tradition, 1921-1943*. Westport, Conn.: Greenwood Press, 1997.

Miller, R. Baxter. *The Art of Imagination of Langston Hughes.* Lexington: University of Kentucky Press, 1989.

Rampersad, Arnold. *The Life of Langston Hughes: 1902-1941.* Vol. 1. New York: Oxford University Press, 1986.

——. *The Life of Langston Hughes: 1941-1967.* Vol. 2. New York: Oxford University Press, 1988.

—Mark Sanders

Zora Neale Hurston

BORN: Eatonville, Florida; January 7, 1891
DIED: Fort Pierce, Florida; January 28, 1960

Hurston depicts the plight and records the language of her people.

TRADITIONS: African American
PRINCIPAL WORKS: *Jonah's Gourd Vine*, 1934; *Mules and Men*, 1935; *Their Eyes Were Watching God*, 1937; *Dust Tracks on a Road*, 1942

Zora Neale Hurston was born in the first incorporated all-black town in America; her father was one of its influential citizens. Her identity was formed in Eatonville; her works clearly show her attachments to that community. When Hurston was nine, her mother died. Hurston was moved among relatives, deprived of a stable home.

She worked to support herself from an early age; at only fourteen she worked as a maid with a touring Gilbert and Sullivan troupe. She later went to night school in Baltimore to catch up on her schooling, to Howard University, and to Barnard College as a scholarship student. She loved learning. Settled in New York in the early 1920's, Hurston filled her life with people who encouraged her work and gave her advice. Some of the most important of these were white: novelist Fanny Hurst and anthropologist Franz Boas, for example. Yet her identity comes from her own people: African American folklore was the focus of her research, and black women's experience informs her best work.

Hurston was influenced by the Harlem Renaissance of the 1920's and is considered one of its stars, but she was not readily accepted in the movement at the time. Protest writers such as Richard Wright and Ralph Ellison found her writing "quaint" and "romantic." She speaks in a clear feminine voice that, if not full of protest, affirms the black woman's identity. Hurston was equally at home with upper-class whites and poor blacks, but she never forgot her heritage.

Hurston's most important works were published during the 1930's: her collection of folklore, *Mules and Men*, in 1935; her novels *Jonah's Gourd Vine* and her masterpiece *Their Eyes Were Watching God* in 1934 and 1937, respectively. An autobiography, *Dust Tracks on a Road*, was published in 1942. She was married and divorced twice.

Throughout her life Hurston was compelled to discover and translate the Southern black, often female, existence. In her collections of folklore, her fiction, her articles, and her life, she presented her people honestly and sympathetically, faithfully recording their language and their beliefs. Not until after her death was the significance of her work fully appreciated. She died in a welfare home in 1960 and was buried in an unmarked grave. In 1973, acclaimed black writer Alice Walker found Hurston's grave and led a revival of interest in her work.

Dust Tracks on a Road

TYPE OF WORK: Autobiography
FIRST PUBLISHED: 1942

Dust Tracks on a Road: An Autobiography was written when Hurston was about fifty years old. The book poignantly describes what it was like to grow up poor, black, and female; it shows an energetic woman who overcomes odds to achieve a liberated, rewarding life. Hurston was born in Eatonville, Florida, America's first incorporated black community. Her father was a driving force in the community; her mother died when she was nine. The liberating force for Hurston was her love of knowledge. While at the black grammar school, she won a reading contest, receiving books that ignited her imagination. In turn, she learned about real life at Joe Clarke's store, the meeting place of the men in town.

After her mother's death, she was moved from place to place. It was her own initiative that released her from her circumstances. When she learned that an actress in a traveling Gilbert and Sullivan troupe was looking for a lady's maid, she approached the woman with "I come to work for you." When her service ended—a service that had been a marvelous education in humanity and the arts—she went back to night high school, then to Howard University and Barnard College.

At Barnard, working under anthropologist Franz Boas, she studied the folklore of her people in Polk County, Florida. This began a lifelong interest

Zora Neale Hurston (Library of Congress)

in the roots of her people. Yet some of Hurston's greatest friends and confidants were the upper-class whites she met both in school and after. Author Fannie Hurst, singer Ethel Waters, and critic Carl Van Vechten were among the many who encouraged her and introduced her to other writers of her times. Hurston at times bemoans her own people and their plight. She sees their disillusionment and oftentimes ill-suited efforts to break out of a stereotype. She lovingly describes the black race as not a race chosen by God but "a collection of people who overslept our time and got caught in the draft."

Hurston's descriptions of her own dedication and hard work inspire the reader to see what a poor African American woman could achieve with forwardness and luck. Her sensitive pictures of her race show people who have the power to overcome obstacles and succeed. Her generous view of humanity and lack of prejudice against anyone because of background or color give the reader a hopeful vision for the future in which love, hope, and hard work make the American Dream possible for anyone.

Their Eyes Were Watching God
TYPE OF WORK: Novel
FIRST PUBLISHED: 1937

Their Eyes Were Watching God is Hurston's most lauded work. It is the story of Janie Crawford Killicks Starks Woods, a thrice-married, twice-widowed woman who learns the hard way: through her own experience. Granddaughter of a slave and daughter of a runaway mother, Janie grows up not realizing her color till she sees a picture of herself among white children. Rather than worry about Janie in her adolescence, her grandmother marries her off to Logan Killicks, an old, narrow-minded, and abusive husband. Hoping for more to life than she has, Janie ends that marriage herself by walking off with Joe Starks, a passerby with a dream, who becomes the mayor of Eatonville, Florida, a new all-black town. Janie reigns as queen of the town, yet she is still unhappily under the control of a jealous, controlling husband.

The town is incensed when, after Starks's death, Janie runs off with Teacake Woods, a young, charming ne'er-do-well. Living with Teacake "on the muck"—picking and planting beans in the Everglades—Janie finds happiness. Teacake truly loves her and cherishes her company, and Janie and Teacake's home is the center of a community of lively, happy, hardworking folks. Janie ends up a widow again. In trying to save Janie from a rabid dog during a flood, Teacake is bitten. In his delirium, he threatens Janie's life, and she must shoot him.

Despite the tragedy in her life, Janie comes across as powerful and self-reliant. She moves from being controlled by men to being assertive and independent. She provides a positive image of the black woman who rises above her circumstances and learns to deal with life on her own terms. After Teacake's death and her trial, she returns to Eatonville with her head high. She is saddened but not defeated; she tells her friend Phoeby that she has "been a delegate to de big 'ssociation of life" and that she has learned that everybody "got tuh find out about livin' fuh theyselves."

Although Hurston's novel received some harsh criticism for being quaint and romantic and was out of print for years, it is now considered an important work for its understanding of the African American folkloric tradition, for its language, and for its female hero, a woman who struggles and successfully finds her own identity.

SUGGESTED READINGS

Awkward, Michael, ed. *New Essays on "Their Eyes Were Watching God."* New York: Cambridge University Press, 1990.

Bloom, Harold, ed. *Zora Neale Hurston's "Their Eyes Were Watching God."* New York: Chelsea House, 1987.

Cronin, Gloria L., ed. *Critical Essays on Zora Neale Hurston.* New York: G. K. Hall, 1998.

Gates, Henry Louis, and Anthony Appiah. *Zora Neale Hurston: Cultural Perspectives Past and Present.* New York: Amistad, 1993.

Hemenway, Robert E. *Zora Neale Hurston: A Literary Biography.* Champaign: University of Illinois Press, 1977.

Howard, Lillie. *Zora Neale Hurston.* Boston: Twayne, 1980.

Lyons, Mary E. *Sorrow's Kitchen: The Life and Folklore of Zora Neale Hurston.* New York: Collier Books, 1990.

Peters, Pearlie Mae Fisher. *The Assertive Woman in Zora Neale Hurston's Fiction, Folklore, and Drama.* New York: Garland, 1998.

Witcover, Paul. *Zora Neale Hurston.* New York: Chelsea House, 1991.

Yanuzzi, Della A. *Zora Neale Hurston: Southern Storyteller.* Springfield, N.J.: Enslow, 1996.

—Janine Rider

David Henry Hwang

BORN: Los Angeles, California; August 11, 1957

Hwang is the first playwright to depict the identity, culture, and history of Chinese Americans in mainstream American theater.

TRADITIONS: Chinese American

PRINCIPAL WORKS: *F.O.B.*, pr. 1978, pb. 1983; *The Dance and the Railroad*, pr. 1981, pb. 1983; *Family Devotions*, pr. 1981, pb. 1983; *M. Butterfly*, pr., pb. 1988; *Bondage*, pr. 1992, pb. 1993; *Golden Child*, pr., pb. 1998

David Henry Hwang is a second-generation Chinese American. From his earliest plays, Hwang has been concerned with the Chinese American experience. Hwang has identified three developmental phases in his early work. His "assimilationist" phase was motivated by the overwhelming desire to be accepted by white American culture. Hwang's first play, *F.O.B.*, exemplifies this first period. Dave, a Chinese American, reacts negatively to a "fresh-off-the-boat" Chinese, Steve, because Steve exhibits all the stereotypic mannerisms that Dave has tried to suppress his entire life.

In college, Hwang lived in an all-Asian dormitory and was caught up in an "isolationist-nationalist" phase. During this phase, Hwang was primarily concerned with writing for a Chinese American audience. This resulted in *The Dance and the Railroad*, which recaptures the history of the Chinese American railroad strike of 1867, and *Family Devotions*, which encourages Chinese Americans to reject negative Western perceptions and remember their Chinese heritage.

After the isolationist phase, Hwang next became interested in the love story. He adapted two classic Japanese love stories and wrote a play without identified Asian characters. Although not successful, this last experiment led directly to Hwang's masterpiece, *M. Butterfly*, in which a French diplomat carries on an affair with a Chinese actress for years, only to discover that "she" is really a man. Identity is explored as Hwang shows how the Frenchman Gallimard falls in love with an Asian stereotype. Gallimard commits suicide at the loss of his lover, a role-reversal of Giacomo Puccini's *Madama Butterfly* (1904). Wanting to advocate a broader forum against sexism and racism in literature, Hwang created *Bondage*, an allegory of love that challenges a variety of prejudices. *Bondage* takes place in a fantasy bondage parlor where domination is subverted when stereotypes are rejected by masked participants.

The historical and cultural identity of Chinese Americans is at the heart of

Hwang's plays, which present a significant exploration of the evolving identity of Asians in a pluralistic society.

David Henry Hwang

Bondage

TYPE OF WORK: Drama
FIRST PRODUCED: 1992; first published, 1993

Bondage, a one-act play set in a fantasy bondage parlor, is an exploration of racial, cultural, and sexual stereotypes. It is presented as an allegory depicting their overwhelming influence in society and offering one alternative for society's progressing beyond them. The play demonstrates Chinese American playwright Hwang's development beyond exclusively Asian American themes to encompass the destructiveness of all stereotyping, be it racial, cultural, or sexual.

Mark, identifiable only as a male, is the client of dominatrix Terri, identifiable only as a female, in a fantasy bondage parlor. Both characters' identities are fully disguised. They are merely a man and a woman who assume the characteristics required for whatever fantasy is suggested. During this encounter, however, both Mark and Terri refuse to accept the stereotypes associated with their fantasy roles.

Terri informs Mark that today he will be a Chinese man and she will be a blonde woman. She immediately characterizes Mark as a horn-rimmed-glasses-wearing engineer afraid of her because she is popular with cowboys and jocks. Mark rejects her Asian stereotypes and, in turn, uses blonde stereotypes to describe her. A personal confrontation ensues because Mark will not accept her ridicule.

This leads to male-female stereotyping, and on to progressive levels of racial stereotyping. As they are unable to resolve this confrontation, they move on to become a white man and a black woman, with underlying stereotyped images of the white liberal. Terri charges that he may try to "play" all races, but she has already "become" all races. Next they assume the roles of Chinese American man and an Asian American woman, exploring inter-cultural stereotypes. Finally they explore Mark's need for penitence as a stereotypical businessman, which drives him to the bondage parlor to be dominated and humiliated in a fantasy world as he dominates and humiliates in the real one. The plight of both men and women, and the roles society forces upon them, dominate the final confrontation. Her resistance having been worn down by Mark's arguing, Terri begins to remove her disguise. She offers Mark his moment of victory, but instead he, too, removes his mask. When he confesses his real love for Terri, she reveals herself—they are as the original fantasy, an Asian man and a blonde woman. Their confrontation has put the stereotypes of their disparate groups behind them. They see each other as individuals and are ready to move beyond their fantasies.

Hwang's optimism that society can move beyond oppressing societal stereotypes pervades *Bondage*. He presents a balanced attack on all stereotyping, showing that regardless of cultural, political, or sexual identity, society will only move forward when all stereotypes are destroyed and people are regarded as individuals.

The Dance and the Railroad
TYPE OF WORK: Drama
FIRST PRODUCED: 1981; first published, 1983

The Dance and the Railroad is a history play based on the Chinese railroad workers' strike of 1867. It reveals a significant event in the Chinese American past, rejecting the stereotype of submissive coolies and depicting assertive men who demanded their rights in spite of great personal risk. Originally intended as a contribution toward the reclaiming of the Chinese American past, it accomplished much broader artistic goals.

Ma, a young Chinese emigrant who has been in America only four weeks, comes to warn Lone, a performer, that the other Chinese do not like his superior attitude. Hired to build the railroad across the Sierras, they are now in the fourth day of a strike against the labor practices of the "white devils."

The Chinese have demanded an eight-hour workday and a fourteen-dollar-a-week increase in pay. Lone is estranged from the other Chinese because he refuses to waste time drinking and gambling and instead practices the traditional Chinese opera. Captivated by Lone's beautiful dance, Ma decides to become a performer when he returns to China a wealthy man. Lone scoffs at Ma's naïve beliefs that America is a place with a mythical Gold Mountain, that his cheating Chinese coworkers are his friends, and that he will ever be able to portray the great Gwan Gung, god of fighters. Lone tells Ma that if he is to succeed he must face reality and willingly accept being shunned by the "already dead" Chinese men. Undaunted by this challenge, Ma begins to practice Chinese opera. Ma is subsequently shocked, however, to learn that if he works hard, he might successfully portray the Second Clown. Lone reveals how he spent eight years in opera school training to play Gwan Gung, only to be "kidnapped" by his parents and sent to the Sierras to work. Ma is determined and practices by spending the night in the "locust" position, a metaphor for the emigrant awakening. Lone returns, reporting that the strike is over. The Chinese have achieved their eight-hour day but only an eight-dollar-a-week raise. Ma finally realizes that, although a few Chinese men in America might achieve their dreams, most become dead to China. Ma and Lone improvise a Chinese opera revealing their voyages to America and experiences on the Gold Mountain. When the mountain fights back, Lone is exhilarated but Ma falls, his spirit broken. Now a realist, Ma returns to work with the "already dead" men, while Lone continues practicing for the Chinese opera.

Hwang contrasts two portraits of emigrant Chinese becoming Americans. Ma loses his innocence, discards his traditions, and joins the "already dead" laborers. Lone adapts Chinese mythology and tradition to his American experience. The Asian community has lauded Hwang's work, praising its depiction of the lives of Chinese Americans.

Family Devotions

TYPE OF WORK: Drama
FIRST PRODUCED: 1981; first published, 1983

Family Devotions was written when Hwang was primarily interested in writing for and about the identity of Asian Americans. The play is autobiographical in that Hwang was raised an evangelical Christian; *Family Devotions* advocates casting off the Western mythology imposed upon Asian cultures.

The play is set in an idealized house with an enclosed patio and tennis court, representing a shallow, materialistic American Dream. The extended families of Ama and Popo, first-generation Chinese Americans, are awaiting the arrival of Di-Gou, their brother whom they have not seen for thirty years and who is arriving from Communist China. As they anticipate Di-Gou's arrival, the women discuss the atrocities of the Communists, whose evil rule they are certain Di-Gou will be grateful to escape. The family descended from the great Chinese Christian evangelist See-goh-poo, and, as a boy, Di-Gou witnessed her miracles, so Ama and Popo anticipate hearing Di-Gou repeat his fervent testimony. When he arrives, however, Di-Gou quietly disavows ever being Christian. Di-Gou confides to Popo's grandson, Chester, that to establish a true American identity, he must believe the stories "written on his face," and these stories reflect many generations.

In act 2 the sisters organize a family devotional and invite Di-Gou to witness for Christ, but a family squabble erupts. Di-Gou is left with the women, who physically force him to submit before their neon cross. They implore him to remember See-goh-poo's miracles. Chester rushes in to rescue Di-Gou, and the scene transforms into a kind of Chinese opera. Di-Gou rises up speaking in tongues, the gas grill bursts into flame, and Chester interprets the revelation: Di-Gou witnessed See-goh-poo give birth out of wedlock, claiming evangelicalism to deceive her family. Di-Gou proclaims that because they now know the truth, their stories are meaningless. The old sisters collapse, dead, and Di-Gou realizes that "No one leaves America." The play ends with Chester standing where Di-Gou first stood, and the "shape of his face begins to change," a metaphor for the beginning acceptance of his Chinese heritage.

Family Devotions is an allegory depicting a cultural awakening of the individual. The world is reversed; "civilized" Christians behave as heathens, and the "heathen" Asian offers wisdom, solace, and love. Hwang calls for Asian Americans to embrace their Asian heritage.

M. Butterfly

TYPE OF WORK: Drama
FIRST PRODUCED: 1988; first published, 1988

M. Butterfly is Hwang's fictionalized account of a real French diplomat who carried on an affair with a Chinese opera singer for twenty years, only to discover she was actually a man. Hwang's compelling drama examines themes of sexual and racial stereotyping, Western imperialism, the role illusion plays in perceptions, and the ability of one person truly to know another.

M. Butterfly contrasts Rene Gallimard with Pinkerton in Giacomo Puccini's *Madama Butterfly* (produced, 1904; published, 1935). Gallimard sees himself as awkward, clumsy at love, but somehow blessed with the utter devotion of Song Liling, a beautiful Oriental woman. Hwang uses the word "Oriental" to convey an exotic, imperialistic view of the East. Gallimard becomes so absorbed with his sexist perception of Asian women that it distorts his thinking. He tests Liling's devotion by neglecting and humiliating her, ultimately forcing her to admit she is his "Butterfly," a character she has publicly denounced.

Unknown to Gallimard, Liling is a Communist agent, manipulating him to extract information about the Vietnam War. At the embassy Gallimard finds increased status because of his Oriental affair. When his analysis of East-West relations, based entirely on his self-delusions, prove wrong, Gallimard is demoted and returned to France. His usefulness spent, Liling is forced to endure hard labor, an official embarrassment because "there are no homosexuals in China." Eventually, the Communists send Liling to France to reestablish his affair with Gallimard. When Gallimard is caught and tried for espionage, it is publicly revealed that Liling is a man. Liling now changes to men's clothing, effecting a complete role-reversal between Liling and Gallimard. Liling becomes the dominant masculine figure while Gallimard becomes the submissive feminine figure. Preferring fantasy to reality, Gallimard becomes "Butterfly," donning Liling's wig and kimono, choosing an honorable death over a dishonorable life.

M. Butterfly demonstrates the dangers inherent in living a life satisfied with shallow stereotypes and misconceptions. Gallimard's singular desire for a submissive Oriental woman was fulfilled only in his mind. It blinded him to every truth about his mistress, refusing even to accept the truth about Liling until he stood naked before him. It first cost him his career, then his wife, then his dignity, then his lover, and finally his life. Even when he is confronted by the truth, Gallimard can only respond that he has "known, and been loved by, the perfect woman."

SUGGESTED READINGS

DiGaetani, John Lewis. "*M. Butterfly:* An Interview with David Henry Hwang." *The Drama Review: A Journal of Performance Studies* 33, no. 3 (Fall, 1989): 141-153.

Gerard, Jeremy. "David Hwang: Riding the Hyphen." *The New York Times Magazine*, March 13, 1988, 44, 88-89.

Hwang, David Henry. Introduction to *FOB and Other Plays.* New York: Plume, 1990.

_____. "'Making His Muscles Work for Himself': An Interview with David Henry Hwang." Interview by Bonnie Lyons. *Literary Review* 42, no. 2 (Winter, 1999): 230.

Skloot, Robert. "Breaking the Butterfly: The Politics of David Henry Hwang." *Modern Drama* 33, no. 1 (March, 1990): 59-66.

Street, Douglas. *David Henry Hwang.* Boise, Idaho: Boise State University Press, 1989.

−Gerald S. Argetsinger

Charles Johnson

BORN: Evanston, Illinois; April 23, 1948

Johnson's philosophical fiction continues an African American literary tradition.

TRADITIONS: African American

PRINCIPAL WORKS: *Faith and the Good Thing*, 1974; *Oxherding Tale*, 1982; *The Sorcerer's Apprentice*, 1986; *Middle Passage*, 1990; *Dreamer*, 1998

Reared in a tight-knit Midwestern black community, Charles Johnson remembers his childhood environment as loving and secure. An only child, he often read to fill up his time. Johnson especially loved comic books and spent hours practicing drawing in hopes of becoming a professional cartoonist. To this end he took a two-year correspondence course and was publishing cartoons and illustrations by the time he completed high school.

At the last minute Johnson decided to attend Southern Illinois University rather than art school. There he became passionately drawn to the study of philosophy and to writing. During his first summer vacation he began to pursue another lifelong interest, the martial arts. Before his undergraduate college days were over he had published a book of his own cartoons, *Black Humor* (1970), had hosted a television series on drawing, and had worked as a reporter for the *Chicago Tribune*. In 1970, he married Joan New, whom he had met two years earlier.

After graduation, Johnson began working as a reporter for the *Illinoisan*; however, he had already decided to become a novelist. Over the next two years, with John Gardner as his mentor, he wrote six "apprentice novels." Finally, in 1974, he published *Faith and the Good Thing*, which he had extensively researched while completing his master's degree in philosophy and writing a thesis on Marxism.

Johnson continued his studies in philosophy at the State University of New York at Stony Brook, this time concentrating on phenomenology. *Oxherding Tale* is a work he intended, he wrote, to be a reply to German novelist Hermann Hesse's *Siddartha* (1922; English translation, 1951). Johnson fashioned *Oxherding* into a "neo-slave narrative for the second half of the twentieth century." A melding of Eastern thought, the American slave experience, and a sharp, witty twentieth-century consciousness, *Oxherding Tale* traces the misadventures of Andrew Hawkins, a privileged slave given the finest education because of his status as the child of the plantation's black butler and the white mistress. Eventually, Andrew leaves home and begins to experience a variety

242

of identities and to test various philosophical stances toward life. His tale culminates with his marriage, his reconciliation with his past, and his final encounter with Soulcatcher, the fugitive slave hunter long on his trail.

By the time *Oxherding Tale* was published, Johnson had accepted an invitation to teach creative writing at the University of Washington. There, he continued to write; in addition to numerous essays, book reviews, and works for television, his credits include a collection of short stories, *The Sorcerer's Apprentice, Being and Race: Black Writing Since 1970* (1988), and his most acclaimed success *Middle Passage*, winner of the National Book Award. Another neo-slave narrative in the style of *Oxherding Tale*, *Middle Passage* continues Johnson's quest to produce entertaining yet seriously philosophical black literature. Johnson also continues his commitment to the martial arts and to Eastern philosophy, especially Buddhism.

Middle Passage
TYPE OF WORK: Novel
FIRST PUBLISHED: 1990

Middle Passage is the story of Rutherford Calhoun's life-changing journey aboard the slaver *Republic* in 1830. Like Johnson's earlier *Oxherding Tale*, this book is narrated by a young black man born into slavery but with a superior education, whose story is rooted in nineteenth century history but whose savvy, humorous voice bespeaks a twentieth century intellectual consciousness.

Rutherford's adventures begin when he stows aboard a ship to escape a woman determined to bring him to the altar. The *Republic*, a slaver, ships out to Africa; there it picks up a special cargo—a hold full of men, women, and children of the mystical Allmuseri tribe. The *Republic*'s captain also secretly brings on board a crate containing the captured Allmuseri god.

Middle Passage blatantly evokes *Moby Dick: Or, The Whale* (1851), "Benito Cereno," and Homer's *Odyssey* (c. 800 B.C., English translation, 1616) among others. Johnson flaunts, mocks, and turns on end these similarities: His dwarfish Captain Falcon is a caricature of the crazed Ahab; the ringleaders of the rebelling Allmuseri are Babo, Fernando, and Atufel; Isadora, Rutherford's intended, knits by day and unravels her work by night to forestall marriage to her new suitor. The *Republic*'s voyage is a darkly comic version of the *Pequod*'s, but one highlighting slavery's role in American history and economy. Whereas Herman Melville's Ishmael asks the philosophical question, "Who ain't a slave?" Johnson's Falcon educates Rutherford in the fundamentals of capitalism by pointing out, "Who ain't up for auction when it comes to it?"

Fittingly, then, Johnson's novel does not end when Falcon dies, the *Republic* sinks, and Rutherford is rescued. Rather, these events deliver Rutherford into the clutches of the *Republic*'s owners, come to check up on their investment.

Also aboard the rescue ship is Isadora and her fiancé, wealthy black New Orleans mobster Papa Zeringue. Once Zeringue is exposed as a part owner of the *Republic*, Isadora is free to marry Rutherford, who joyfully embraces marriage as an emotional haven in a cannibalistic world.

Middle Passage charts Rutherford's growth from a self-serving opportunist to a responsible man who values the ties that link human beings. His passage from a worldview based on multiplicity, individualism, dualism, and linearity to acceptance of the Allmuseri concept of "unity of being" opens him up to love, compassion, and commitment.

Rutherford's growth into this new identity seems also to comment on Johnson's identity as a sophisticated black writer navigating his way through African American, American, Western, and Eastern traditions. Johnson calls *Middle Passage* his attempt to fill a literary void by producing "philosophical black literature." An admirer of writers such as Thomas Mann, Jean-Paul Sartre, Hermann Hesse, Herman Melville, and Ralph Ellison, who "understood instinctively that fiction and philosophy were sister disciplines," Johnson weds, in this work, his own interests in philosophy, African American history, and fiction.

In *Middle Passage*, Johnson reminds readers that the received American epic (literary and historical) has an African American counterpart, and he adds a new dimension to the slave narrative tradition by creating an African American narrator who speaks in a formidably intellectual voice. Johnson also insists that Rutherford be taken seriously simply as a human being engaged in exploring fundamental underpinnings of the human condition. Johnson won the 1990 National Book Award for *Middle Passage*.

SUGGESTED READINGS

Byrd, Rudolph, ed. *I Call Myself an Artist: Writings by and About Charles Johnson.* Bloomington: Indiana University Press, 1999.

Coleman, J. W. "Charles Johnson's Quest for Black Freedom in *Oxherding Tale.*" *African American Review* 29, no. 4 (Winter, 1995): 631-644.

Johnson, Charles. "An Interview with Charles Johnson." Interview by Jonathan Little. *Contemporary Literature* 34, no. 12 (Summer, 1993): 158-182.

Keneally, Thomas. Review of *Middle Passage*, by Charles Johnson. *The New York Times Book Review,* July 1, 1990, 8.

Rushdy, Ashraf. "The Phenomenology of the Allmuseri." *African American Review* 26 (Fall, 1992): 373-394.

Scott, D. M. "Interrogating Identity: Appropriation and Transformation in *Middle Passage.*" *African American Review* 29, no. 4 (Winter, 1995): 645-655.

Travis, M. A. "*Beloved* and *Middle Passage:* Race, Narrative, and the Critics' Essentialism." *Narrative* 2, no. 3 (October, 1994): 179-200.

—Grace McEntee

James Weldon Johnson

BORN: Jacksonville, Florida; June 17, 1871
DIED: Wiscasset, Maine; June 26, 1938

*One of the first to celebrate African American art forms, Johnson was a major
figure in the Harlem Renaissance.*

TRADITIONS: African American

PRINCIPAL WORKS: *The Autobiography of an Ex-Coloured Man,* 1912; *The Book of
American Negro Poetry,* 1922 (editor); *The Book of American Negro Spirituals,*
1925 (editor); *God's Trombones: Seven Sermons in Verse,* 1927; *Along This Way,*
1933; *Saint Peter Relates an Incident: Selected Poems,* 1935

James Weldon Johnson was born in Jacksonville, was graduated from Atlanta
University in 1894, and went on to become one of the most versatile artists
of his time. In addition to expressing his artistic talents, he led a successful
professional life and was an
influential civil rights advocate. After his graduation
in 1894, Johnson became
principal of Stanton School
and edited a newspaper,
the *Daily American.* He advocated civil rights in his
articles in a time that saw a
dramatic rise in the number
of lynchings. He thus as-
sumed a public role in the
African American commu-
nity. Encouraged by his
brother Rosamond, Johnson
and his brother went to New
York in 1899 to work on a
musical career. Their most
lasting achievement of that
period is the song "Lift
Every Voice and Sing," also
known as the African
American national anthem.
After having been ap-
pointed consul in Vene-

James Weldon Johnson (Library of Congress)

245

zuela and Nicaragua, Johnson, after publication of *The Autobiography of an Ex-Coloured Man*, decided to attempt to support himself through literary work. He returned to New York to begin writing an influential column for the *New York Age*, commenting on literary matters and encouraging black literary activity. He published *The Book of American Negro Poetry* three years before Alain Locke's anthology *The New Negro* (1925) officially ushered in the Harlem Renaissance.

Beginning in 1916, Johnson was field secretary for the National Association for the Advancement of Colored People (NAACP), organizing new branches and looking into matters of racial injustice nationwide. In 1920, he became the first African American secretary of the NAACP, a post he would hold until 1930. Johnson saw his civil rights work and his artistic activity as complementary, believing that the production of great works of art would improve African Americans' position in society. Johnson contributed major work to that effort with the publication of *God's Trombones*, bringing the language of the African American church into the realm of literature. Weldon also collected two volumes of African American spirituals, which made clear that this expression of African American folk spirit belonged to the world of art. His death in a car accident in 1938 interrupted Johnson in his wide-ranging efforts.

Along This Way

TYPE OF WORK: Autobiography
FIRST PUBLISHED: 1933

Johnson claimed that one of the reasons for publishing his autobiography, *Along This Way*, was to finally make clear that his novel *The Autobiography of an Ex-Coloured Man* (1912) was not a record of his life. A public figure as important as Johnson hardly needed, however, a justification for adding another book to the growing shelf of autobiographies of distinguished African Americans, such as Frederick Douglass, Booker T. Washington, and W. E. B. Du Bois. In a controlled and often ironic narrative tone, Johnson not only provides insights into his life and times but also focuses on African American accomplishments in the hostile social climate that he battled against all his life.

Despite a middle-class upbringing, a university degree, and immediate success first as a school principal, in passing the Florida bar examination—the first African American to do so—and then as songwriter, writer, consul, and civil rights activist, Johnson always committed himself to the cause of African Americans. When on university vacation, he spent three months teaching African American farmers' children in rural Georgia, realizing "that they were me, and I was they; that a force stronger than blood made us one." Accordingly, all his artistic work was committed to improving the social situation of African Americans and to exploring African American art forms. When embarking on his composing and songwriting career, he "began to grope toward a realization of the American Negro's cultural background and his creative folk-art." In much of his poetry, too, Johnson built on African American folk traditions. He did so because he believed in the uniqueness of the African American heritage, based as it was on a deep spirituality. Thus, he implies that African Americans are a main resource for the United States in matters of artistry and spirituality, and that, in turn, the United States will be measured by how it treats African Americans. He pithily summarizes this belief in saying "that in large measure the race question involves the saving of black America's body and white America's soul."

A considerable part of the book is devoted to Johnson's fight for racial justice and his time in the leadership of the National Association for the Advancement of Colored People. Johnson reveals explicitly that his program for improving the social status of African Americans, despite his own artistic, legal, and political efforts, is really a moral one: "The only kind of revolution that would have an immediately significant effect on the American Negro's status would be a moral revolution." As *Along This Way* makes clear, Johnson did his best on all fronts.

The Autobiography of an Ex-Coloured Man
TYPE OF WORK: Novel
FIRST PUBLISHED: 1912

The Autobiography of an Ex-Coloured Man was first published anonymously in 1912, but only became a success when republished in 1927 at the height of the Harlem Renaissance. The novel chronicles the coming-of-age of its unnamed protagonist, who switches back and forth between ethnic identities until he finally decides to pass as a European American. Its most striking feature might well be that it calls the notion of ethnic identity into question.

In order to explore ethnic identity, Johnson has his protagonist experience both sides of the "color line," to use the famous phrase by W. E. B. Du Bois. Growing up believing himself European American, as the white-looking child of a light-skinned African American mother and a European American father, the protagonist finds out in school that he is African American. Having harbored prejudice against African Americans, he now becomes an object of prejudice. Once over this initial shock, he resolves to become famous in the service of African Americans. In order to learn about his mother's heritage, he leaves for the South, where he often finds himself an outsider to African American society. He knows little of African American folk customs, so at first he reacts to African Americans ambiguously. In this way, Johnson shows that the culture of one's upbringing is a more important factor in determining one's outlook on other cultures than ethnic bloodlines are.

After losing his money in the South, the protagonist eventually embarks on a musical career, which takes him to New York. He discovers ragtime there and is fascinated by it, renewing his resolve to become famous, and intending to do so through African American music. After a sojourn in Europe, he returns to the South in order to learn more about the roots of African American music, which he calls "a mine of material" when visiting a religious meeting at which spirituals are sung. The reader discovers that the protagonist's interest in African American culture is mainly commercial. He nevertheless often comments enthusiastically on African American contributions to American culture. The protagonist gives up his idea of becoming famous through African American music, however, after witnessing a lynching. He returns North, marries a European American woman, and becomes a white businessman. In the end, he wishes he had followed his musical inclinations, which are connected to his African American heritage, instead of achieving material success. Thus, the novel shows that a hostile social climate can bring people to forsake their heritage, but also that ethnic identity is partly a matter of choice.

Saint Peter Relates an Incident
Type of work: Poetry
First published: 1935

Saint Peter Relates an Incident: Selected Poems and *God's Trombones* (1927) mark the culmination of Johnson's poetic work. His most famous poems appear in *Saint Peter Relates an Incident,* including the title poem, "O Black and Unknown Bards," and "Lift Every Voice and Sing."

"Saint Peter Relates an Incident of the Resurrection Day," originally published in 1930, was written in response to the visit by mothers of highly decorated World War I soldiers to their sons' graves in France. The State Department, which sponsored the visit, sent white mothers in one ship and African American mothers in another, second-class ship. The poem imagines Saint Peter telling the assembled angels of Heaven an incident occurring on Judgment Day. The dead are called from their graves, and white war veterans, among them members of the Ku Klux Klan, gather together in order to escort the Unknown Soldier to Heaven. Once they liberate him from his grave, they are shocked to find that he is black and debate whether they should bury him again. Until the white war veterans knew the Unknown Soldier's color, they intended to honor him; his color alone turns their admiration into hatred. The Unknown Soldier marches triumphantly into Heaven, while, it is implied, the war veterans dismayed by his skin color end up in Hell. Johnson points out the bitter irony and absurdity of drawing a color line even after death, particularly when death was incurred in the service of one's country.

"O Black and Unknown Bards" originally appeared in *Fifty Years and Other*

Poems (1917). The title refers to the unknown creators of the spirituals, a musical form that Johnson regarded as artistic work of the first rank, a point he makes by comparing it with the creations of classical composers. Incorporating titles of actual spirituals, such as "Steal Away to Jesus" and "Go Down, Moses," into the poem, Johnson pays homage to African American folk art, admiring its spiritual and artistic accomplishments, and bridges the gap between folk art forms and so-called high art.

"Lift Every Voice and Sing," perhaps the work which has done most to keep Johnson's name alive, was originally composed as a tribute to Abraham Lincoln's birthday and set to music. It is still known as the African American national anthem. Inspirational in nature, the poem makes no direct reference to ethnicity but refers metaphorically to hardships endured by African Americans while also celebrating liberties won in hard struggle. The third and last stanza reminds the listeners to remain faithful to God and ends on a patriotic note, which claims the United States as African Americans' "native land."

SUGGESTED READINGS

Butterfield, Stephen. *Black Autobiography in America.* Amherst: University of Massachusetts Press, 1974.

Fleming, Robert E. *James Weldon Johnson.* Boston: Twayne, 1987.

Levy, Eugene. *James Weldon Johnson: Black Leader, Black Voice.* Chicago: University of Chicago Press, 1973.

Phylon 32 (Winter, 1971): 330-402.

Price, Kenneth M., and Lawrence J. Oliver, eds. *Critical Essays on James Weldon Johnson.* New York: G. K. Hall, 1997.

Redmond, Eugene B. *Drumvoices: The Mission of Afro-American Poetry.* Garden City, N.J.: Anchor Press, 1976.

Stepto, Robert B. *From Behind the Veil: A Study of Afro-American Narrative.* Champaign: University of Illinois Press, 1979.

Sundquist, Eric J. *The Hammers of Creation: Folk Culture in Modern African-American Fiction.* Athens: University of Georgia Press, 1992.

Wagner, Jean. *Black Poets of the United States.* Champaign: University of Illinois Press, 1973.

Wisner-Broyles, Laura A., ed. *Poetry Criticism: Excerpts from Criticism of the Works of the Most Significant and Widely Studied Poets of World Literature.* Vol. 24. Detroit: Gale Research, 1999.

—Martin Japtok

Gayl Jones

BORN: Lexington, Kentucky; November 23, 1949

Jones's conventional gothic novels and short stories are among the most intense psychological portrayals of black female characters in African American literature.

TRADITIONS: African American

PRINCIPAL WORKS: *Chile Woman,* pr. 1973, pb. 1974; *Corregidora,* 1975; *Eva's Man,* 1976; *White Rat,* 1977; *Song of Anninho,* 1981; *The Hermit-Woman,* 1983; *Xarque and Other Poems,* 1985; *Liberating Voices: Oral Tradition in African American Literature,* 1991; *The Healing,* 1998

Poet, novelist, essayist, short-story writer, and teacher, Gayl Jones is best known for the intensity and probing nature of her gothic tales, which mix the conventions of the gothic with radically unconventional worlds of madness, sexuality, and violence. Jones began writing seriously at age seven under the encouraging and guiding influence of her grandmother, her mother, and her high school Spanish teacher, Anna Dodd. Later, her mentors would be Michael Harper and William Meredith at Brown University, where she earned two degrees in creative writing. She published her first and best-known novel, *Corregidora,* while still at Brown.

No stranger to the art of writing and storytelling, Jones grew up in a household of female creative writers: Her grandmother wrote plays for church production. Jones's mother, Lucille, started writing in fifth grade and read stories she had written to Jones and her brother. It is therefore not surprising that stories, storytelling, and family history are the source of most of the material for her fiction.

In addition to her distinction as teller of intense stories about insanity and the psychological effects of violence on black women, another characteristic of Jones's art is her consistent use of the first person for her protagonists. Claiming neither "political compulsions nor moral compulsions," Jones is first and foremost interested in the "psychology of characters" and therefore seeks to examine their "puzzles," as she states, by simply letting her characters "tell their stories." Her interest in the character as storyteller permits her to evoke oral history and engage the African American tradition of storytelling, which she accomplishes in her novels *Corregidora* and *Eva's Man.*

Corregidora, a historical novel, is what Jones calls a blues narrative. The novel examines the psychological effects of slavery and sexual abuse on three generations of women, particularly Ursa, a professional blues singer. *Eva's*

Man, Jones's more provocative and controversial second novel, explores the psychological effects of violence. Eva Medina Canada, the protagonist-narrator, tells in confusing but gripping detail the story of her violent reaction to her victimization in a male-dominated society. Jones continues her thematic concerns with *White Rat,* a volume of twelve short stories, and *Song of Anninho,* a long narrative poem. In addition to her fiction and essay writing, Jones teaches full-time, writes poetry, and conducts research.

Eva's Man
TYPE OF WORK: Novel
FIRST PUBLISHED: 1976

Eva's Man, Jones's provocative second novel, is a psychological tale of repression, manipulation, and suffering. It is a gothic story of madness—Eva's madness—and the psychological effects of violence on black women. From her prison asylum room, where she has been incarcerated for five years for poisoning, then castrating, her lover, Eva Medina Canada, the psychotic title character, narrates the events which led up to her bizarre and violent act. Although she has maintained a steadfast and defiant silence in response to the grinding interrogation of the male judicial authorities—the police and psychiatrists—Eva readily tells her story to the reader. Through time and space intrusions, many flashbacks and a combination of dreams, fantasies, memories, interrogation, and exchanges between herself and her cellmate, Elvira, Eva tells everything except her motive.

In the unsequential narrative, Eva's story delineates unequivocally men's malevolence and women's natural acceptance of a destiny inevitably circumscribed by this malevolence. Eva's appropriating of and identification with the story of Queen Bee, the femme fatale whose love, like a deadly sting, kills off every man with whom she falls in love, suggests that women resign themselves to a female destiny. This horrid fatalism blames and punishes women for their sexuality. Paradoxically, since the drone is always at the service of the queen bee, it is women who have power to affirm or deny manhood. Aligning herself with the queen bee, Eva kills Davis, the drone, rather than submit to his excessive domination.

For Eva the lessons in the violent consequences of womanhood and female sexuality began early. Prepubescent Freddy, a neighbor boy, initiates her sexually with a dirty Popsicle stick. Her mother's lover, Tyrone, makes her feel him. She sees her father punish her mother's infidelity with rape. Cousin Alphonse solicits sex from her, and a thumbless man harasses her sexually. Moses Tribbs propositions her, thereby provoking her attack on him with a pocket knife. Her fifty-five-year-old husband James, out of jealousy, disallows a telephone in the house. Finally, Davis, her lover, imprisons and uses her for five days. To each of these men, Eva (like other women characters in the novel, including her mother) exists merely as an object to satisfy insatiable male sexual needs. In response to this objectification and violence by men, Eva remains steadfastly silent, choosing neither to explain her extreme action nor to defend herself.

Apart from the bizarreness of Eva's brutal act, which delineates the level of her madness, it is perhaps the exclusive use of the first-person narrative voice and the lack of authorial intrusion or questioning of Eva's viewpoint that make *Eva's Man* controversial and successful.

SUGGESTED READINGS

Coser, Stelamaris. *Bridging the Americas: The Literatures of Paule Marshall, Toni Morrison and Gayl Jones.* Philadelphia: Temple University Press, 1994.

Davidson, C. M. "Love 'em and Lynch 'em: The Castration Motif in Gayl Jones's *Eva's Man.*" *African American Review* 29 (Fall, 1995): 393-410.

Dixon, Melvin. *Ride out the Wilderness.* Chicago: University of Illinois Press, 1987.

Evans, Mari, ed. *Black Women Writers: 1950-1980.* Garden City, N.Y.: Doubleday, 1984.

Plummer, William. "Beyond Healing." *People Weekly* 49 (March 16, 1998): 81-82.

Robinson, Sally. *Engendering the Subject.* Albany: State University of New York Press, 1991.

—Pamela J. Olubunmi Smith

Cynthia Lynn Kadohata

BORN: Chicago, Illinois; July 2, 1956

Kadohata is best known for her portrayal of a Japanese American family in her first novel, The Floating World.

TRADITIONS: Japanese American
PRINCIPAL WORKS: *The Floating World*, 1989; *In the Heart of the Valley of Love*, 1992; *The Glass Mountains*, 1995

Cynthia Lynn Kadohata aspired to be a journalist after she was graduated from college, believing that only nonfiction can express the truth. Her parents, as were other Japanese Americans, were uprooted during World War II and traveled extensively across the country in search of work. Kadohata's keen observation of landscape and people during these long drives prepared her for her later career.

Kadohata changed her plans for the future after she was seriously injured in an automobile accident. While recuperating, she read extensively and discovered the power of fiction, its ability to say what could not be said otherwise. She tried her hand at writing short stories, and, after several rejections, one of her stories was accepted by *The New Yorker*. She felt encouraged to devote her life to writing fiction.

Kadohata's two attempts at obtaining formal instruction in creative writing were of little use to her. She found her own observations and travels to be more useful than any theoretical discussions. In her first novel, *The Floating World*, Kadohata drew upon her own experiences of moving with her family from various cities on the Pacific coast to Arkansas. The protagonist and narrator, Olivia Osaka, is a third-generation Japanese American whose years of growing up are typical of all adolescents. The novel was well received and commended for its portrayal of a Japanese American migrant family. The success of the novel enabled her to win awards from the Whiting Foundation and the National Endowment for the Arts.

In the Heart of the Valley of Love, Kadohata's second novel, depicts Los Angeles in the 1950's. Her picture of grim and bleak life in the years to come is based on the implications of the changing demographics in California in the 1990's. Living in a period when a widening chasm between the classes breeds discontent and lawlessness, the protagonist, Francie, a young woman of Asian-African American ancestry, undergoes traumatic experiences. She loses her parents and then her surrogate parents, but eventually finds love, hope, and the possibility of renewal. She expresses Kadohata's optimism about the survival of a multicultural society in the future.

Kadohata is clearly influenced by writers such as Maxine Hong Kingston and Amy Tan, who draw upon their Chinese heritage. She adds another dimension to the multicultural experience by adding the Japanese American perspective.

The Floating World

TYPE OF WORK: Novel
FIRST PUBLISHED: 1989

The Floating World deals with the theme of identity at two levels. The narrator, Olivia Osaka, a girl of twelve at the beginning of this episodic novel, is, like all adolescents, trying to understand the world around her. In her case, the problems normally associated with growing up are further complicated by the fact that her parents are of Japanese origin. Thus Olivia has to find her place not just as an adult but as an American of Japanese descent.

The experiences recounted by Olivia take place in the 1950's and 1960's. The internment camps for the Japanese Americans had been disbanded soon after World War II, but the effects of their dislocation were still discernible. The title of the novel comes from the Japanese word *ukiyo*–the floating world–the world of gas station attendants, restaurants, and temporary jobs encountered by the Osaka family. Charles Osaka is constantly on the move with his wife and four children–Olivia and three sons–to seek better opportunities.

Olivia discovers that Charlie is not her biological father and that her charming, graceful mother still mourns the loss of her first love. Olivia is baffled by her mother's unhappiness, for she cannot understand why the love of a decent man like Charlie is not enough for her mother. Like all children in families with marital tensions, Olivia wonders if she and her brothers are responsible for the unhappiness of their parents.

Obasan, Olivia's grandmother, lives with them for some years before her death. For Olivia, she becomes the link with her Japanese heritage. She is fascinated yet repelled by the seventy-three-year-old tyrant. Olivia enjoys her grandmother's fantastic tales of growing up in Japan, but she abhors her strict, Japanese ways of disciplining the children. She hates Obasan while she is alive, but Olivia realizes later that the memories of her grandmother's stories and the observations in her diaries are invaluable in helping her understand the lives of her parents and of the Japanese American community.

In Gibson, Arkansas, the family stays long enough for Olivia to finish high school. During this period, she experiences her first love, and begins to appreciate the hardships endured by the Japanese Americans. By the time she leaves for Los Angeles, she has learned certain truths about herself and her relationship to her community. She recognizes the fears and uncertainties that govern her parents' lives but has confidence in her own ability to overcome these uncertainties.

Olivia's narrative comes to an end with her decision to go to college. She has turned twenty-one and her years in Los Angeles have given her time to learn independence, to make her own mistakes, and to come to terms with the memories of Obasan and her biological father. With the acceptance of her past and her hyphenated identity, Olivia seems ready to take her place in American society.

In the Heart of the Valley of Love
TYPE OF WORK: Novel
FIRST PUBLISHED: 1992

In the Heart of the Valley of Love is a futuristic novel depicting life in Los Angeles in the 2050's. Narrated by Francie, who comes to stay with her aunt in Los Angeles after she loses her African American father and Japanese mother to cancer, the novel portrays the decline of the once-prosperous city.

The picture that Francie draws of Los Angeles in the 2050's is clearly based on the demographical changes in California and the widening chasm between the rich and the poor in the 1990's. Kadohata envisions a bleak city where the nonwhites and poor whites make up 64 percent of the population and where extreme pollution causes unusual and unheard-of diseases. Shortages of all essential commodities have led to rationing of water and gas; corruption and lawlessness among officials is widespread. The city is clearly divided into the areas of haves and have-nots, and rioting by unhappy citizens is commonplace.

It is no surprise, then, that this city of despair is inhabited by "expressionless people." Young people lead undisciplined lives in the absence of responsible adults in their lives. They tattoo their faces and their bodies—a way of "obliterating themselves," according to the narrator.

Francie, too, is affected by the times. Her adoptive family is disintegrated after Rohn, her aunt's boyfriend, disappears. It is suspected that he has been arrested by the authorities. As her aunt risks her life and devotes all her time to tracing him, Francie drifts, like her young peers. She joins a community college where there are several other men and women in their twenties and thirties keeping themselves occupied in aimless activities. Eventually, she overcomes her cynical approach to love and life in general, for amid the ruins she sees signs of renewal of the land.

Francie observes at the end of the novel: "I didn't know whether, a hundred years from now, this would be called The Dark Century or The Century of Light. Though others had already declared it the former, I hoped it would turn out to be the latter." Her comment does little to diminish the chilling picture of a possible future for Los Angeles.

SUGGESTED READINGS

Kakutani, Michiko. "Growing up Rootless in an Immigrant Family." *The New York Times,* June 30, 1989, C15.

Park, You-me, and Gayle Wald. "Native Daughters in the Promised Land: Gender, Race, and the Question of Separate Spheres." *American Literature* 70, no. 3 (September, 1998): 607.

Pearlman, Mickey. *Listen to Their Voices: Twenty Interviews with Women Who Write.* New York: W. W. Norton, 1993.

See, Lisa. "Cynthia Kadohata." *Publishers Weekly* 239 (August 3, 1992): 48-49.

—Leela Kapai

Adrienne Kennedy

BORN: Pittsburgh, Pennsylvania; September 13, 1931

Kennedy's surrealist plays are leading examples of African American drama.

TRADITIONS: African American
PRINCIPAL WORKS: *A Rat's Mass*, pr. 1966, pb. 1968; *Cities in Bezique*, pb. 1969; *Funnyhouse of a Negro*, pr. 1962, pb. 1969; *The Lennon Play: In His Own Write*, pr. 1967, pb. 1969 (with John Lennon and Victor Spinetti); *A Lesson in a Dead Language*, pr., pb. 1968; *Sun: A Poem for Malcolm X Inspired by His Murder*, pr. 1968, pb. 1971; *A Beast's Story*, pr., pb. 1969; *Boats*, pr. 1969; *An Evening with Dead Essex*, pr. 1973; *A Movie Star Has to Star in Black and White*, pr. 1976; *A Lancashire Lad*, pr. 1980; *Orestes and Electra*, pr. 1980; *Black Children's Day*, pr. 1980; *People Who Led to My Plays*, 1987; *Adrienne Kennedy in One Act*, 1988; *Deadly Triplets: A Theatre Mystery and Journal*, 1990; *The Alexander Plays*, pb. 1992; *June and Jean in Concert*, pr. 1995

Adrienne Kennedy's plays baffle and entice theater critics. In Kennedy, critics recognize a singularly able writer whose surrealism equals that of Tom Stoppard and Amiri Baraka. Edward Albee's early recognition of Kennedy's ability encouraged the yet-unpublished playwright to persist in her writing and led to the production of her *Funnyhouse of a Negro*.

Raised in a multiethnic neighborhood in Cleveland, Ohio, where her father, Cornell Wallace Hawkins, was an executive secretary for the Young Men's Christian Association and her mother, Etta Haugabook Hawkins, was a teacher, Kennedy was secure in her identity. She grew up associating with her neighbors: blacks, Jews, Italians, eastern Europeans. Where she lived, these people existed harmoniously, so Adrienne was not exposed to a racially motivated identity crisis until she entered Ohio State University in Columbus in 1949. There Kennedy felt isolated and inferior. Columbus's restaurants were still segregated, and there was little interaction between blacks and whites. By the time she was graduated in 1953, her anger and her detestation of prejudice had eaten away at her in ways that would shape her future writing career.

Kennedy married Joseph Kennedy shortly after graduation and followed him to New York City, where they both attended Columbia University. She studied creative writing there from 1954 until 1956. In 1958, she studied at the American Theatre Wing, then at the New School for Social Research, and finally at Edward Albee's Circle-in-the-Square School in 1962, where she was the only black student. Albee's encouragement led to Kennedy's continuing her writing career.

Her drama examines the inner struggles people encounter as they cope with their identities in relation to the outside forces that confront them. Kennedy's plays are essentially without plot. Her leading characters have multiple personalities, reflecting aspects of their identities. She relies heavily on the use of masks, each reflecting the different identities of her characters and suggesting elements of African art and culture as well.

Funnyhouse of a Negro

TYPE OF WORK: Drama
FIRST PRODUCED: 1962; first published, 1969

The struggle of the individual with internalized social and cultural forces is the focal point of most of Adrienne Kennedy's plays. In particular, she focuses on the internal conflict of the African American, whose existence is a result of the violent blending of European and African cultures. This conflict in *Funnyhouse of a Negro* is imaged in the Negro-Sarah's idolatrous love of her fair-skinned mother and rejection of her black father. The mother's whiteness has driven her insane; the father's darkness has tied him to revolution and bloodshed. Sarah's eventual escape is suicide.

The play is set in Sarah's space. The characters in the play are views of herself, or they are inspired by the objects in her room. The space is filled with relics of European civilization: dusty books, pictures of castles and monarchs, the bust of Queen Victoria. Sarah's occupation is writing, the geometric placement of words on white paper. The space is also a coffin; the white material of the curtain looks as though it has been "gnawed by rats." Throughout the play the space becomes more confining as the walls drop down. Eventually it becomes the jungle, overgrown and wild. In the context of the play's imagery of death, the jungle represents the earth's reclamation of the body.

Adrienne Kennedy

On another level, the play is set within a "funnyhouse," an "amusement park house of horrors." Raymond and the Landlady are representations of the two grinning minstrel faces outside the funnyhouse. They are white society mocking the Negro's confusion. The bald heads and dropping walls are cheap effects designed to create confusion and fear; the mirrors in Raymond's room conceal true reflections, as distorted funnyhouse mirrors do.

Kennedy is also a woman writer, and the play makes a statement about the roles of black women and white women in society. The mother was light-skinned and beautiful by European standards. There was no destiny for her in society except madness: To be a light-skinned woman is to invite the rape of black men. Sarah is dating a white man, and this seems to give her some power in the scene with Raymond when she is the Duchess of Hapsburg. It is Raymond, however, who is asking the questions and who has control over the environment. Even the white female characters in the play who represent powerful figures are victims of hair loss; they too are unable to escape the dark man who pursues them.

In the playwright's view, the world is a disturbing place. The lure of power is held out to women, when in fact they are powerless. For the Negro, to be assimilated into white society is to go mad or self-destruct.

Funnyhouse of a Negro invites the viewer into the mind of a very confused young black woman. The characters of the play are identified as facets of herself. She sees herself as omnipotent (Jesus), powerful (Queen Victoria, the Duchess of Hapsburg), and revolutionary (Patrice Lumumba). According to the dream logic of the play, these diverse characters all suffer from the conflict between their father, a black man, and their mother, a light-complexioned black woman who was raped and driven to insanity. The characters evoke the era of European colonialism, the zealotry of Christian missionaries, and the subsequent search for liberation by the peoples of Africa.

A Rat's Mass

TYPE OF WORK: Drama
FIRST PRODUCED: 1966; first published, 1968

A Rat's Mass is a play about the negative aspects of the black experience, about prejudice and hatred and rejection, about being an outsider with no hope of ever belonging, and about the failure of traditional institutions to offer any solutions to the problem. Brother Rat and Sister Rat represent the black population, Rosemary the white society that subjugates and oppresses, and the Procession of holy figures the uncaring, impersonal church, which offers neither succor nor forgiveness.

For Brother and Sister Rat, the pain of living black in a white world is realized in their adoration of Rosemary, the white child who is all that they can never be—"a descendant of the Pope and Julius Caesar and the Virgin Mary." Rosemary is the source of their feelings of rejection ("Colored people are not Catholics, are they?"), the instigator of their sin ("Rosemary said if I loved her I would do what she said"), the reminder of their guilt ("I will never atone you"). Clad in her white Communion dress, Rosemary is both the unattainable ideal and the avenging angel.

Perhaps what is most theatrical—and sometimes most frustrating to audiences about *A Rat's Mass* is the surrealistic quality of the play. The set, composed as it is of two black chains, a red aisle runner, and candles, evokes images of a Black Mass and forbidden rituals, creating inevitable unease in the audience. The main characters, who are described as "two pale Negro children," are part rat, part human, and as their despair mounts and their hope dies, they sound more and more like rats, less and less human. Adrienne Kennedy's choice of rats as representative of a maligned and mistreated minority is especially apt: Rats—unlike mice—evoke no sympathy, elicit only disgust and the desire to exterminate them, and conjure up images of filth and degradation, which are violently juxtaposed to the Holy Family and their entourage and Rosemary in her white dress. Most startling of the visual images in the play is the finale, in which the Holy Procession—composed of the familiar biblical figures who grace every Nativity scene ever displayed—guns down the fleeing Brother Rat and Sister Rat. This nightmarish ending provides strong reinforcement for one of the play's more pervasive ideas: that the organized church is responsible in large part for racism and hatred and indeed can be directly implicated in some of the deaths of oppressed peoples. The biblical characters so long held to be symbols of salvation and redemption become in this play the agents of destruction for a pair of innocent children, whose only fault is their color and their desire to emulate and be accepted by the dominant race and culture.

Like most of Adrienne Kennedy's plays, *A Rat's Mass* is a curious blend of monologue and dream vision, informed by highly evocative symbolism and incantatory dialogue, laced with references to mythical and historical figures. Neither her most ambitious nor her most important work, the play nevertheless is a good example of the kind of work that has earned Kennedy the acclaim of theater critics, scholars, and audiences. Like her better-known plays, *A Rat's Mass* is concerned with the anguish of not belonging, with the pain of rejection.

SUGGESTED READINGS

Betsko, Kathleen, and Rachel Konig. "Adrienne Kennedy." In *Interviews with Contemporary Women Playwrights*. New York: William Morrow, 1987.

Blau, Herbert. "The American Dream in American Gothic: The Plays of Sam Shepard and Adrienne Kennedy." *Modern Drama* 27 (December, 1984): 520-539.

Bryant-Jackson, Paul K., and Lois More Overbeck, eds. *Intersecting Boundaries: The Theatre of Adrienne Kennedy.* Minneapolis: University of Minnesota Press, 1992.

Cohn, Ruby. *New American Dramatists: 1960-1990.* New York: Grove, 1982.

Kennedy, Adrienne. "An Interview with Adrienne Kennedy." Interview by Elin Diamond. *Studies in American Drama, 1945-Present* 4 (1989): 143-157.

————. "A MELUS Interview with Adrienne Kennedy." Interview by Wolfgang Binder. *MELUS* 12 (Fall, 1985): 99-108.

Meigs, Susan E. "No Place Like the Funnyhouse: The Struggle for Identity in Three Adrienne Kennedy Plays." In *Modern American Drama: The Female Canon,* edited by June Schlueter. Rutherford, N.J.: Fairleigh Dickinson University Press, 1990.

Posnock, Ross. *Color and Culture: Black Writers and the Making of the Modern Intellectual.* Cambridge, Mass.: Harvard University Press, 1998.

Sollors, Werner. "Owls and Rats in the American Funnyhouse." *American Literature: A Journal of Literary History, Criticism, and Bibliography* 63 (September, 1991): 507-532.

Tener, Robert. "Theatre of Identity: Adrienne Kennedy's Portrait of the Black Woman." *Studies in Black Literature* 6 (1975): 1-5.

—*R. Baird Shuman/Kathryn Ervin Williams/E. D. Huntley*

Indexes

Author Index

Title Index

Ethnic Identity List